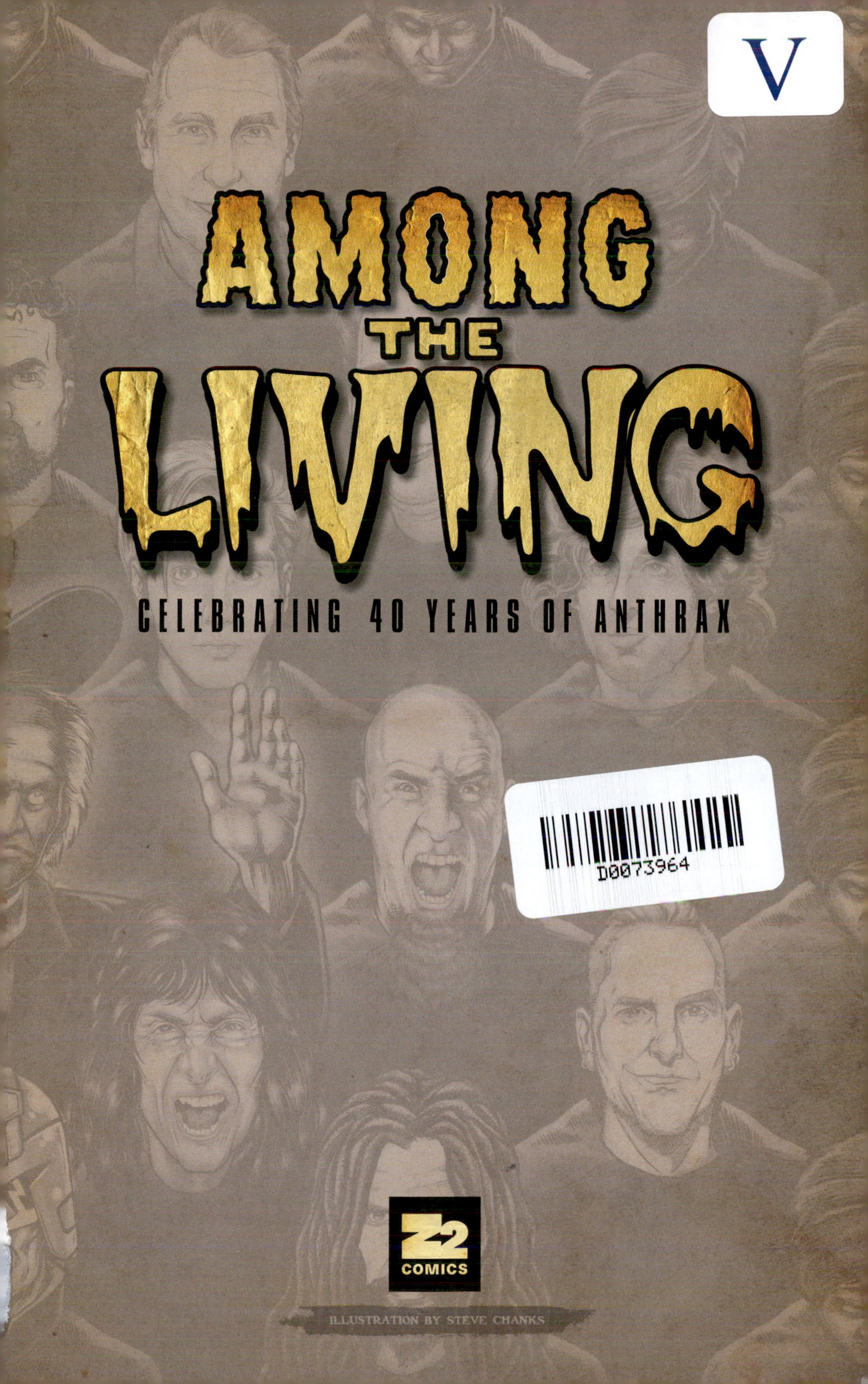

AMONG THE LIVING

CELEBRATING 40 YEARS OF ANTHRAX

Z2 COMICS

ILLUSTRATION BY STEVE CHANKS

PUBLISHERS Joshua Frankel & Sridhar Reddy
CFO & GENERAL COUNSEL Kevin Meek
SENIOR VICE PRESIDENT Josh Bernstein
V.P., PUBLIC RELATIONS & MARKETING Jeremy Atkins
V.P., DIGITAL Anthony Lauletta
V.P., OPERATIONS Dominique Rosés
ARTIST LIAISON Jess Lechtenberg
PRODUCTION DESIGN DIRECTOR Courtney Menard
DESIGN DIRECTOR Tyler Boss
SENIOR DIGITAL MARKETING ASSOCIATE Rebecca Cicione

© Anthrax licensed by Global Merchandising Services Limited. All rights reserved. No similarity between any of the names, characters, persons, and/or institutions in this Graphic Novel with those of any living or dead person or institution is intended, and any such similarity which may exist is purely coincidental. No part of this publication may be reproduced, stored in a retrieval system or transmitted in any form or by any means, electronic, mechanical, photocopying, recording or otherwise, without prior permission of Global Merchandising Services Limited. First printing May 2021. Printed in Canada.

Copyright © 1977, 2021 Rebellion.

Judge Dredd, Judge Death, the Dark Judges, and all other characters are Copyright © Rebellion 1977, 2021. 2000 AD, Judge Dredd, Judge Death, and I Am The Law are trademarks of Rebellion and are registered trademarks in certain jurisdictions. All Rights Reserved.

The stories, characters and incidents featured in this publication are entirely fictional.

Judge Dredd created by John Wagner and Carlos Ezquerra.

Published under license from Rebellion. www.2000AD.com

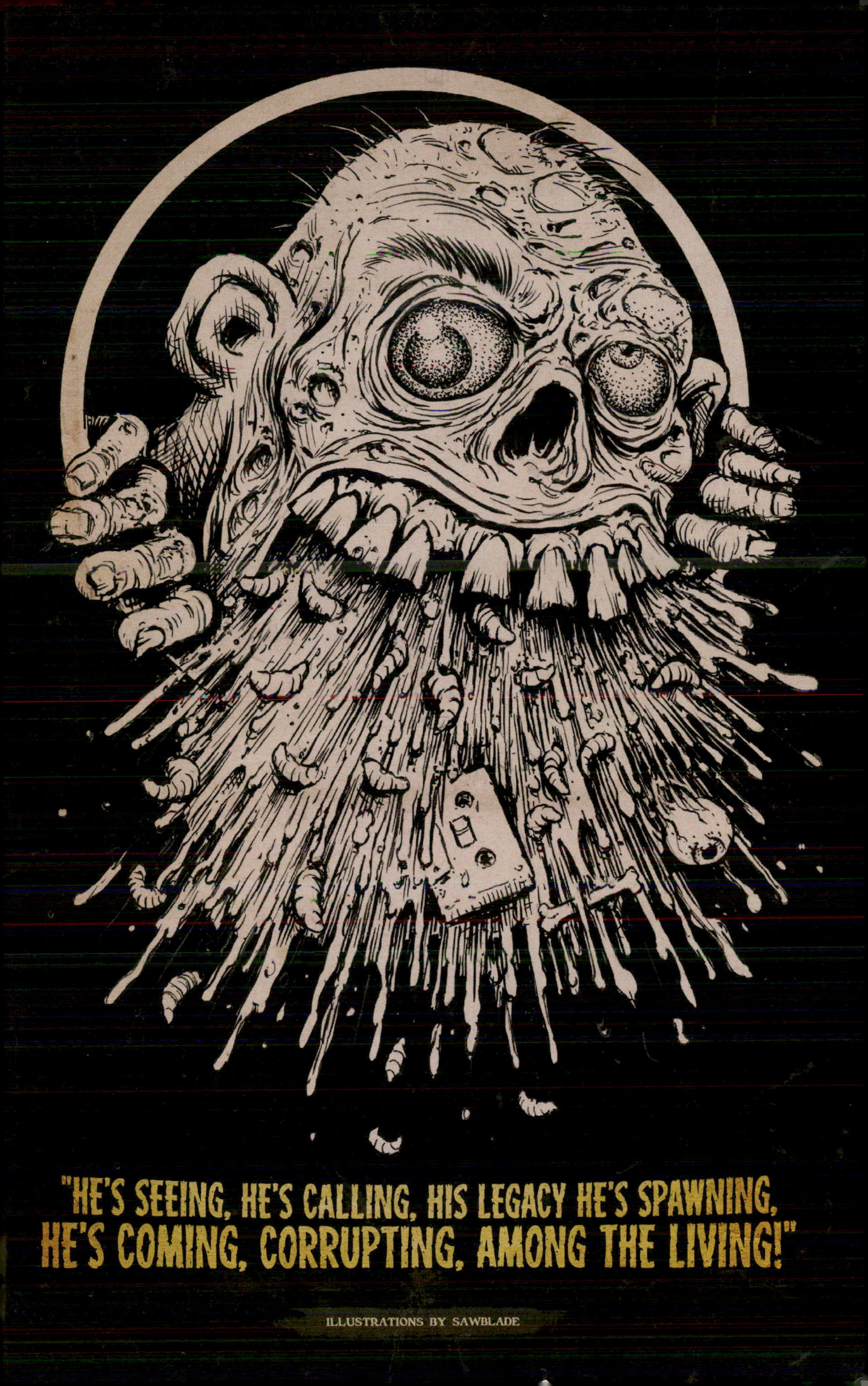

"HE'S SEEING, HE'S CALLING, HIS LEGACY HE'S SPAWNING,
HE'S COMING, CORRUPTING, AMONG THE LIVING!"

ILLUSTRATIONS BY SAWBLADE

AMONG THE LIVING

CELEBRATING 40 YEARS OF ANTHRAX

EDITED BY
IAN SATTLER

LETTERED BY
ANDWORLD DESIGN

ALBUM COVER BY
J.G. JONES

JUDGE DREDD COVER BY
CHARLIE BENANTE

VINTAGE COVER BY
ERIC POWELL

THE NEW NOT MAN BY
GREG NICOTERO

DESIGN BY
JOSH BERNSTEIN

EXECUTIVE PRODUCERS
SCOTT IAN + MIKE MONTERULO

THIS BOOK IS DEDICATED TO THE LOVING MEMORY OF MARSHA ZAZULA

ILLUSTRATION BY SAWBLADE

CONTRIBUTORS

FOREWORD
WRITER: JOEY BELLADONNA

NOT MAN'S INTRODUCTION
WRITER: JIMMY PALMIOTTI ARTIST: NELSON

AMONG THE LIVING
WRITER: BRIAN POSEHN ARTISTS: SCOTT KOBLISH + ALADDIN COLLAR

CAUGHT IN A MOSH
EDITOR: RYAN CADY WRITERS: GERARD WAY + MIKEY WAY
ARTISTS: DARICK ROBERTSON + PHILLIP SEVY + ALADDIN COLLAR

I AM THE LAW
WRITER: SCOTT IAN ARTISTS: CHRIS WESTON + ALADDIN COLLAR

EFILNIKUFESIN (N.F.L.)
WRITERS: RICK REMENDER + JOE TROHMAN ARTISTS: ROLAND BOSCHI + DAN BROWN

A SKELETON IN THE CLOSET
WRITER: COREY TAYLOR ARTIST: MAAN HOUSE

INDIANS
WRITER: GRANT MORRISON ARTISTS: FREDDIE WILLIAMS II + ANDREW DALHOUSE

ONE WORLD
WRITER: FRANK BELLO ARTISTS: ANDY BELANGER + TATTO CABALLERO

A.D.I./HORROR OF IT ALL
WRITER: BRIAN AZZARELLO ARTIST: DAVE JOHNSON

IMITATION OF LIFE
WRITER: ROB ZOMBIE ARTISTS: ERIK RODRIGUEZ + STEVE CHANKS

COVER AND PRINT GALLERY
ARTISTS: J.G. JONES + ERIC POWELL + GREG NICOTERO
CHARLIE BENANTE + BRIAN EWING + JOSH BERNSTEIN

SPECIAL THANKS

CHARLIE BENANTE + SCOTT IAN + FRANK BELLO + JOEY BELLADONNA
STEPHEN KING, MISSI CALLAZZO, JON DONAIS, REBELLION U.K., ESP GUITARS
GLOBAL MERCHANDISING SERVICES, NECA, METROPRO, UNIVERSAL RECORDS, MEGAFORCE RECORDS
MONSTER ENERGY & TIM DRALLE, HEIDI ROBINSON-FITZGERALD, DON BRAUTIGAM, RYAN CADY

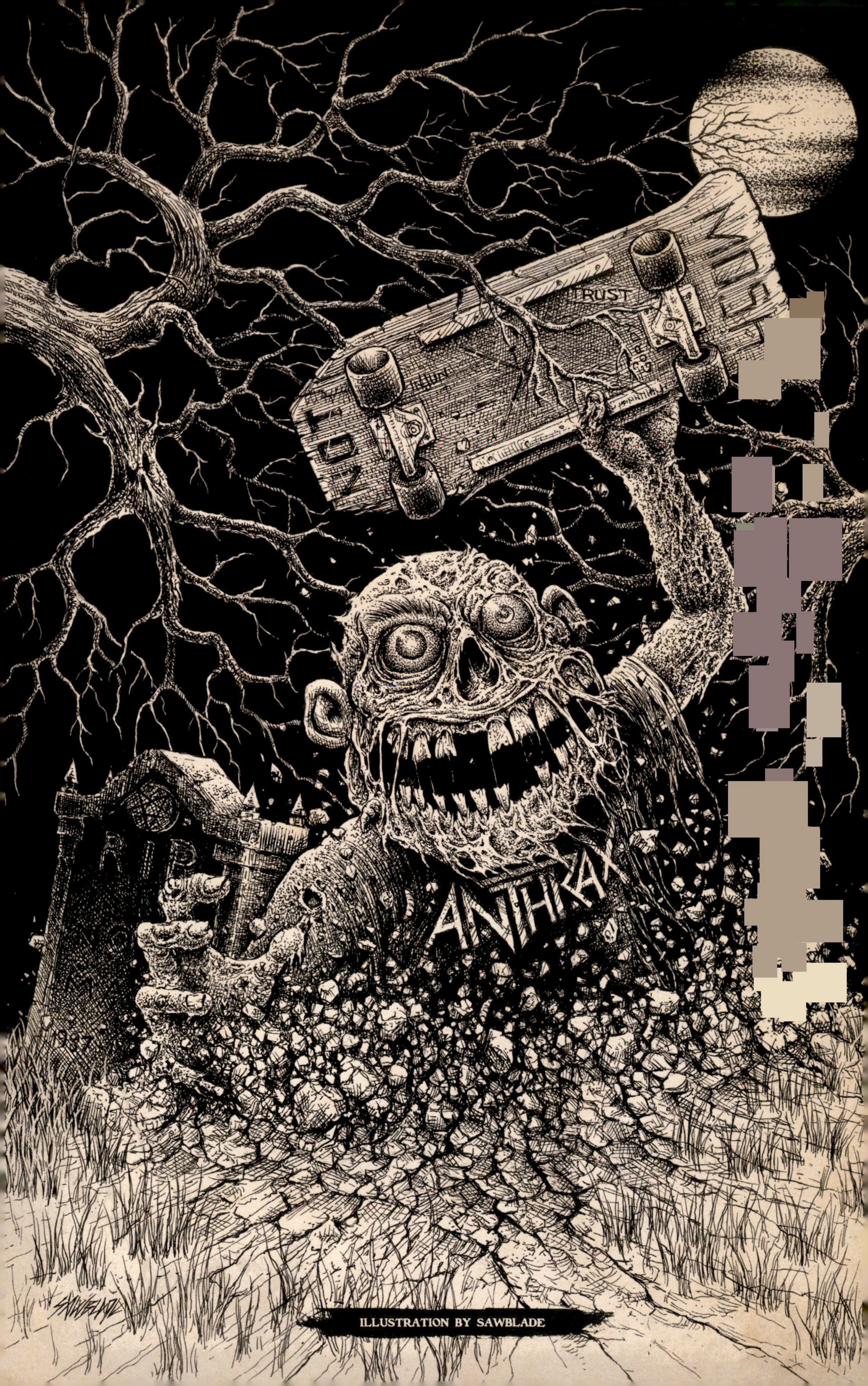
RUST
ANTHRAX

ILLUSTRATION BY SAWBLADE

FOREWORD

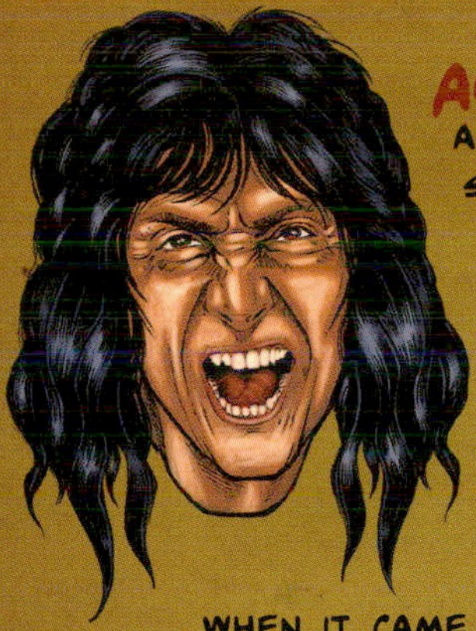

AMONG THE LIVING WAS MY SECOND ALBUM WITH ANTHRAX. MUSICALLY, IT WAS AN EVOLUTION FROM *SPREADING THE DISEASE,* AND RECORDING IT WAS LIKE GETTING INTO A MILITARY FIGHTER JET...WE ALL STRAPPED OURSELVES IN FOR THE FASTER SONGS AND THE FASTER LYRICS THAT TOOK US INTO A HEAVIER, THRASH WORLD. IT FELT LIKE WE WERE A BRAND NEW BAND, WE HAD A NEW VISION, AND THAT ALBUM SET A TONE FOR US AS A GROUP. *AMONG THE LIVING* WAS OUR FIRST GOLD ALBUM, AND WAS THE ALBUM THAT TOOK US TO ANOTHER LEVEL.

WHEN IT CAME TO OUR MUSIC, WE WERE SERIOUS, MORE SERIOUS THAN ANYONE COULD IMAGINE. BUT, AT THE SAME TIME, I THINK THAT WHAT SEPARATED US FROM OTHER BANDS - AND IN A GOOD WAY - WAS THAT PEOPLE SAW US AS A FUN BAND. WE WORE THE SHORTS, WE WERE VERY DIFFERENT FROM EACH OTHER, IT WAS OBVIOUS THAT WE WERE ALL HAVING A GOOD TIME, SO PEOPLE STARTED TO SEE US AS CHARACTERS, EVEN *MAD MAGAZINE'S* MORT DRUCKER DREW A CARICATURE OF US FOR OUR *STATE OF EUPHORIA* ALBUM.

SO, NOW 34 YEARS LATER, TO SEE *AMONG THE LIVING* CELEBRATED AS A GRAPHIC NOVEL, PUT TOGETHER BY SOME OF THE MOST TALENTED WRITERS AND ARTISTS IN THE WORLDS OF MUSIC AND COMIC BOOKS, IS AS MIND-BLOWING AS IT IS THE PERFECT LINK BETWEEN THE WORLDS OF ANTHRAX'S MUSIC AND COMIC BOOKS. THESE ARTISTS PUT THEIR OWN SPIN ON THE ALBUM'S NINE SONGS, WRITING OR ILLUSTRATING *WHAT THE SONG SAID TO THEM.* AND WHAT AN AWESOME GANG: ROB ZOMBIE, COREY TAYLOR, *THE WALKING DEAD'S* GREG NICOTERO, JOE TROHMAN, BRIAN AZZARELLO, DAVE JOHNSON, GRANT MORRISON, FREDDIE WILLIAMS II, RICK REMENDER, BRIAN POSEHN, GERARD AND MIKEY WAY, JIMMY PALMIOTTI, CHRIS WESTON, MAAN HOUSE, JG JONES, ROLAND BOSCHI, NELSON, ERIC POWELL, SCOTT KOBLISH, ERIK RODRIGUEZ, DARICK ROBERTSON, STEVE CHANKS, ANDY BELANGER, TATTO CABALLERO, DIEGO RODRIGUEZ, ALADDIN COLLAR, DAN BROWN, ANDREW DALHOUSE AND ANTHRAX'S OWN FRANK BELLO AND SCOTT IAN, WHO EACH WROTE A STORYLINE FOR TWO OF THE SONGS, AND CHARLIE BENANTE WHO DID AN ORIGINAL ILLUSTRATION FOR THE BOOK. AND IF THAT'S NOT ENOUGH, OUR MASCOT, THE NOT MAN, NEWLY DESIGNED BY GREG NICOTERO, NARRATED THE WHOLE SHEBANG.

I KNOW I SPEAK FOR THE ENTIRE BAND WHEN I OFFER MY SINCERE THANKS TO ALL OF THE INCREDIBLE PEOPLE WHO MADE THIS A REALITY, THOSE NAMED ABOVE, AS WELL AS OUR GOOD FRIEND JOSH BERNSTEIN AND THE TEAM AT Z2 COMICS, OUR MANAGER MIKE MONTERULO FOR HELPING PUT THIS TOGETHER, AND A BIG SHOUT-OUT TO JON DONIAS. MOST OF ALL, HERE'S TO EACH AND EVERY ONE OF YOU, OUR FANS...WITHOUT YOU, NEITHER *AMONG THE LIVING* NOR THE LAST 40 YEARS WOULD HAVE HAPPENED THE WAY THEY HAVE.

JOEY BELLADONNA, 2021

ILLUSTRATION BY STEVE CHANKS

FOLLOW ME OR DIE!

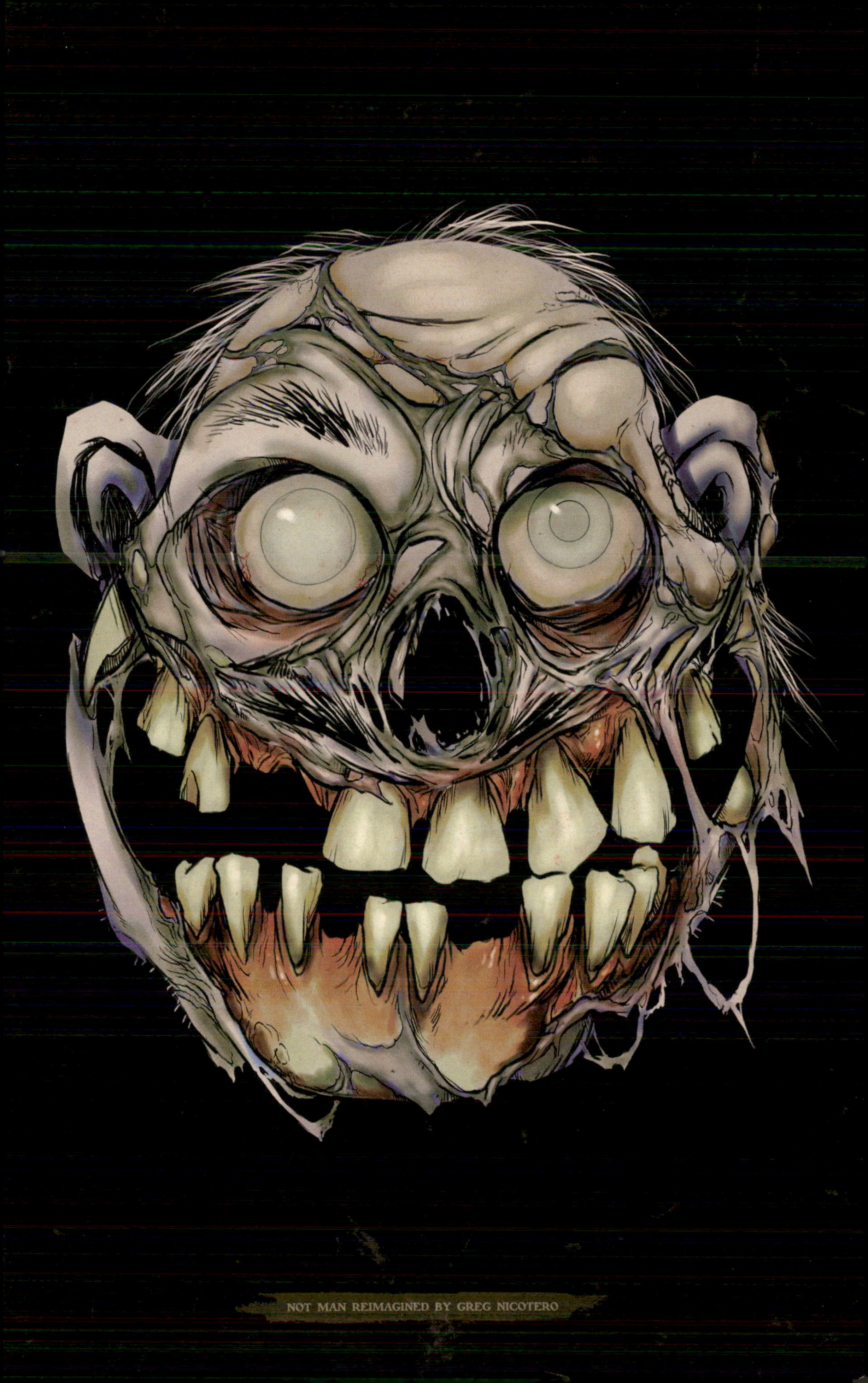

NOT MAN REIMAGINED BY GREG NICOTERO

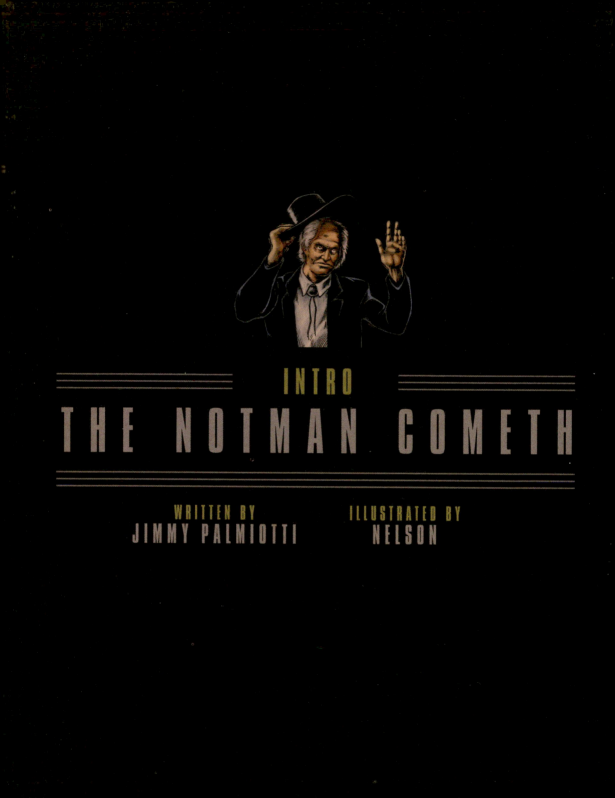

INTRO

THE NOTMAN COMETH

WRITTEN BY
JIMMY PALMIOTTI

ILLUSTRATED BY
NELSON

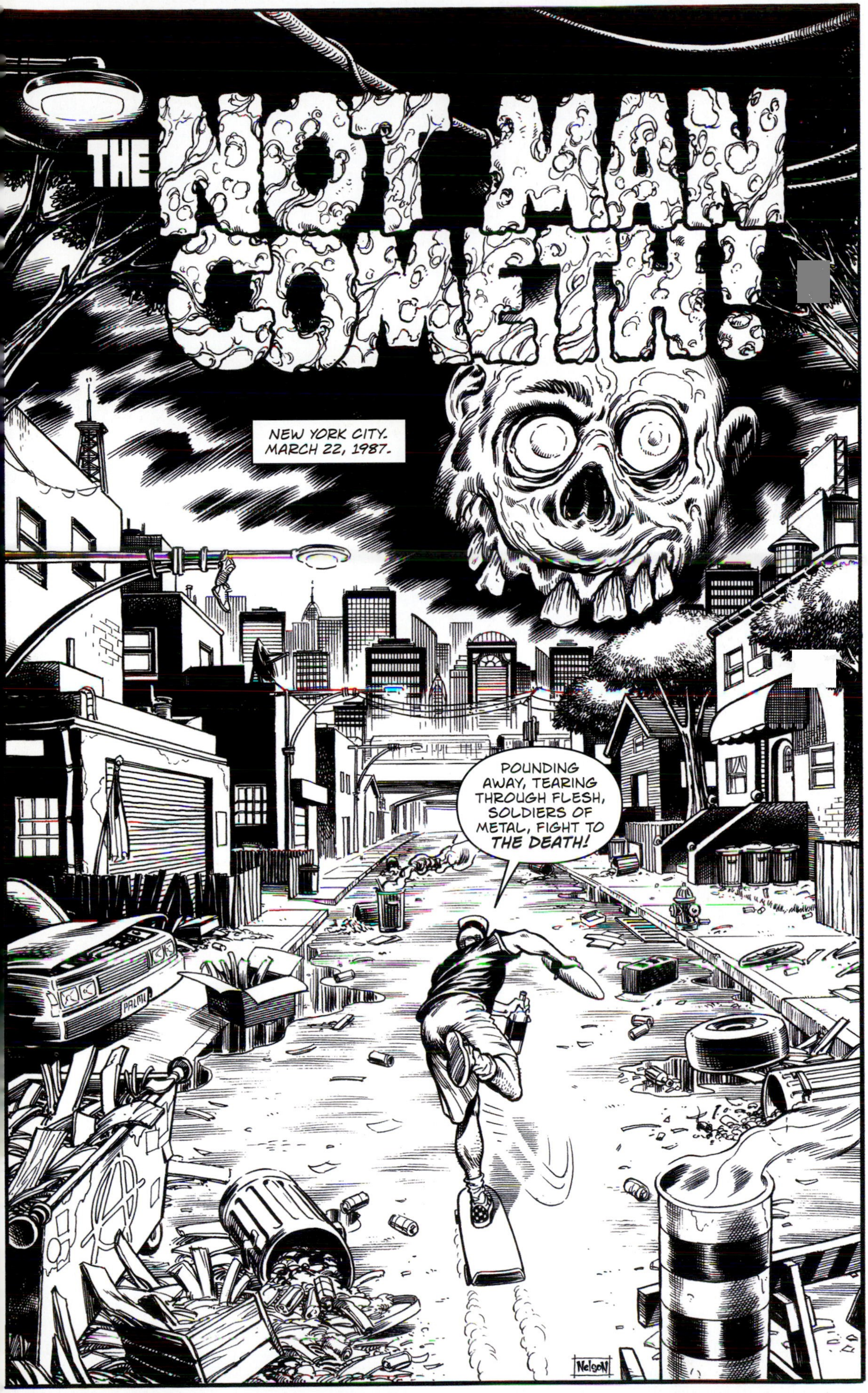
THE NOT MAN COMETH!
NEW YORK CITY. MARCH 22, 1987.
POUNDING AWAY, TEARING THROUGH FLESH, SOLDIERS OF METAL, FIGHT TO THE DEATH!
NELSON

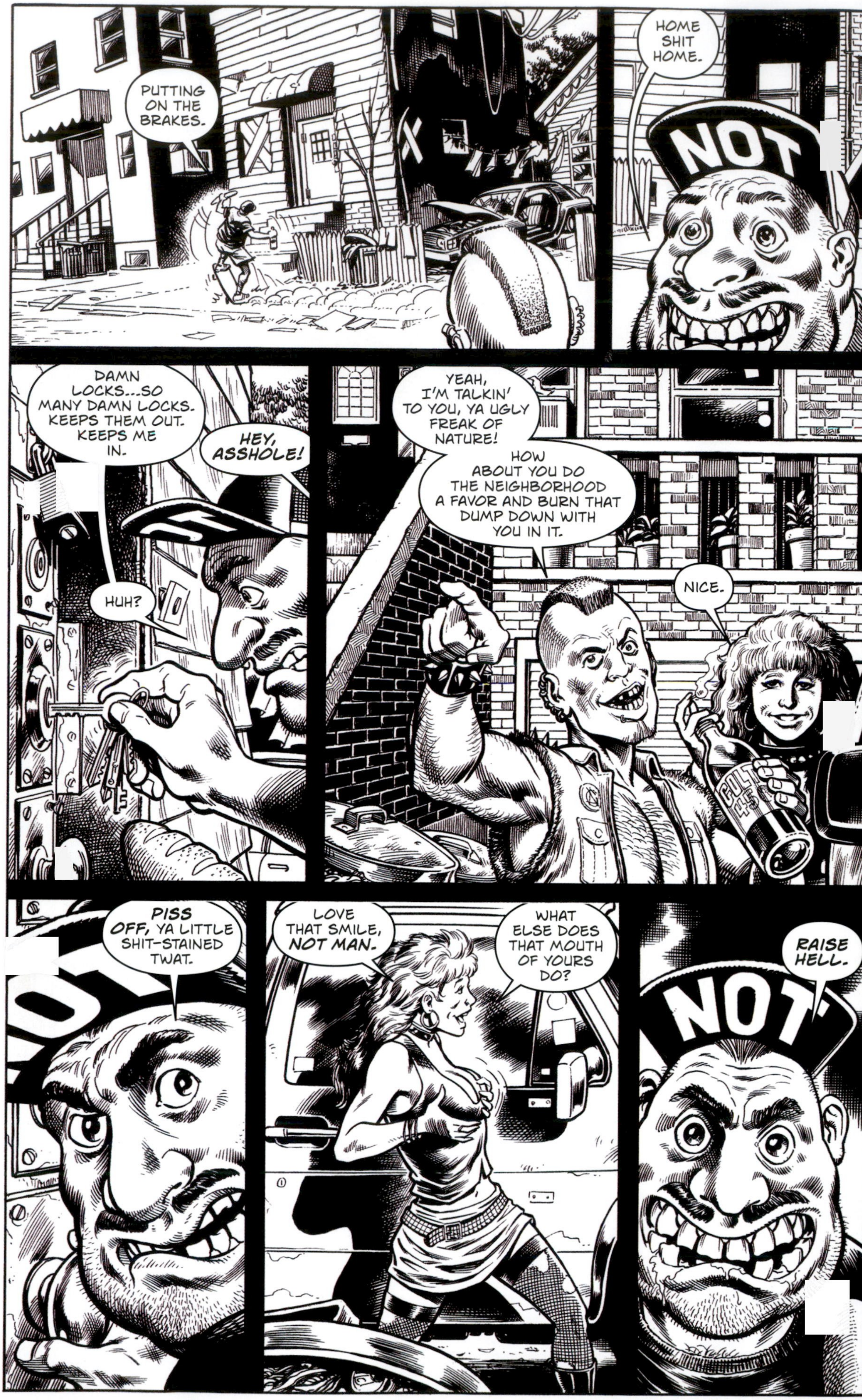
PUTTING ON THE BRAKES.
HOME SHIT HOME.
NOT
DAMN LOCKS...SO MANY DAMN LOCKS. KEEPS THEM OUT. KEEPS ME IN.
HEY, ASSHOLE!
HUH?
YEAH, I'M TALKIN' TO YOU, YA UGLY FREAK OF NATURE!
HOW ABOUT YOU DO THE NEIGHBORHOOD A FAVOR AND BURN THAT DUMP DOWN WITH YOU IN IT.
NICE.
PISS OFF, YA LITTLE SHIT-STAINED TWAT.
LOVE THAT SMILE, NOT MAN.
WHAT ELSE DOES THAT MOUTH OF YOURS DO?
RAISE HELL.
NOT

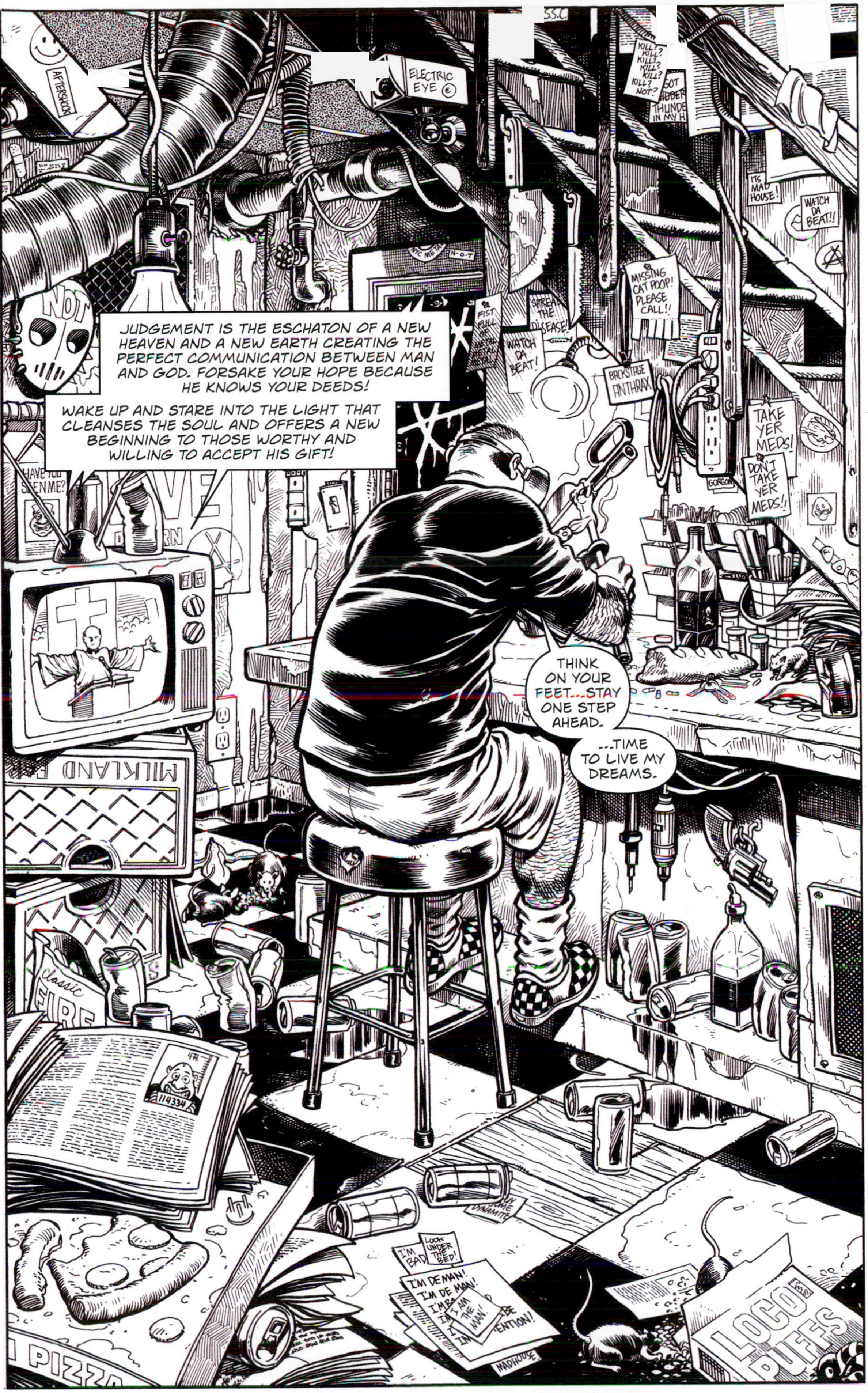
JUDGEMENT IS THE ESCHATON OF A NEW HEAVEN AND A NEW EARTH CREATING THE PERFECT COMMUNICATION BETWEEN MAN AND GOD. FORSAKE YOUR HOPE BECAUSE HE KNOWS YOUR DEEDS!
WAKE UP AND STARE INTO THE LIGHT THAT CLEANSES THE SOUL AND OFFERS A NEW BEGINNING TO THOSE WORTHY AND WILLING TO ACCEPT HIS GIFT!
THINK ON YOUR FEET...STAY ONE STEP AHEAD.
...TIME TO LIVE MY DREAMS.
AFTERSHOCK
ELECTRIC EYE
NOT
KILL? KILL? KILL? KILL? KILL? NOT?
ITS MAD HOUSE!
WATCH DA BEAT!!
MISSING CAT POOP! PLEASE CALL!!
WATCH DA BEAT!
BACKSTAGE FINTHRAX
TAKE YER MEDS!
DON'T TAKE YER MEDS!!
HAVE YOU SEEN ME?
MILKLAND
CLASSIC
114334
I'M BAD
LOOK UNDER THE BED!
I'M DE MAN!
I'M DE MAN!
I'M THE MAN!
MADHOUSE
LOCO PUFFS
PIZZA

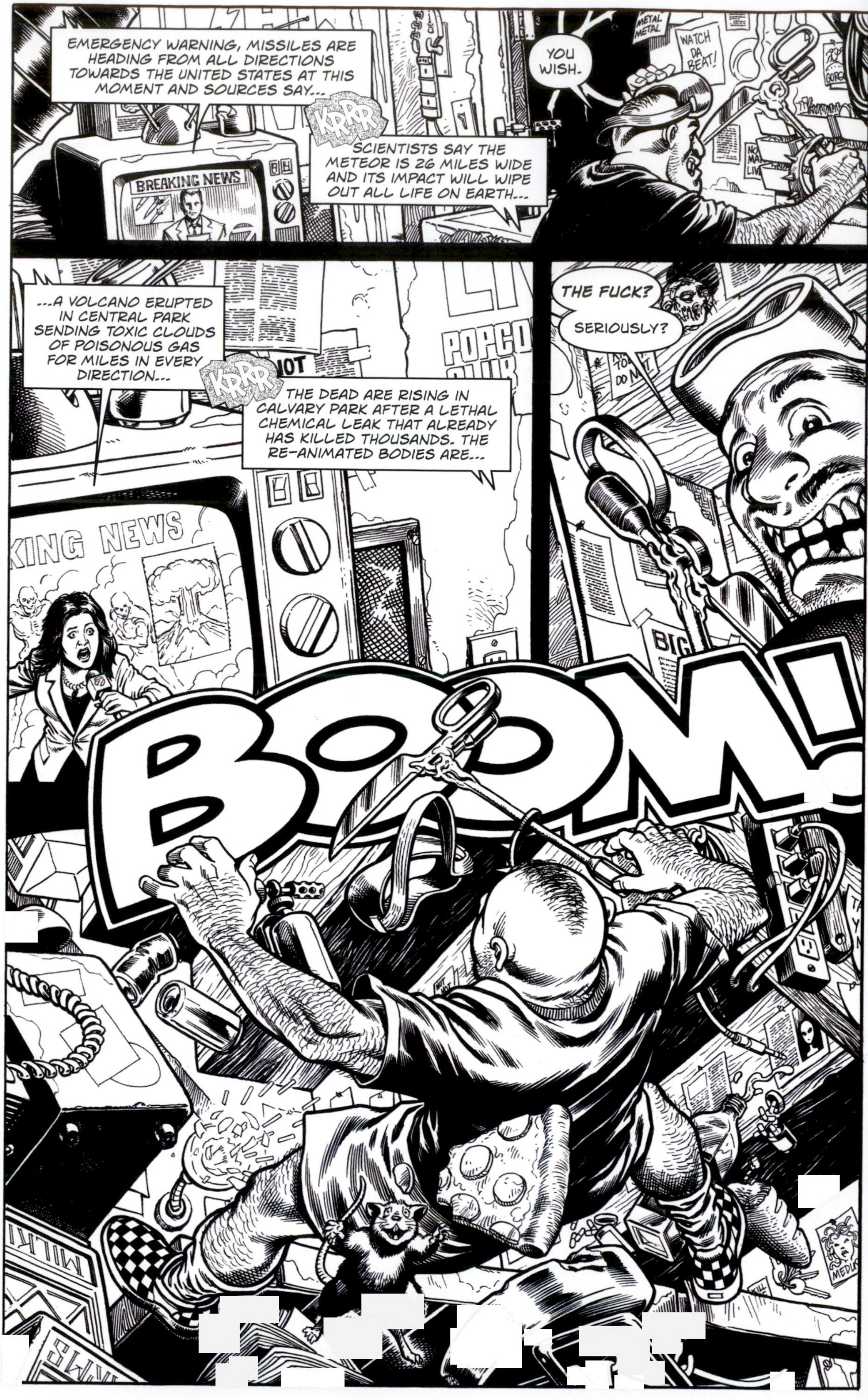
EMERGENCY WARNING, MISSILES ARE HEADING FROM ALL DIRECTIONS TOWARDS THE UNITED STATES AT THIS MOMENT AND SOURCES SAY...
KRRR
SCIENTISTS SAY THE METEOR IS 26 MILES WIDE AND ITS IMPACT WILL WIPE OUT ALL LIFE ON EARTH...
YOU WISH.
...A VOLCANO ERUPTED IN CENTRAL PARK SENDING TOXIC CLOUDS OF POISONOUS GAS FOR MILES IN EVERY DIRECTION...
KRRR
THE DEAD ARE RISING IN CALVARY PARK AFTER A LETHAL CHEMICAL LEAK THAT ALREADY HAS KILLED THOUSANDS. THE RE-ANIMATED BODIES ARE...
THE FUCK?
SERIOUSLY?
BOOM!

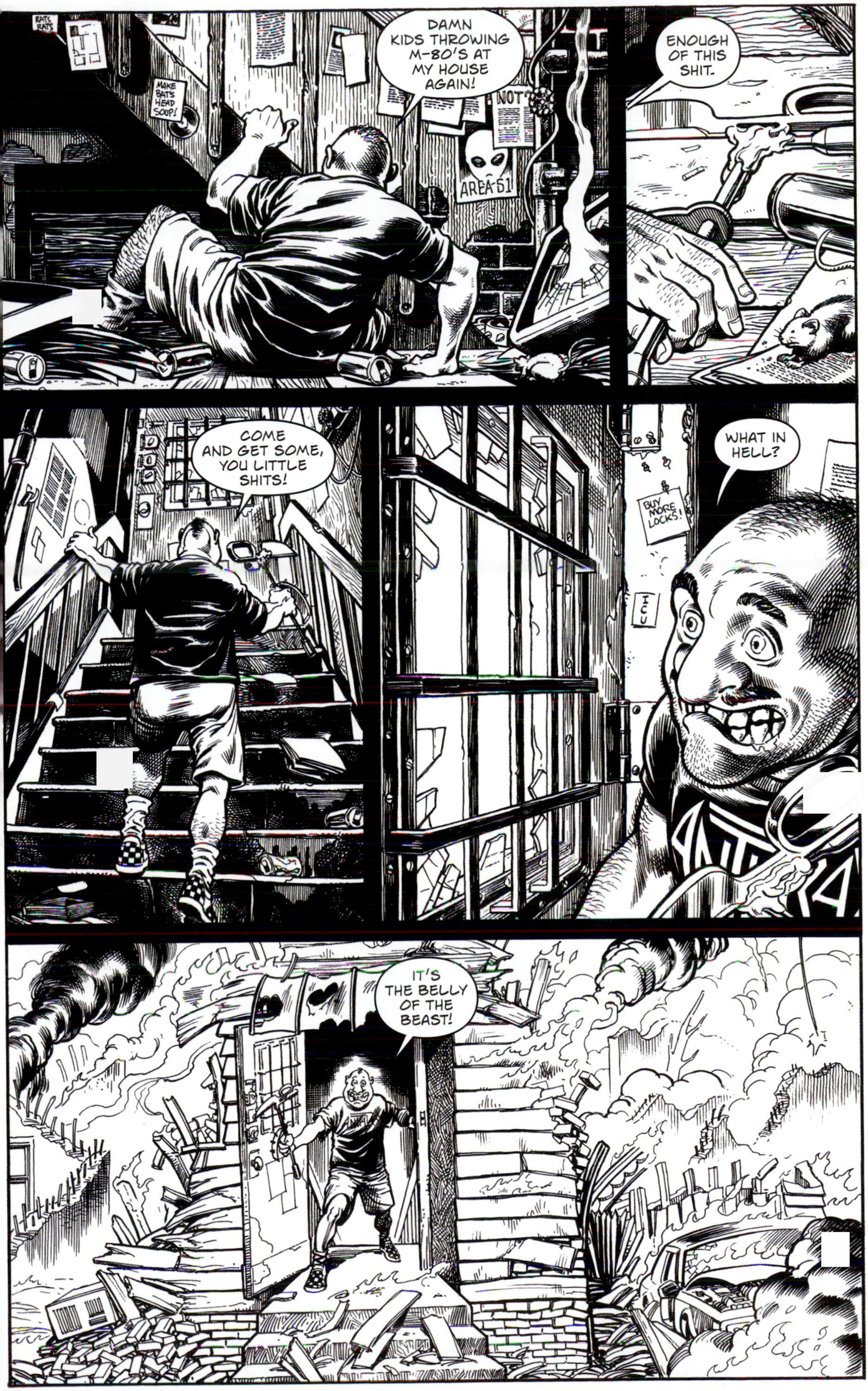

MAKE BATS HEAD SOUP!
DAMN KIDS THROWING M-80'S AT MY HOUSE AGAIN!
AREA 51
ENOUGH OF THIS SHIT.
COME AND GET SOME, YOU LITTLE SHITS!
BUY MORE LOCKS!
WHAT IN HELL?
IT'S THE BELLY OF THE BEAST!

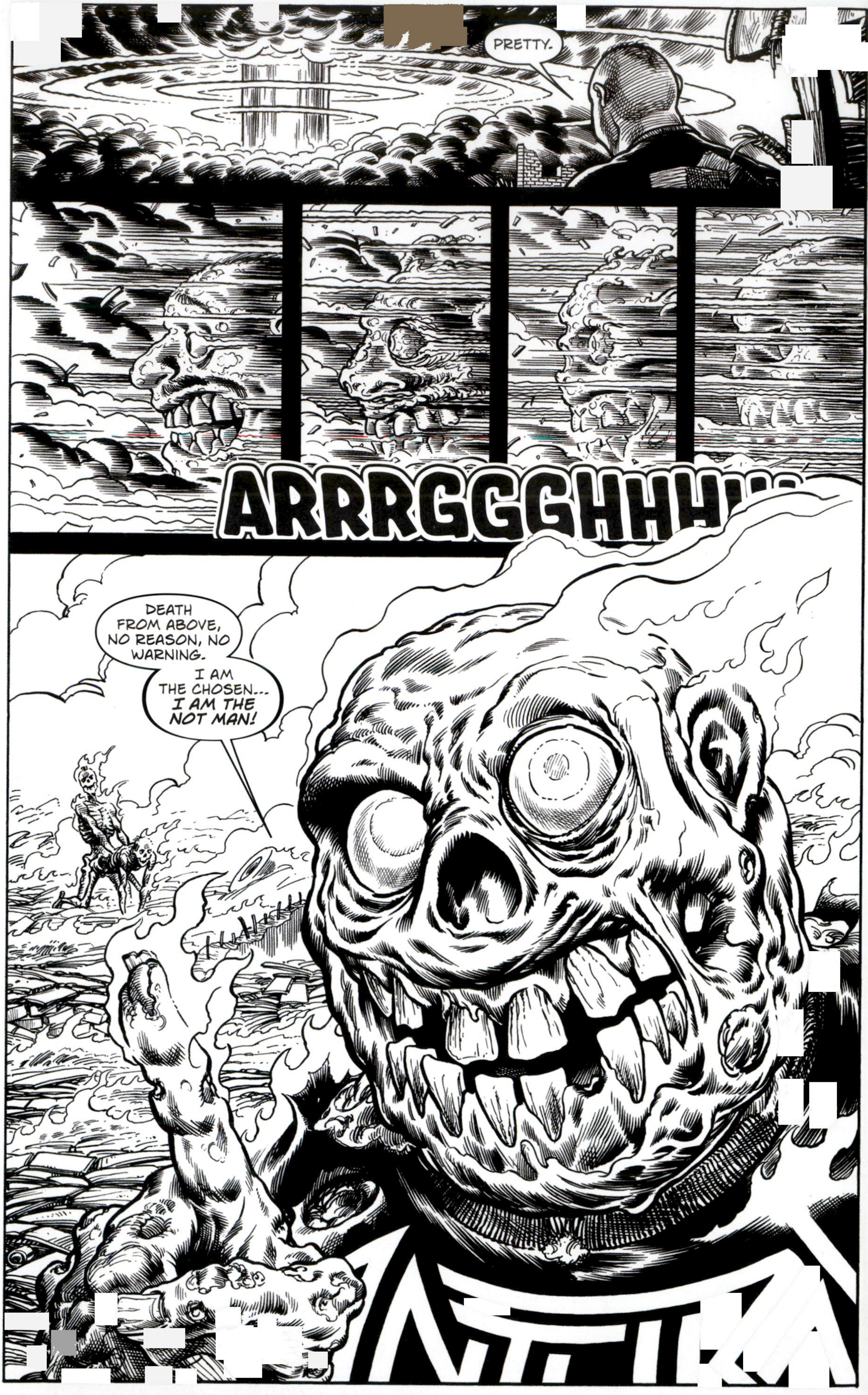
PRETTY.
ARRRGGGHHH
DEATH FROM ABOVE, NO REASON, NO WARNING.
I AM THE CHOSEN... *I AM THE NOT MAN!*

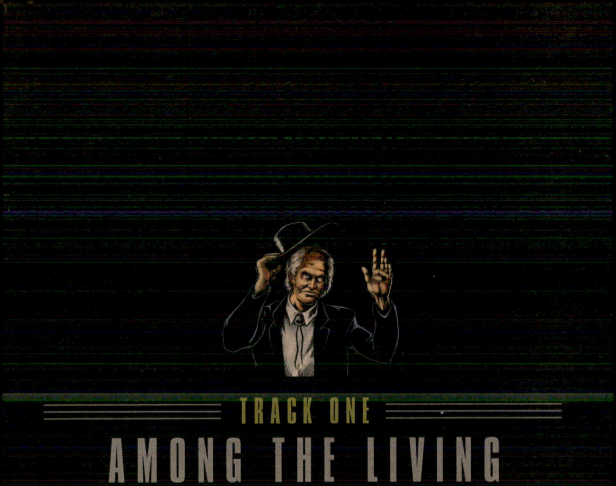

TRACK ONE
AMONG THE LIVING

WRITTEN BY
BRIAN POSEHN

ILLUSTRATED BY
SCOTT KOBLISH

COLORED BY
ALADDIN COLLAR

"IT'S TIME TO TAKE A STAND FOR
WHAT YOU ARE WILLING TO FIGHT FOR!"

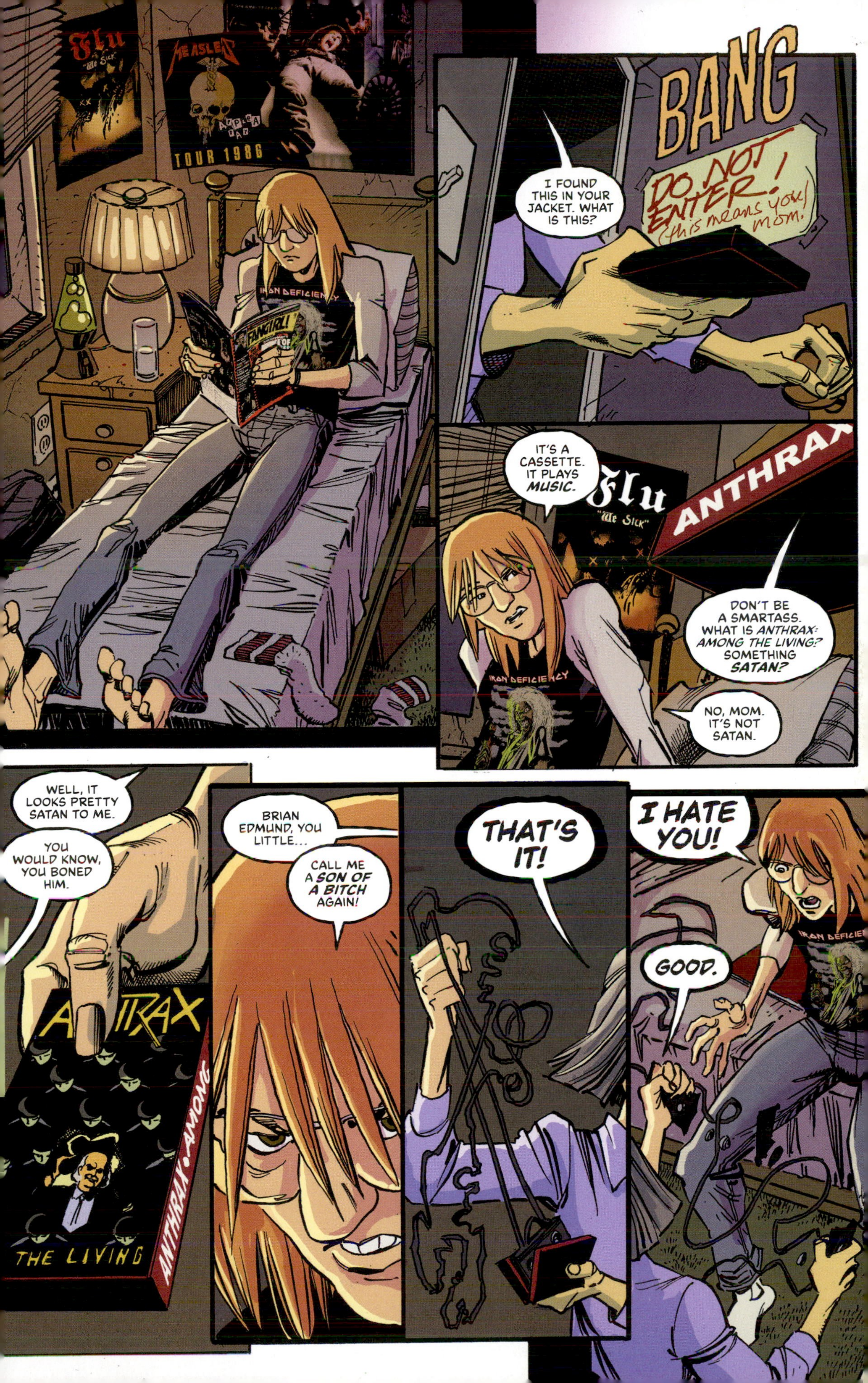

Flu
"We Sick"
MEASLES
TOUR 1986
IRON DEFICIENCY
FANGIRL!
BANG
I FOUND THIS IN YOUR JACKET. WHAT IS THIS?
DO NOT ENTER! (this means you! mom.)
IT'S A CASSETTE. IT PLAYS *MUSIC*.
ANTHRAX
DON'T BE A SMARTASS. WHAT IS *ANTHRAX: AMONG THE LIVING?* SOMETHING *SATAN?*
NO, MOM. IT'S NOT SATAN.
WELL, IT LOOKS PRETTY SATAN TO ME.
YOU WOULD KNOW, YOU BONED HIM.
ANTHRAX
THE LIVING
ANTHRAX • AMONG
BRIAN EDMUND, YOU LITTLE...
CALL ME A *SON OF A BITCH* AGAIN!
THAT'S IT!
I HATE YOU!
GOOD.

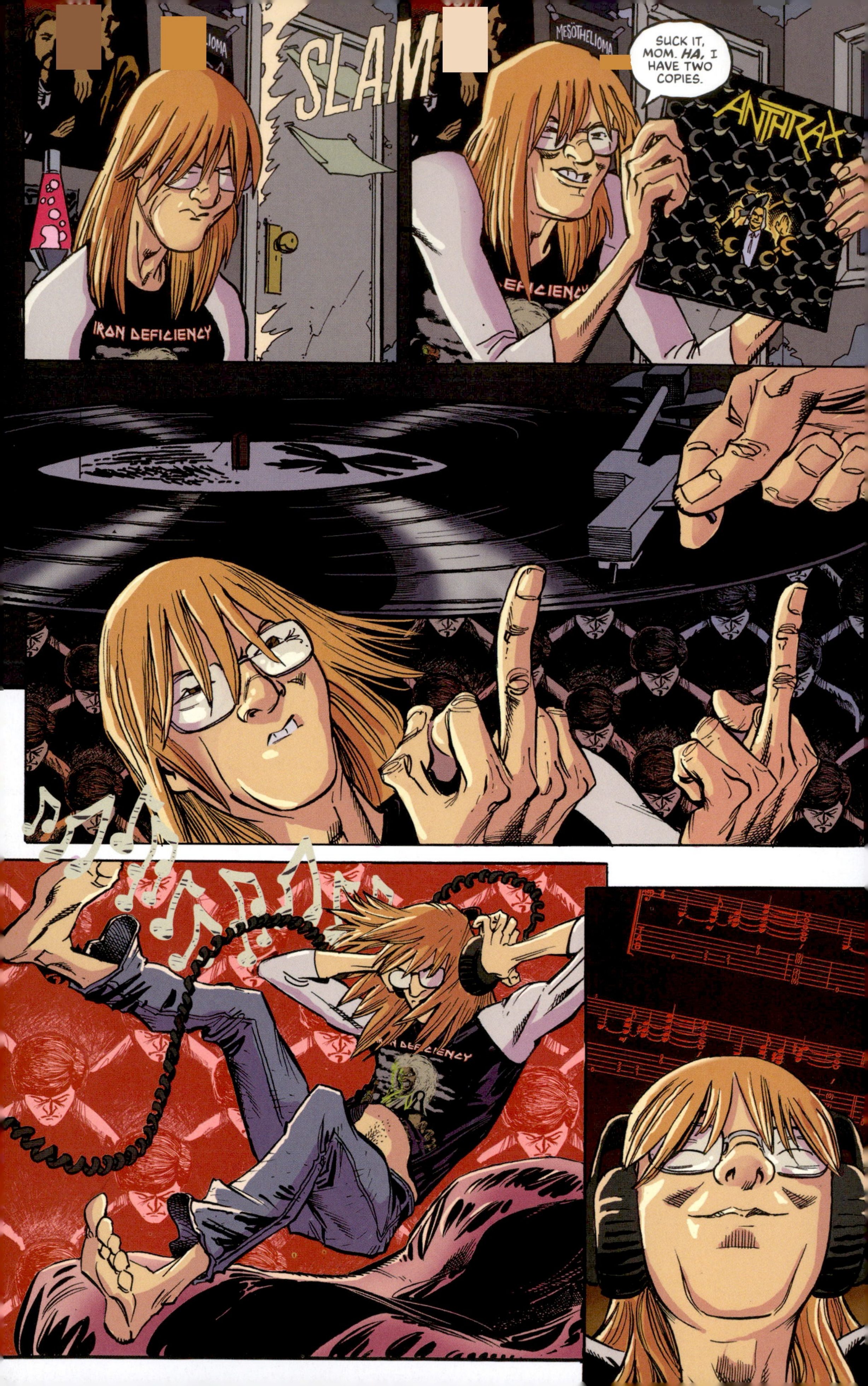
SLAM
IRON DEFICIENCY
MESÖTHELIOMA
SUCK IT, MOM. HA, I HAVE TWO COPIES.
ANTHRAX
IRON DEFICIENCY

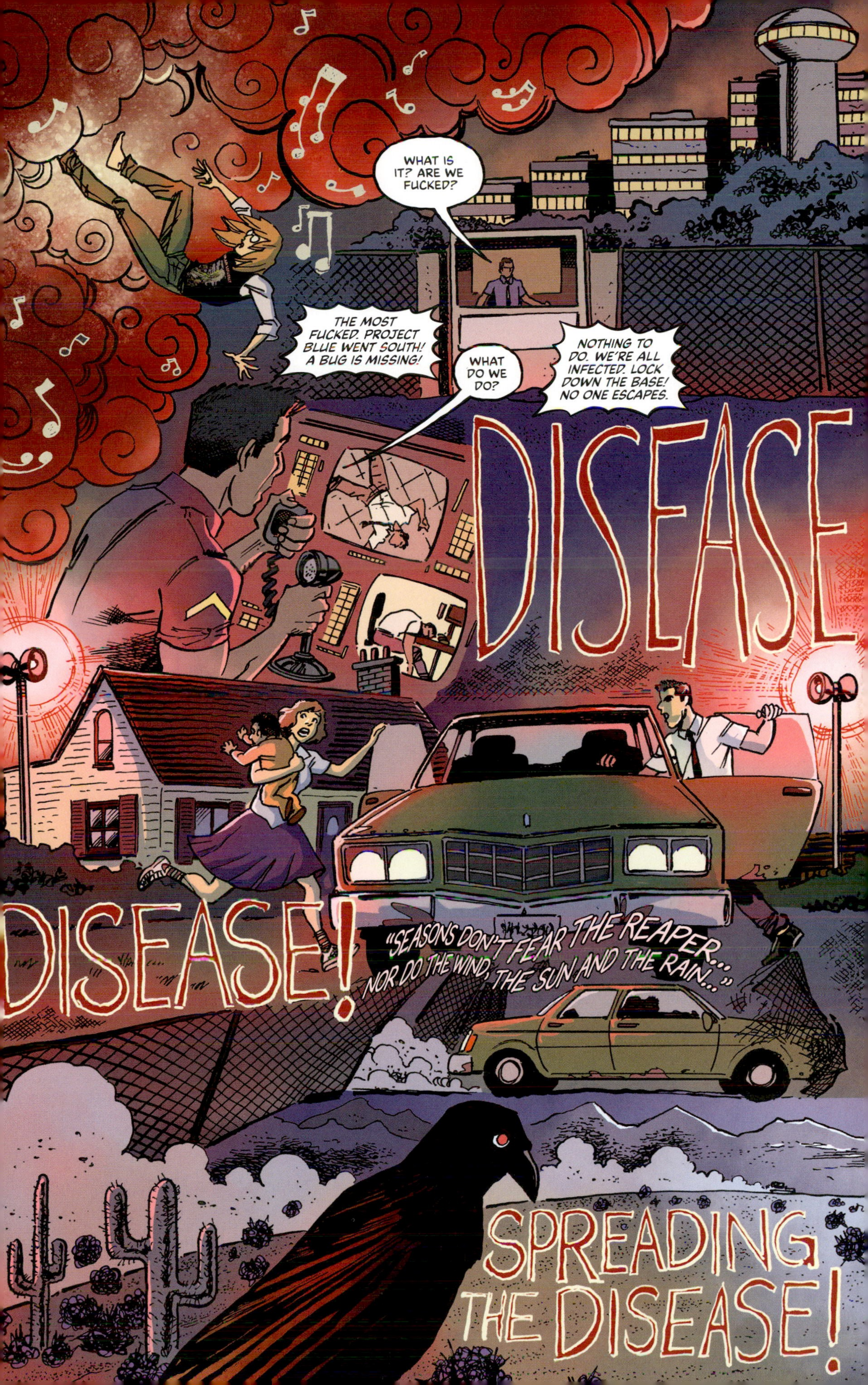
WHAT IS IT? ARE WE FUCKED?
THE MOST FUCKED. PROJECT BLUE WENT SOUTH! A BUG IS MISSING!
WHAT DO WE DO?
NOTHING TO DO. WE'RE ALL INFECTED. LOCK DOWN THE BASE! NO ONE ESCAPES.
DISEASE
DISEASE!
"SEASONS DON'T FEAR THE REAPER... NOR DO THE WIND, THE SUN AND THE RAIN..."
SPREADING THE DISEASE!

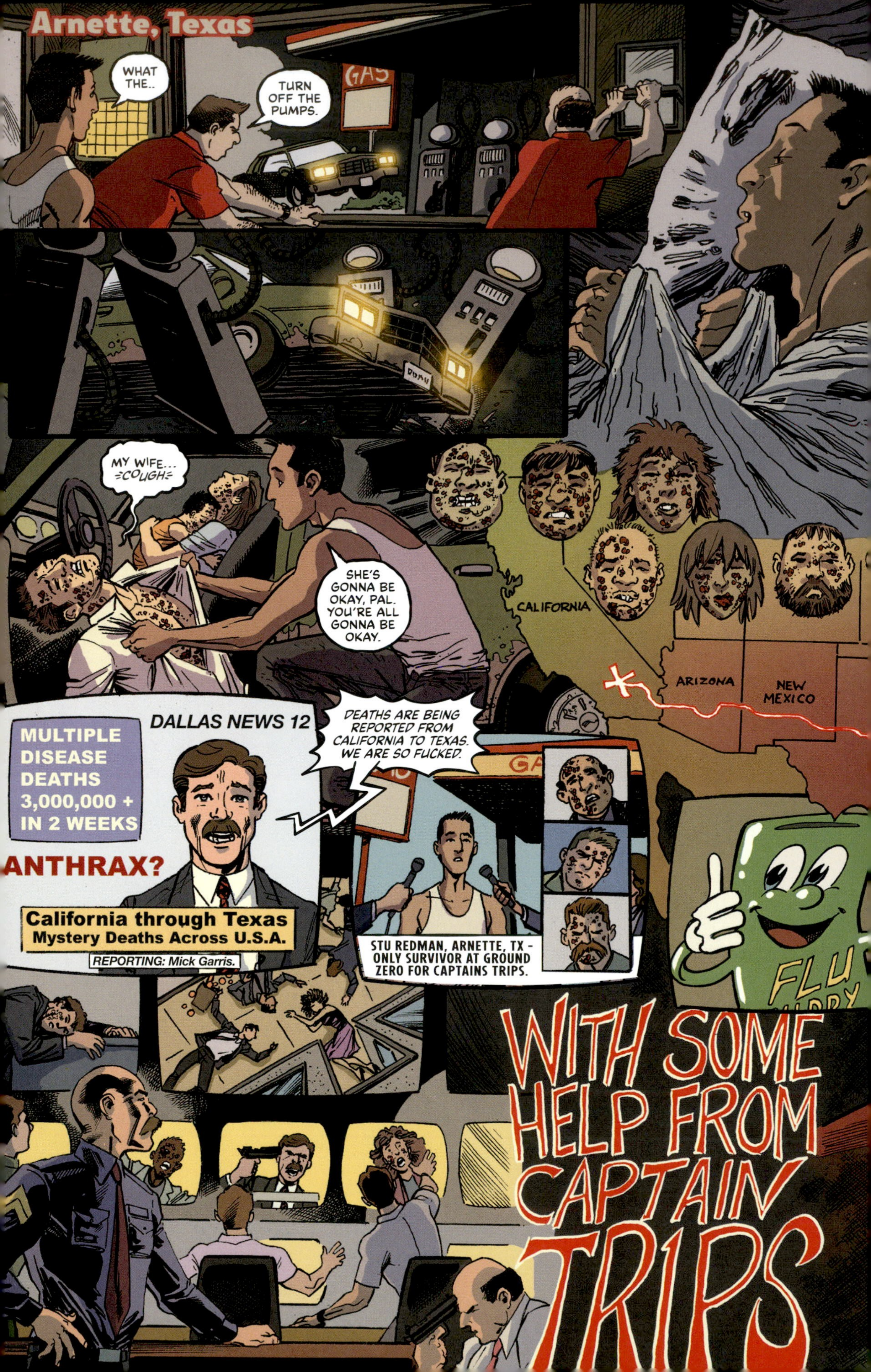
Arnette, Texas
WHAT THE..
TURN OFF THE PUMPS.
GAS
MY WIFE... =COUGH=
SHE'S GONNA BE OKAY, PAL. YOU'RE ALL GONNA BE OKAY.
CALIFORNIA
ARIZONA
NEW MEXICO
DALLAS NEWS 12
MULTIPLE DISEASE DEATHS 3,000,000 + IN 2 WEEKS
ANTHRAX?
California through Texas
Mystery Deaths Across U.S.A.
REPORTING: Mick Garris.
DEATHS ARE BEING REPORTED FROM CALIFORNIA TO TEXAS. WE ARE SO FUCKED.
STU REDMAN, ARNETTE, TX - ONLY SURVIVOR AT GROUND ZERO FOR CAPTAINS TRIPS.
FLU
WITH SOME HELP FROM CAPTAIN TRIPS

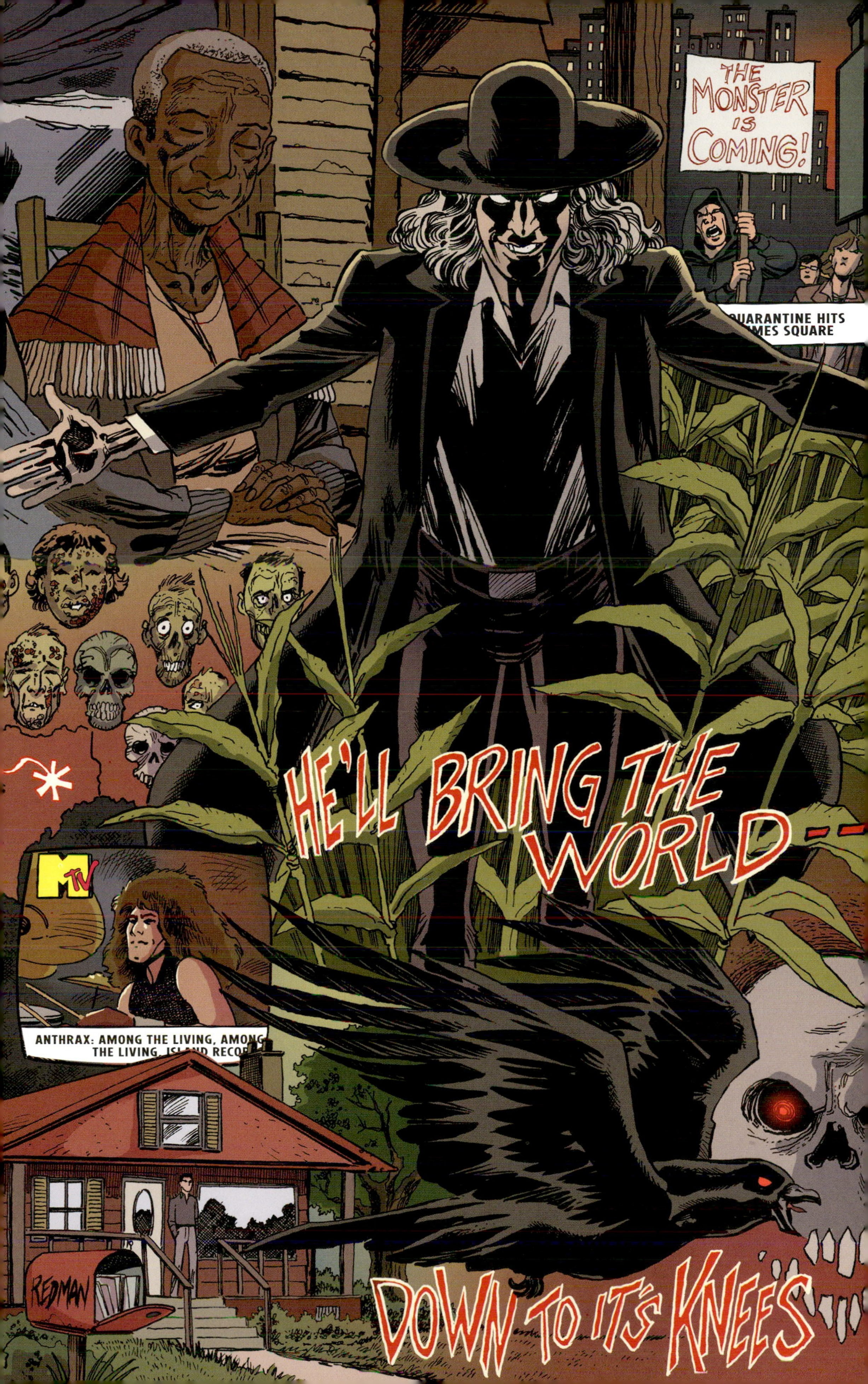
THE MONSTER IS COMING!
QUARANTINE HITS
MES SQUARE
HE'LL BRING THE WORLD--
MTV
ANTHRAX: AMONG THE LIVING, AMONG THE LIVING, ISLAND RECO
REDMAN
DOWN TO IT'S KNEES

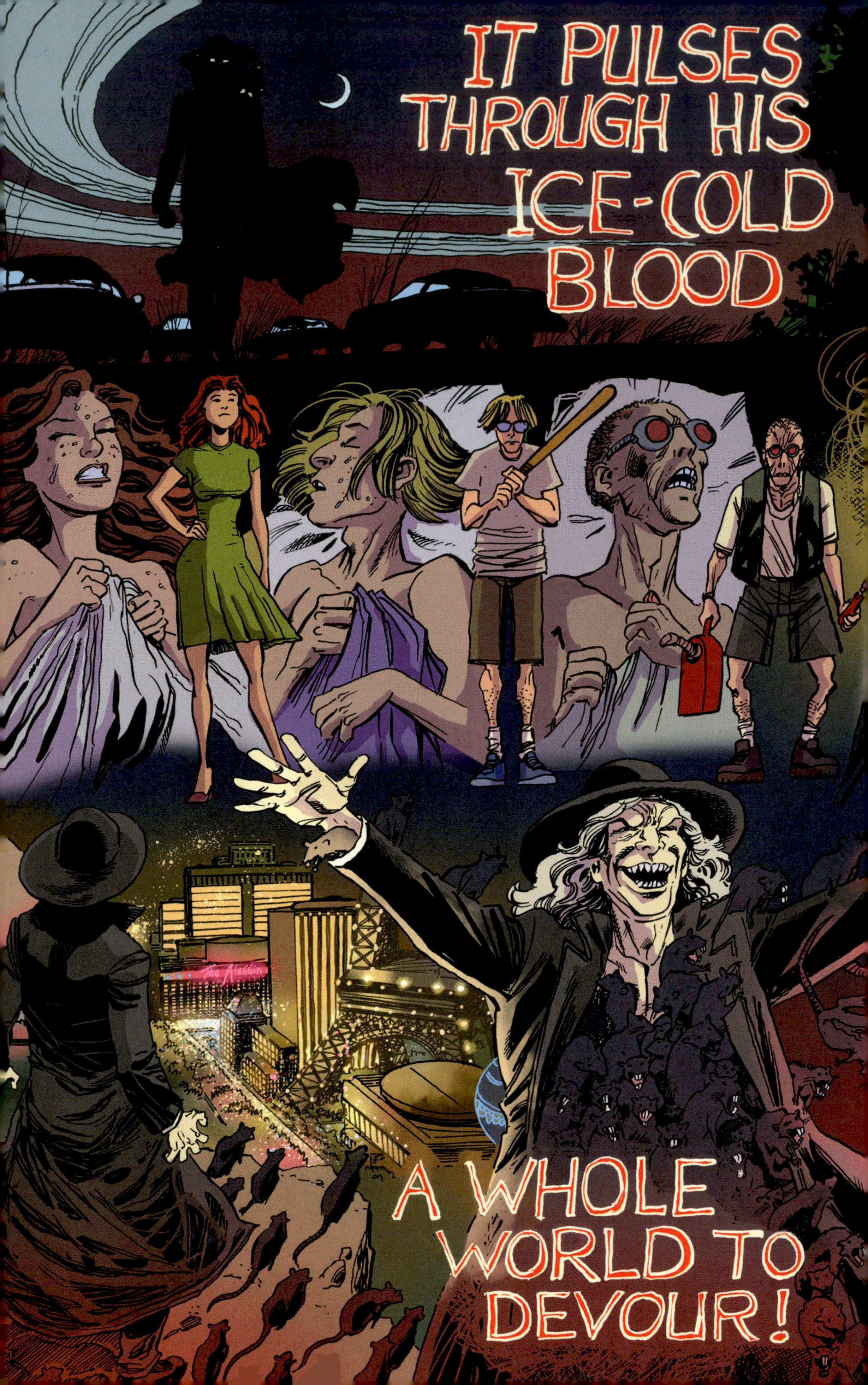
IT PULSES THROUGH HIS ICE-COLD BLOOD
A WHOLE WORLD TO DEVOUR!

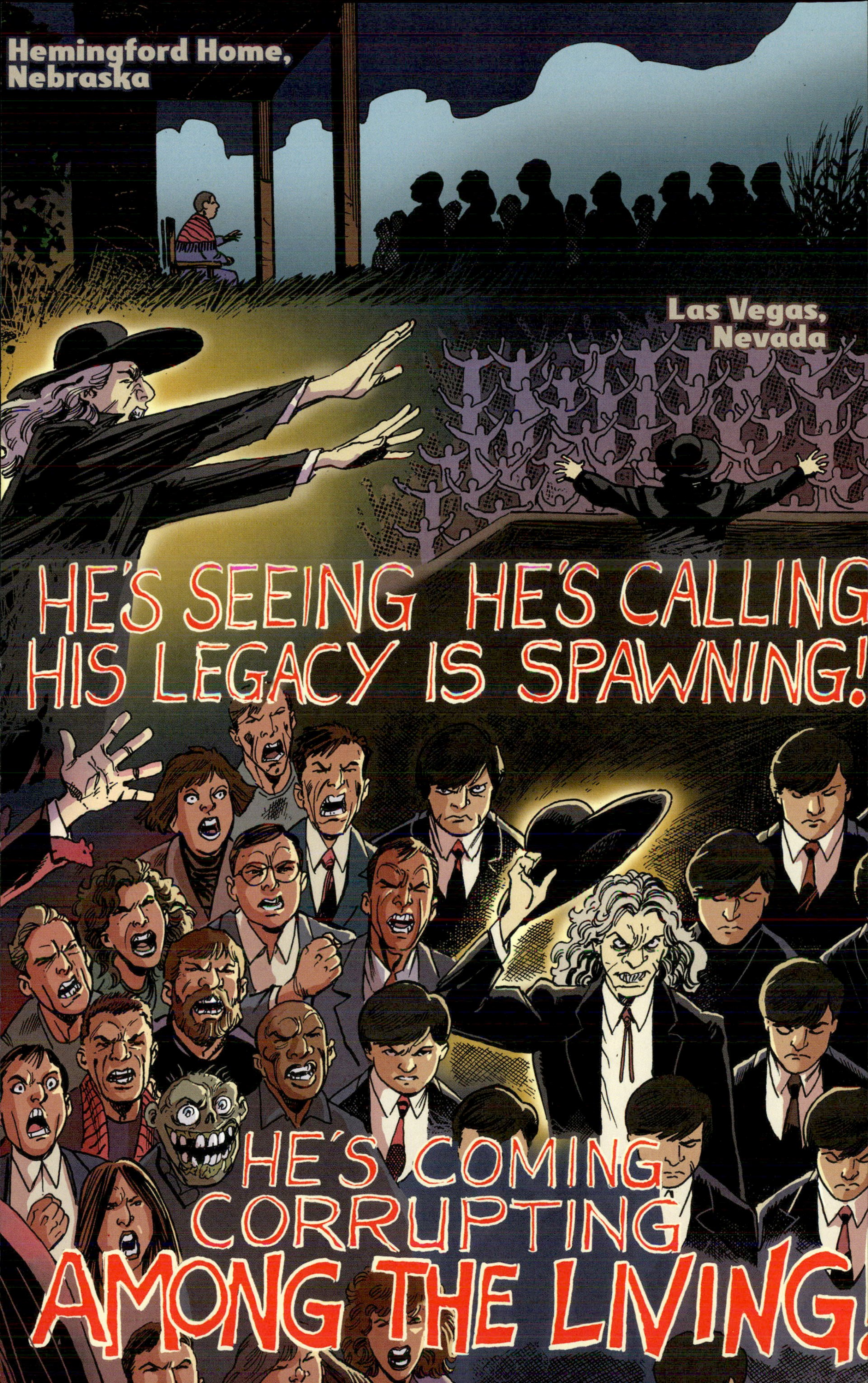
Hemingford Home, Nebraska
Las Vegas, Nevada
HE'S SEEING HE'S CALLING
HIS LEGACY IS SPAWNING!
HE'S COMING
CORRUPTING
AMONG THE LIVING!

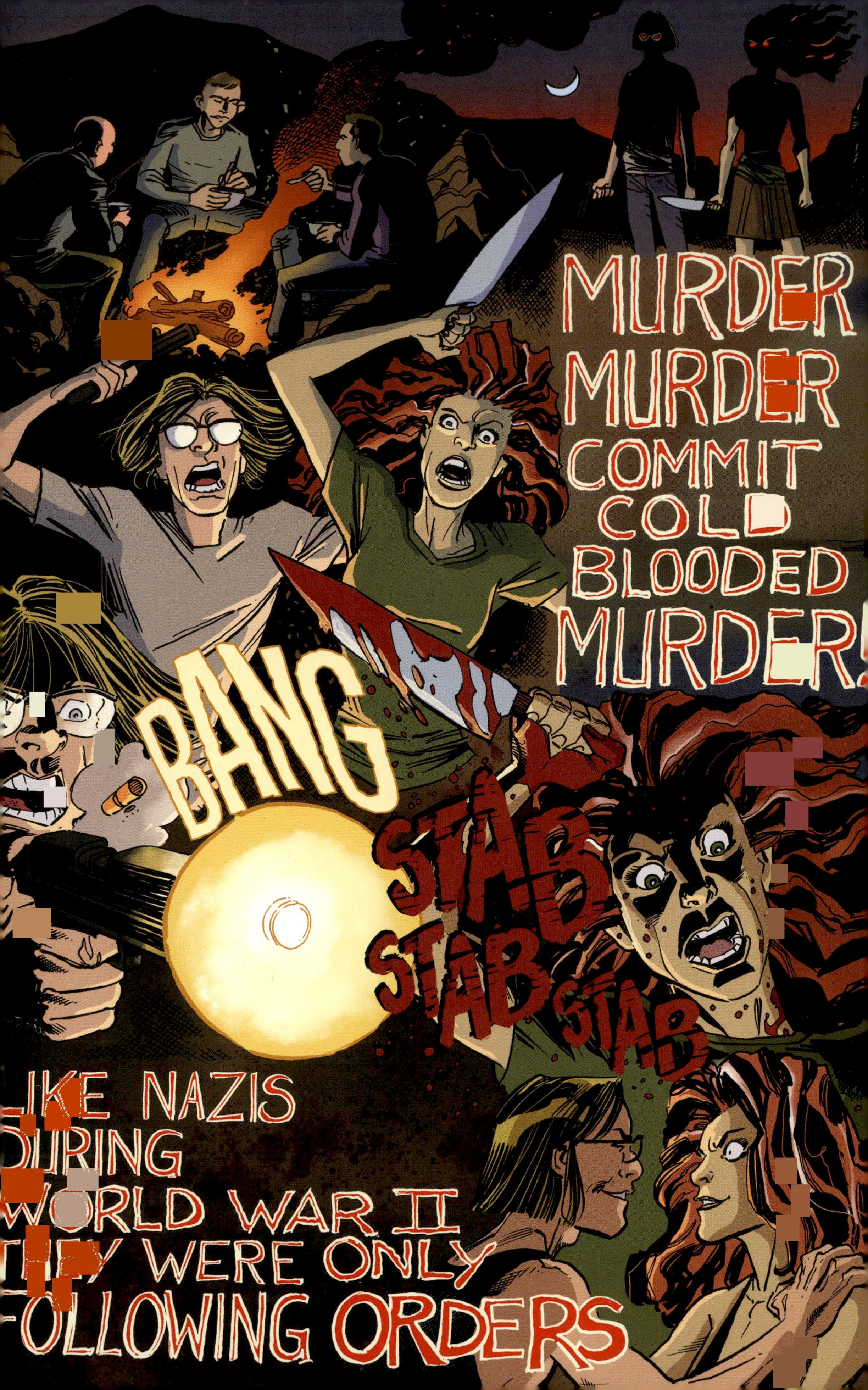
MURDER
MURDER
COMMIT
COLD
BLOODED
MURDER!
BANG
STAB
STAB
STAB
STAB
LIKE NAZIS
DURING
WORLD WAR II
THEY WERE ONLY
FOLLOWING ORDERS

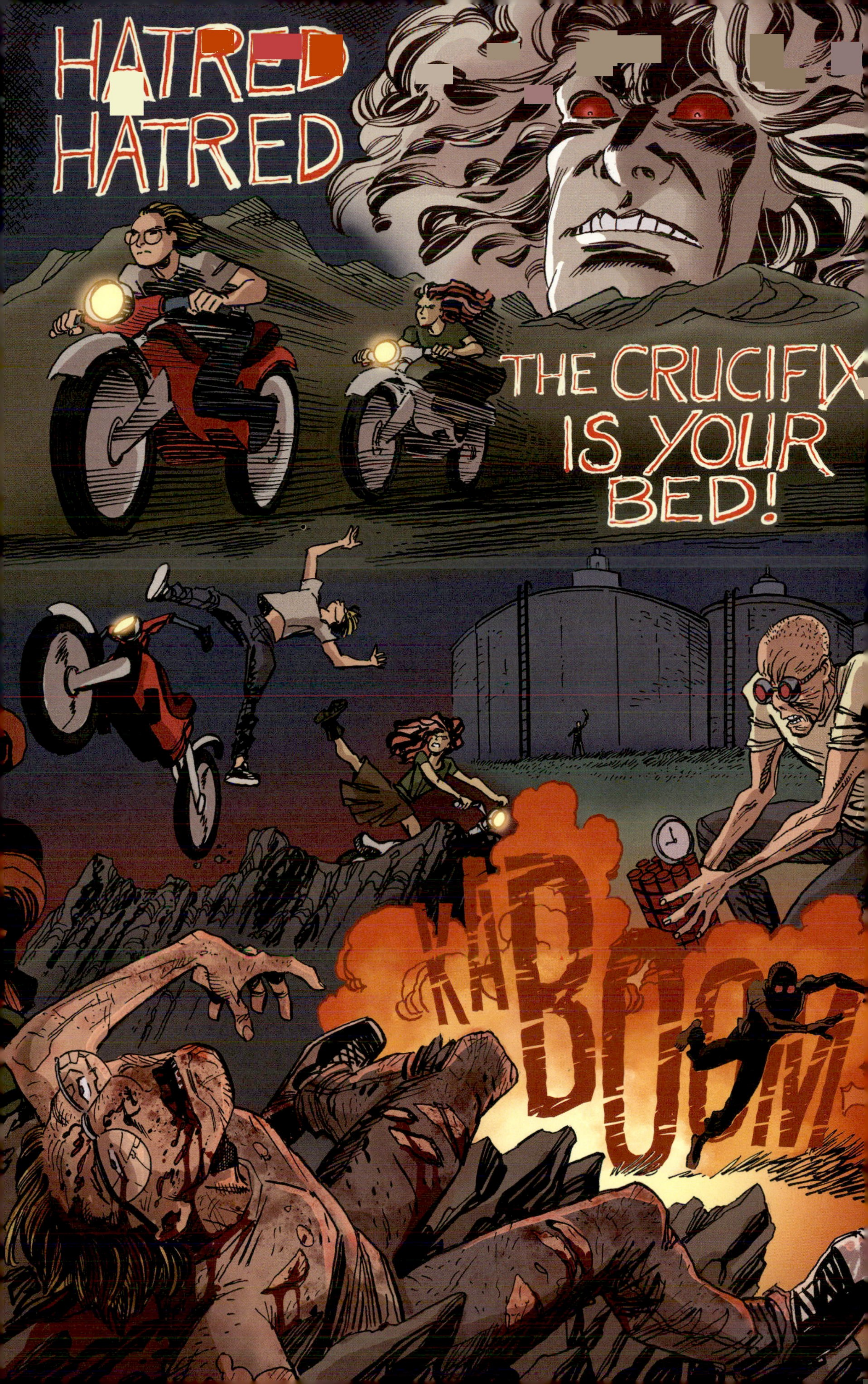
HATRED
HATRED
THE CRUCIFIX IS YOUR BED!
KHBOOM

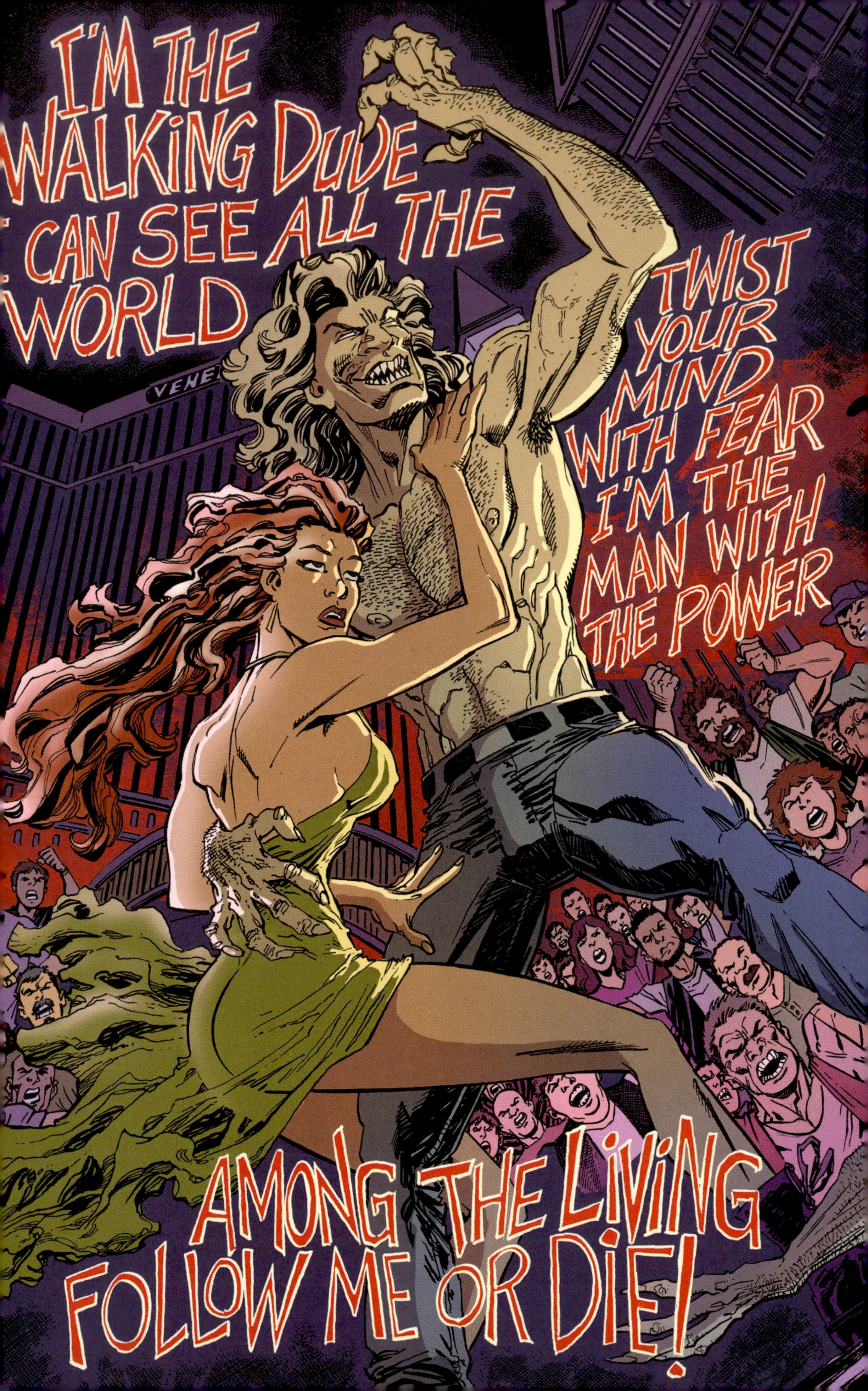
I'M THE WALKING DUDE
CAN SEE ALL THE WORLD
TWIST YOUR MIND WITH FEAR
I'M THE MAN WITH THE POWER
AMONG THE LIVING
FOLLOW ME OR DIE!

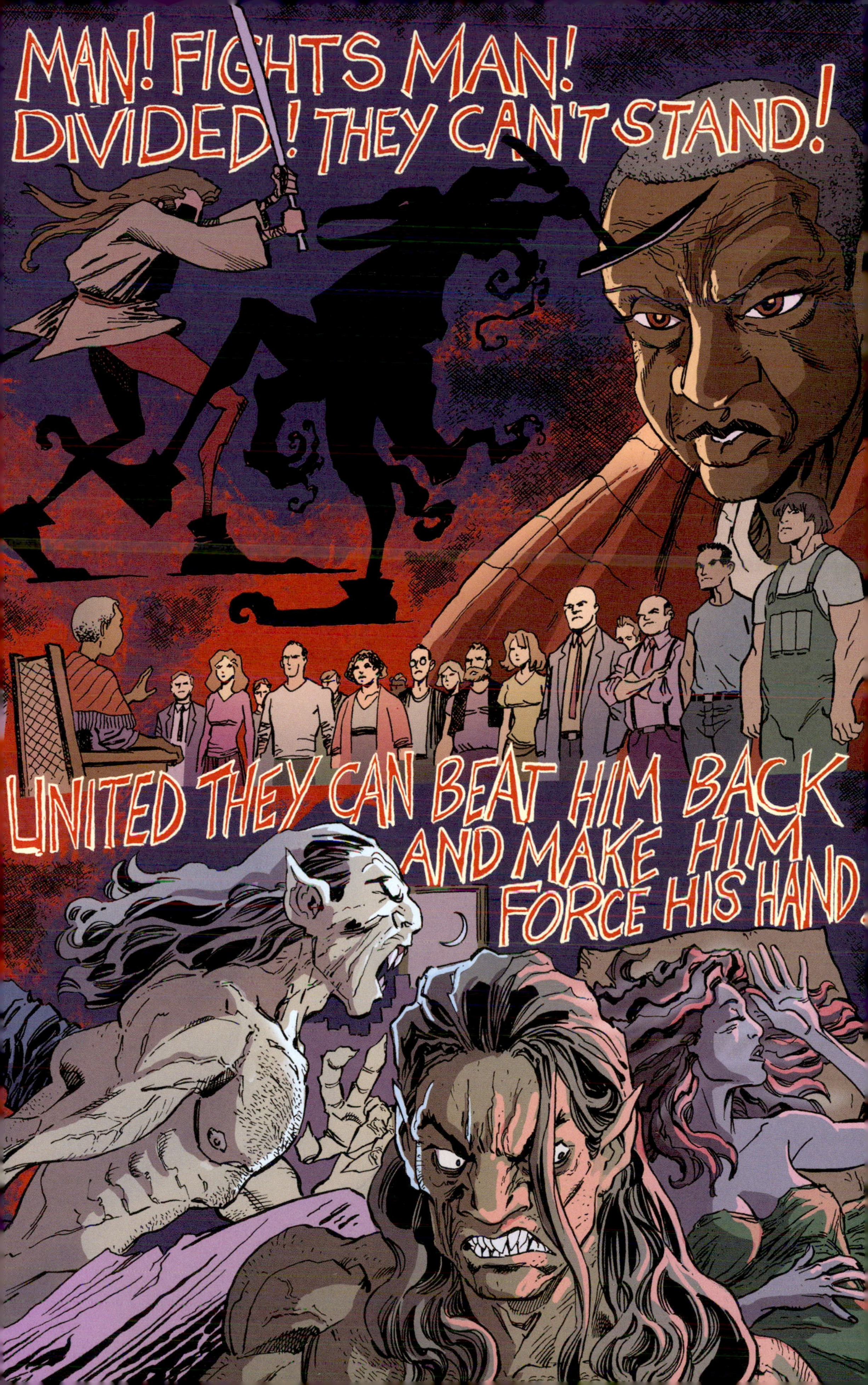
MAN! FIGHTS MAN!
DIVIDED! THEY CAN'T STAND!
UNITED THEY CAN BEAT HIM BACK
AND MAKE HIM
FORCE HIS HAND.

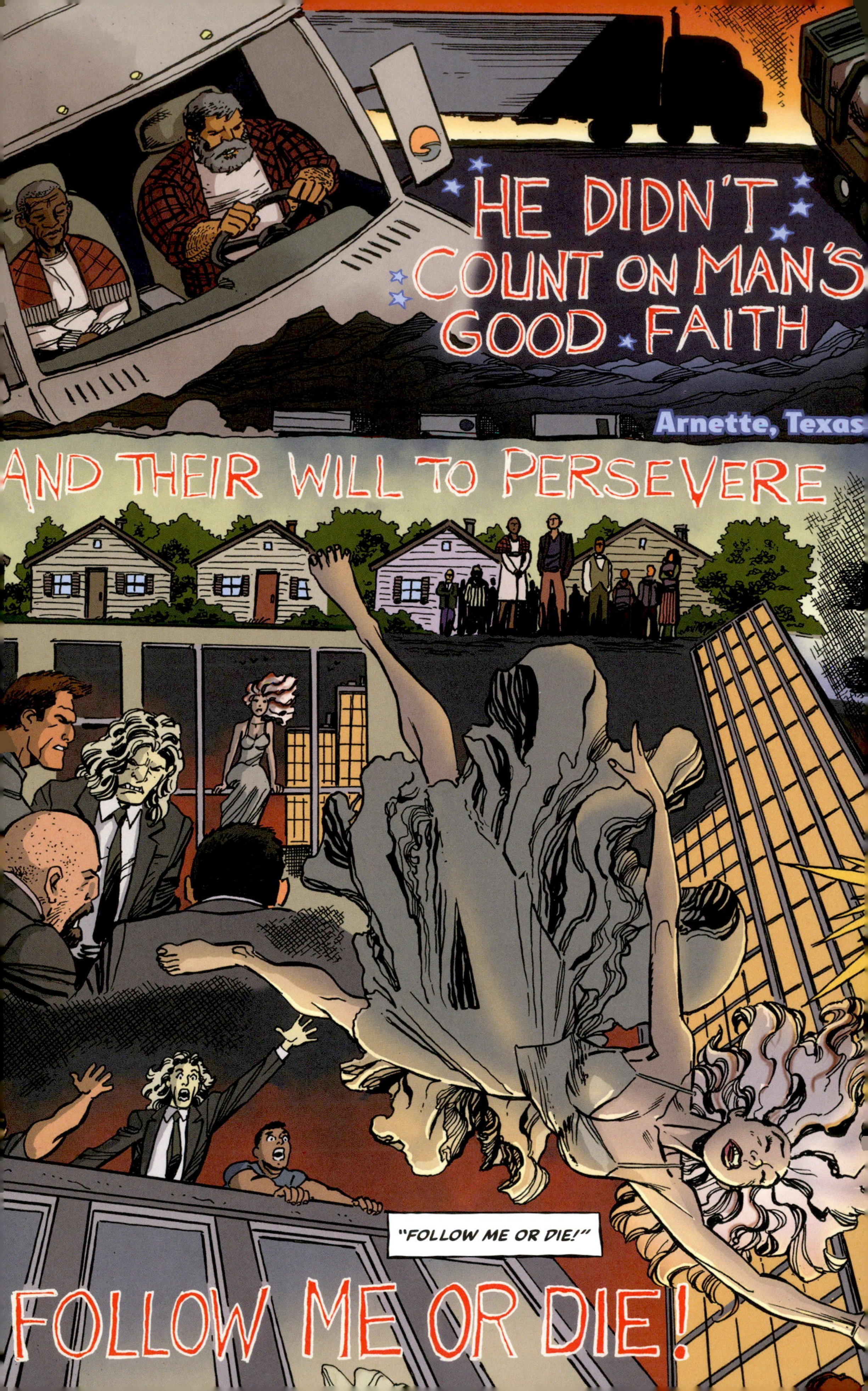
HE DIDN'T COUNT ON MAN'S GOOD FAITH
Arnette, Texas
AND THEIR WILL TO PERSEVERE
"FOLLOW ME OR DIE!"
FOLLOW ME OR DIE!

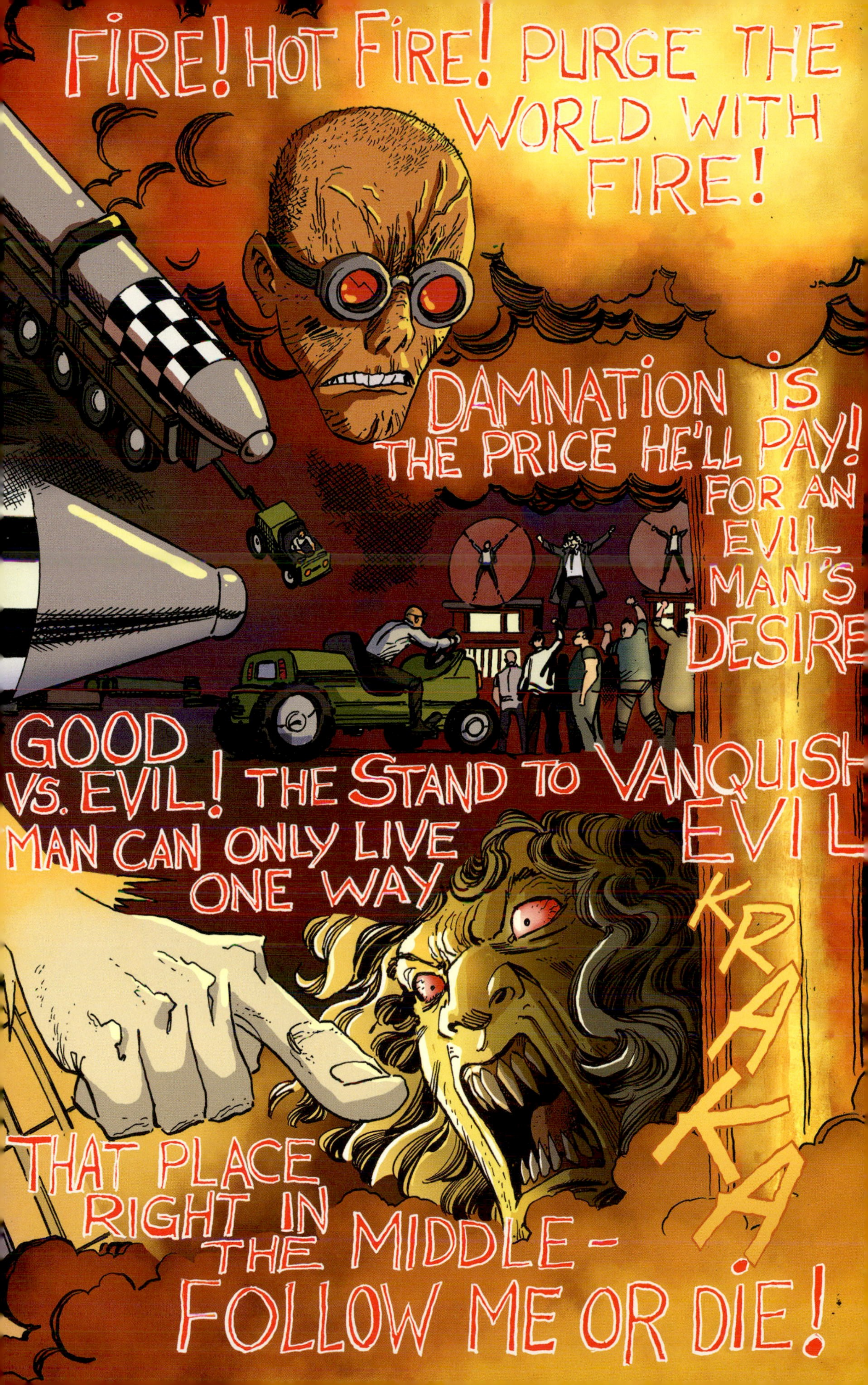
FIRE! HOT FIRE! PURGE THE WORLD WITH FIRE!
DAMNATION IS THE PRICE HE'LL PAY! FOR AN EVIL MAN'S DESIRE
GOOD VS. EVIL! THE STAND TO VANQUISH EVIL
MAN CAN ONLY LIVE ONE WAY
KRAKA
THAT PLACE RIGHT IN THE MIDDLE -
FOLLOW ME OR DIE!

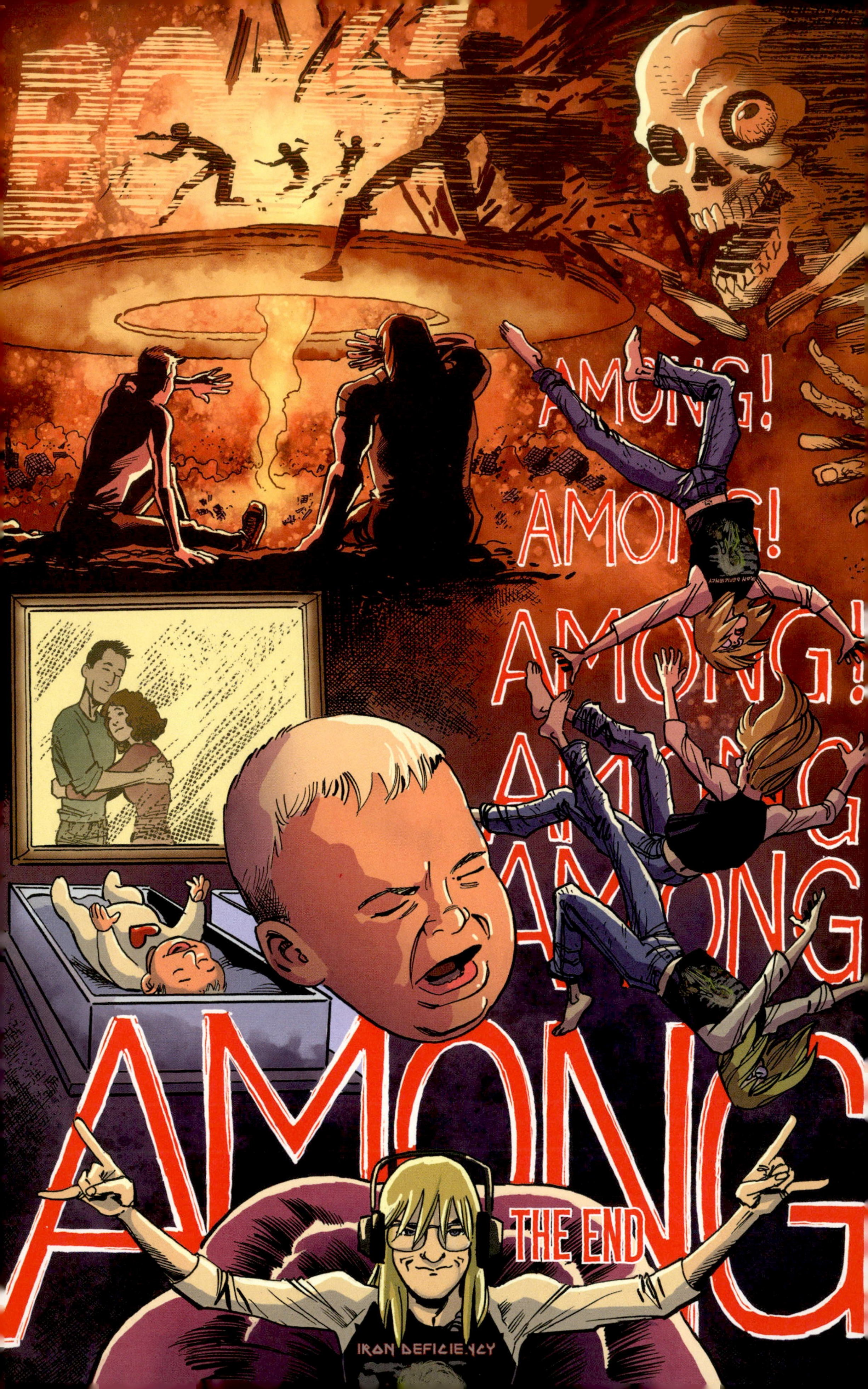
AMONG!
AMONG!
AMONG!
AMONG
AMONG
AMONG
AMONG
THE END
IRON DEFICIENCY

TRACK TWO
CAUGHT IN A MOSH

WRITTEN BY
GERARD WAY
&
MIKEY WAY

ILLUSTRATED BY
DARICK ROBERTSON
&
PHILLIP SEVY

COLORED BY
ALADDIN COLLAR

"WHICH ONE OF THESE WORDS
DON'T YOU UNDERSTAND?"

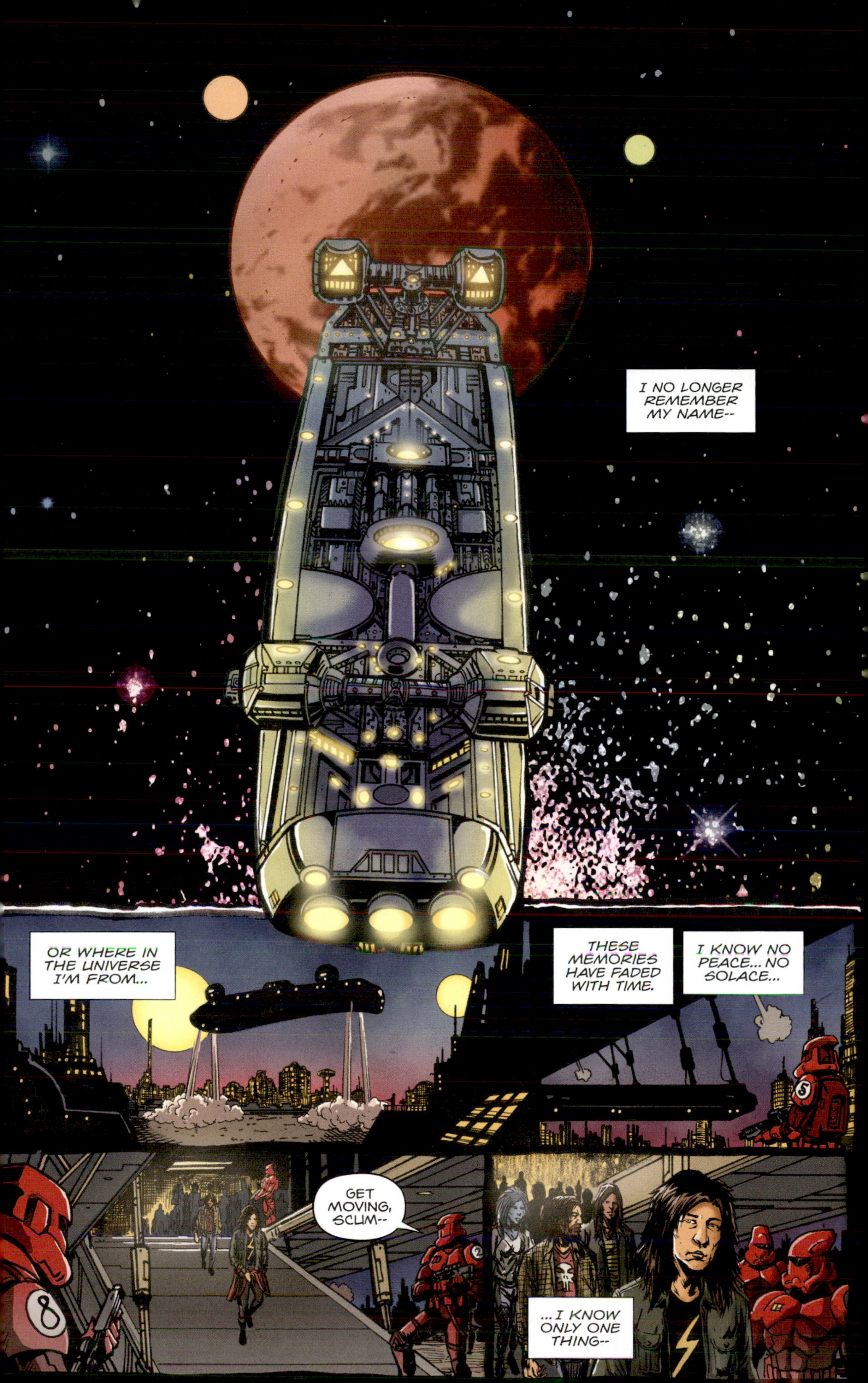
I NO LONGER REMEMBER MY NAME--
OR WHERE IN THE UNIVERSE I'M FROM...
THESE MEMORIES HAVE FADED WITH TIME.
I KNOW NO PEACE... NO SOLACE...
GET MOVING, SCUM--
...I KNOW ONLY ONE THING--

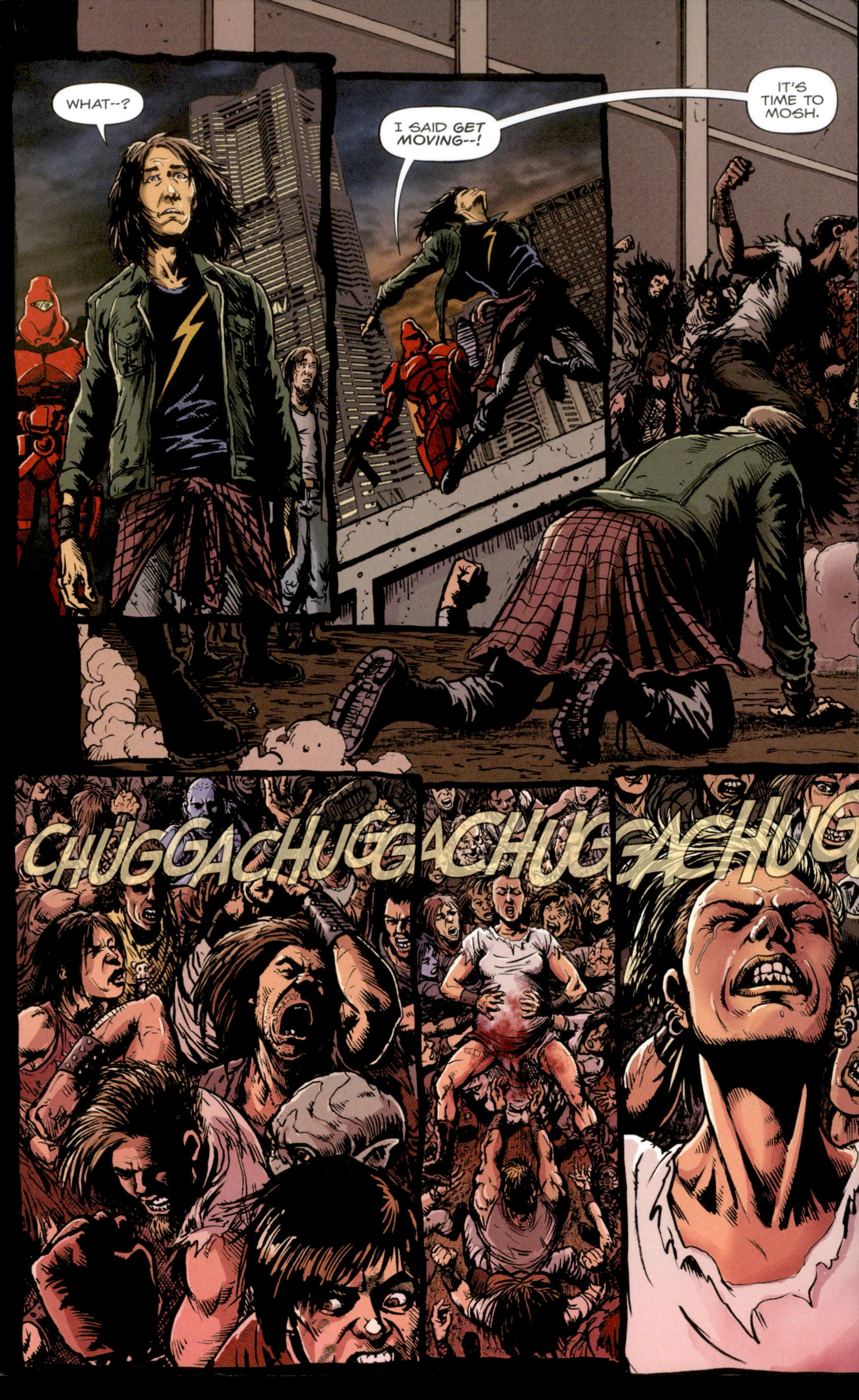
WHAT--?
I SAID GET MOVING--!
IT'S TIME TO MOSH.
CHUGGACHUGGACHUGGACHUG

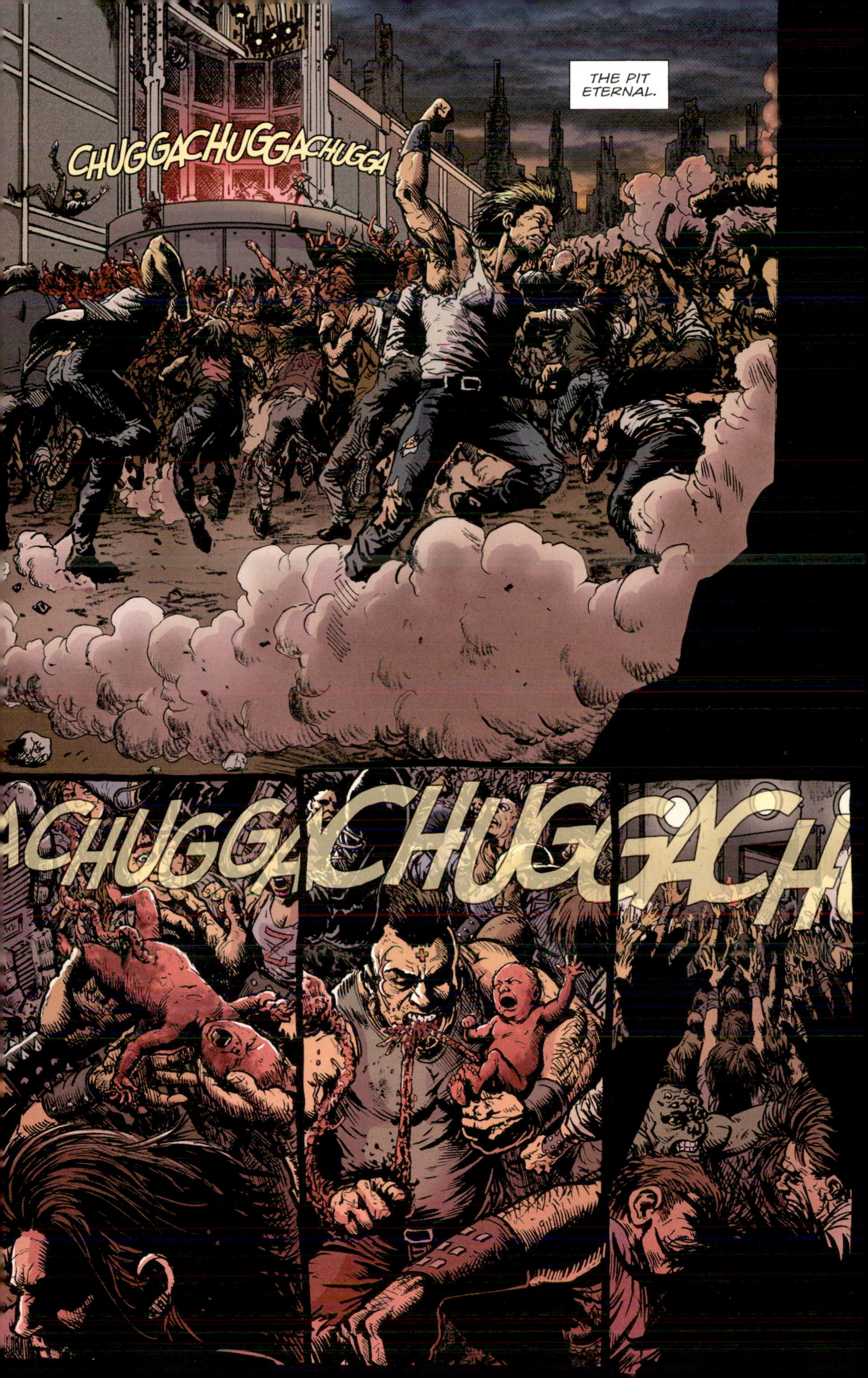
THE PIT ETERNAL.
CHUGGACHUGGACHUGGA
ACHUGGACHUGGACH

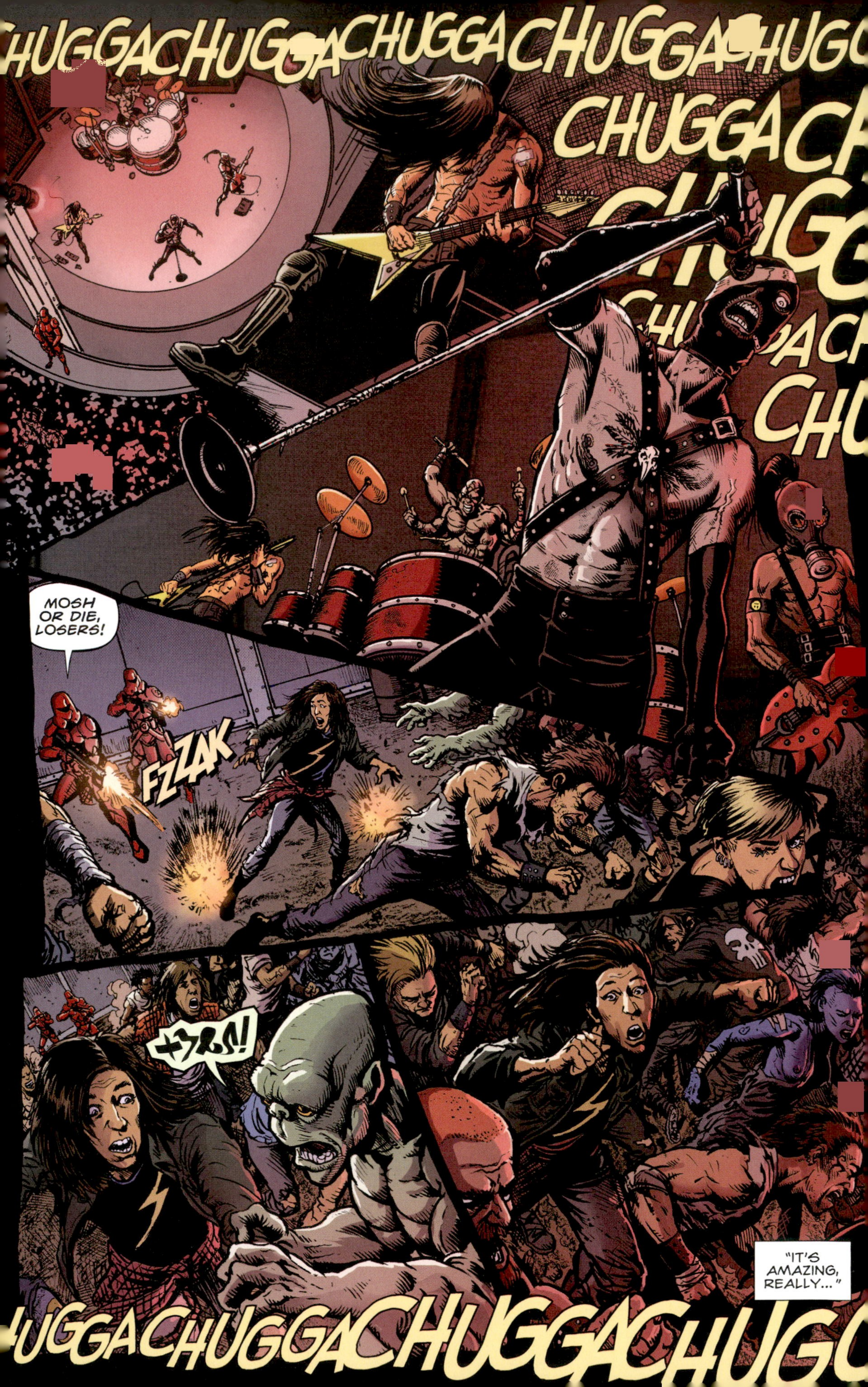
CHUGGACHUGGACHUGGACHUGGACHUG
CHUGGACH
MOSH OR DIE, LOSERS!
FZZAK
"IT'S AMAZING, REALLY..."
UGGACHUGGACHUGGACHUG

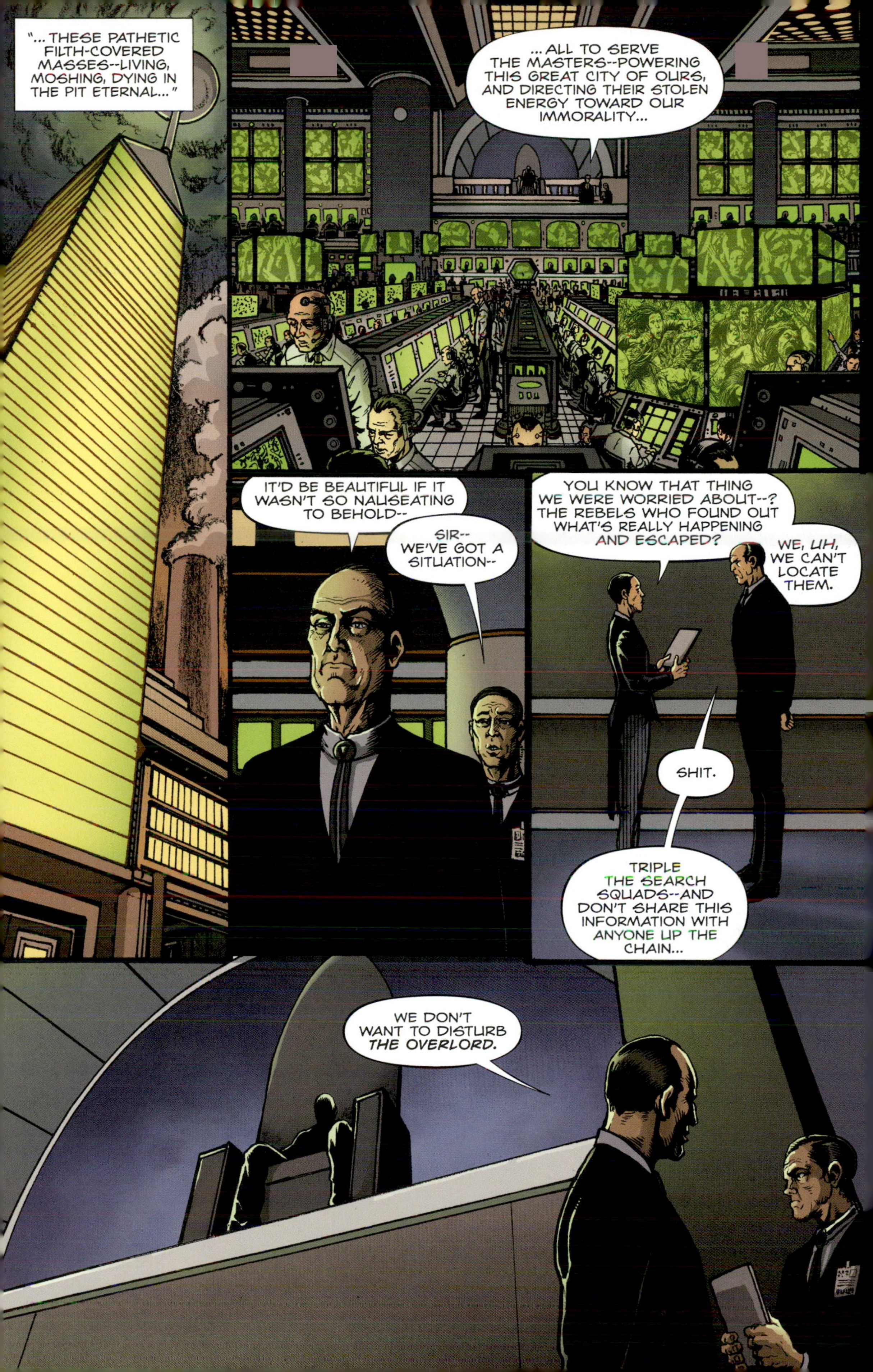
"...THESE PATHETIC FILTH-COVERED MASSES--LIVING, MOSHING, DYING IN THE PIT ETERNAL..."
...ALL TO SERVE THE MASTERS--POWERING THIS GREAT CITY OF OURS, AND DIRECTING THEIR STOLEN ENERGY TOWARD OUR IMMORALITY...
IT'D BE BEAUTIFUL IF IT WASN'T SO NAUSEATING TO BEHOLD--
SIR-- WE'VE GOT A SITUATION--
YOU KNOW THAT THING WE WERE WORRIED ABOUT--? THE REBELS WHO FOUND OUT WHAT'S REALLY HAPPENING AND ESCAPED?
WE, UH, WE CAN'T LOCATE THEM.
SHIT.
TRIPLE THE SEARCH SQUADS--AND DON'T SHARE THIS INFORMATION WITH ANYONE UP THE CHAIN...
WE DON'T WANT TO DISTURB THE OVERLORD.

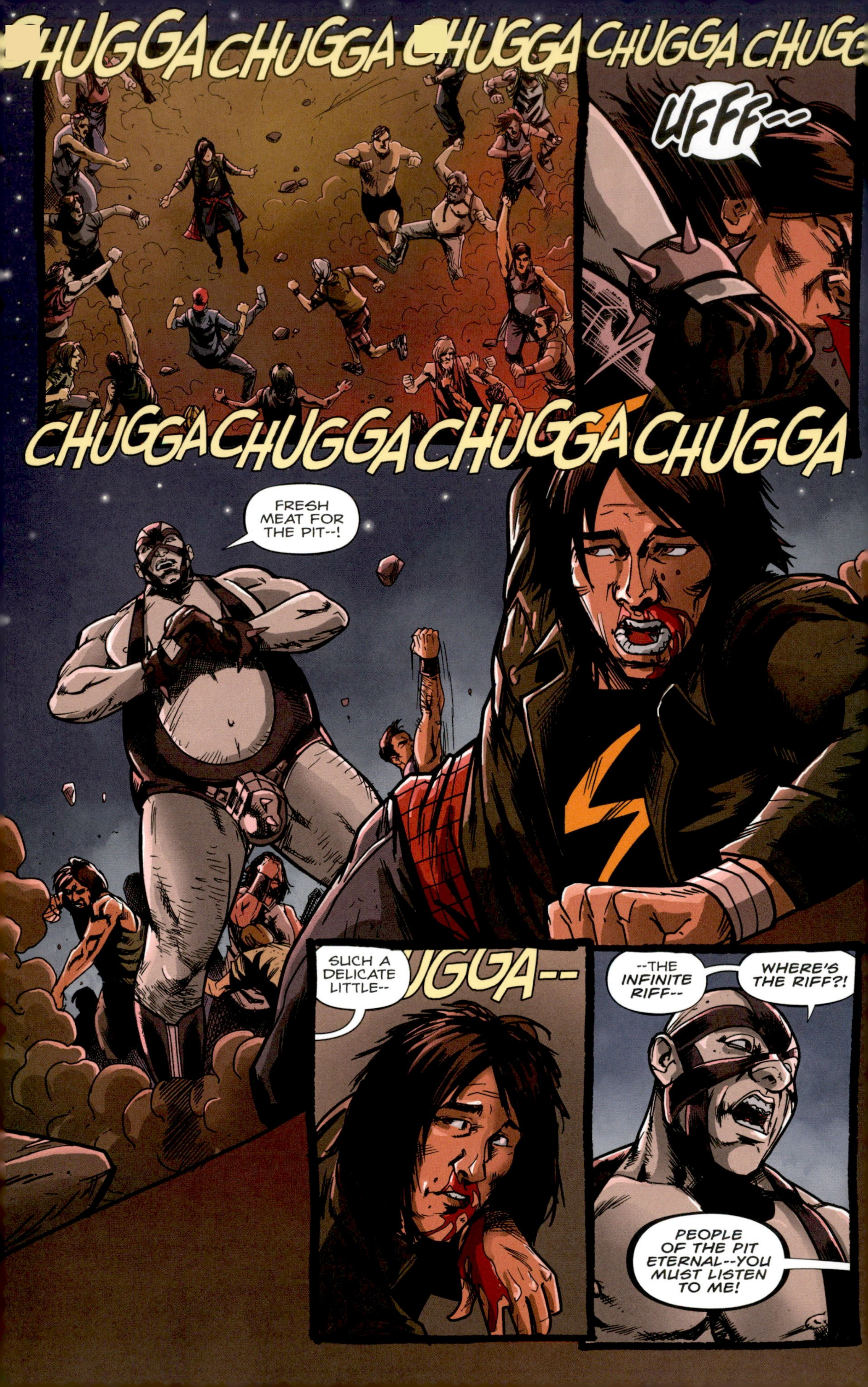
CHUGGA CHUGGA CHUGGA CHUGGA CHUGG
UFFF--
CHUGGA CHUGGA CHUGGA CHUGGA
FRESH MEAT FOR THE PIT--!
SUCH A DELICATE LITTLE--
UGGA--
--THE INFINITE RIFF--
WHERE'S THE RIFF?!
PEOPLE OF THE PIT ETERNAL--YOU MUST LISTEN TO ME!

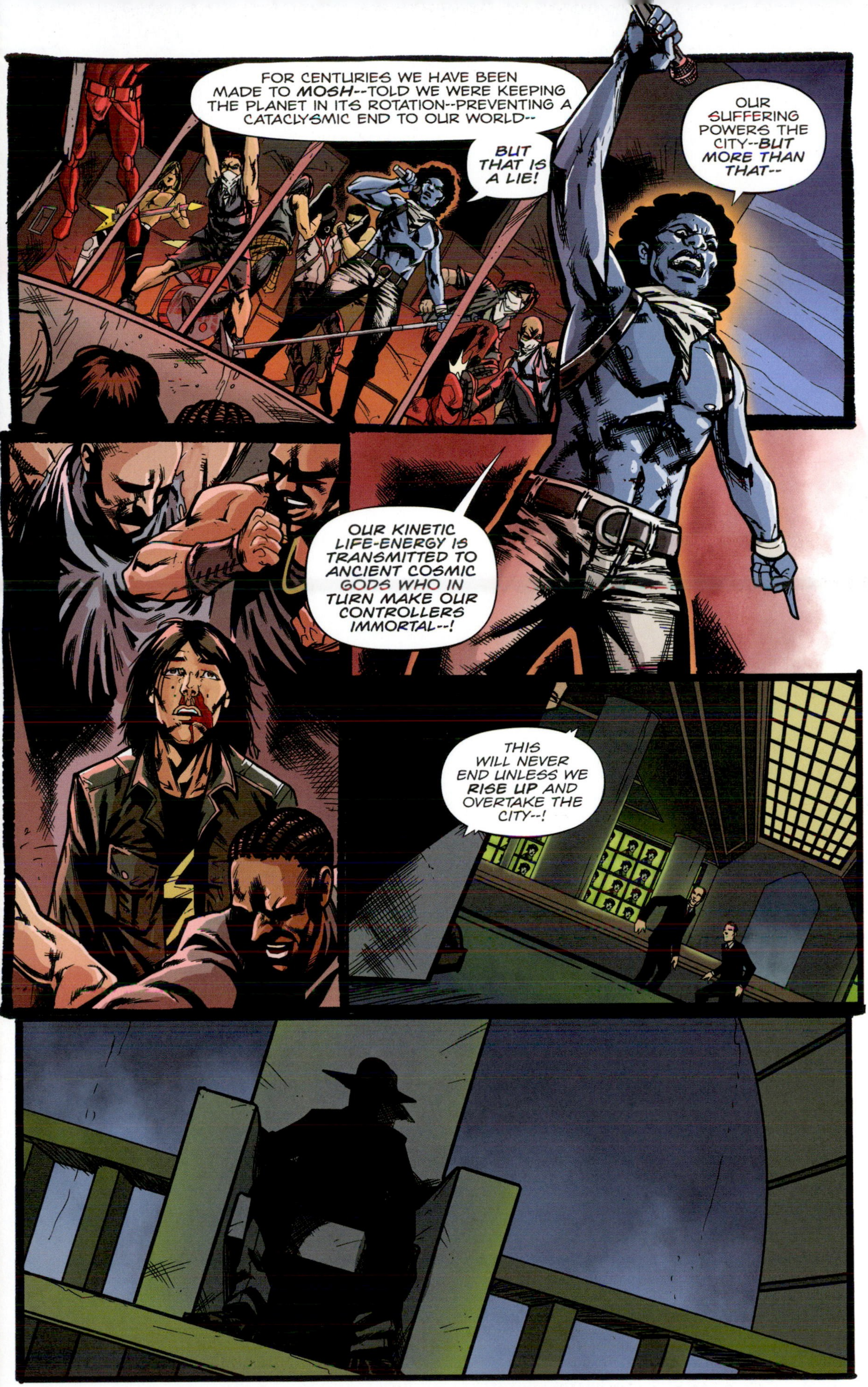
FOR CENTURIES WE HAVE BEEN MADE TO MOSH--TOLD WE WERE KEEPING THE PLANET IN ITS ROTATION--PREVENTING A CATACLYSMIC END TO OUR WORLD--
BUT THAT IS A LIE!
OUR SUFFERING POWERS THE CITY--BUT MORE THAN THAT--
OUR KINETIC LIFE-ENERGY IS TRANSMITTED TO ANCIENT COSMIC GODS WHO IN TURN MAKE OUR CONTROLLERS IMMORTAL--!
THIS WILL NEVER END UNLESS WE RISE UP AND OVERTAKE THE CITY--!

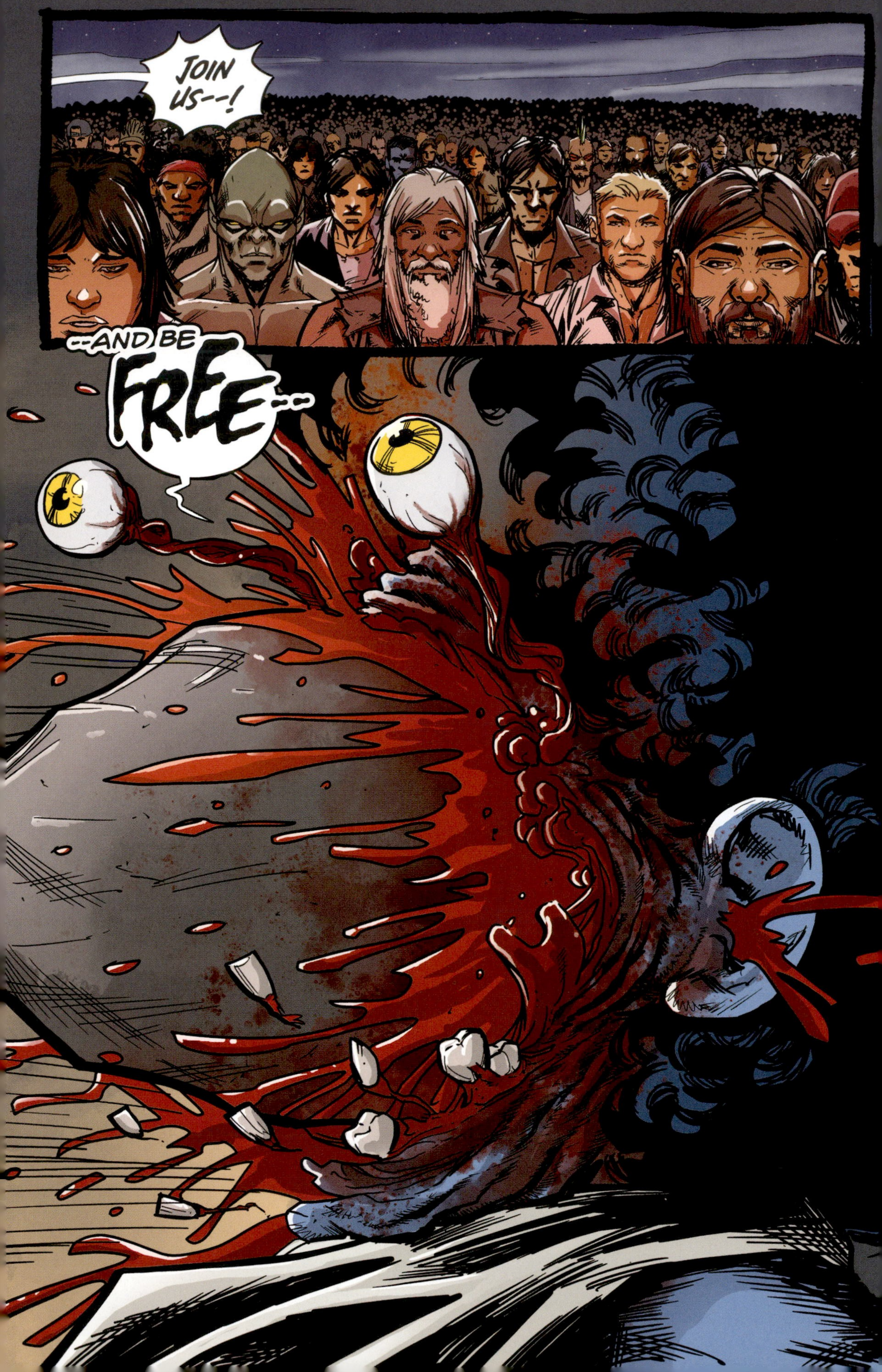
JOIN US--!
--AND BE FREE--

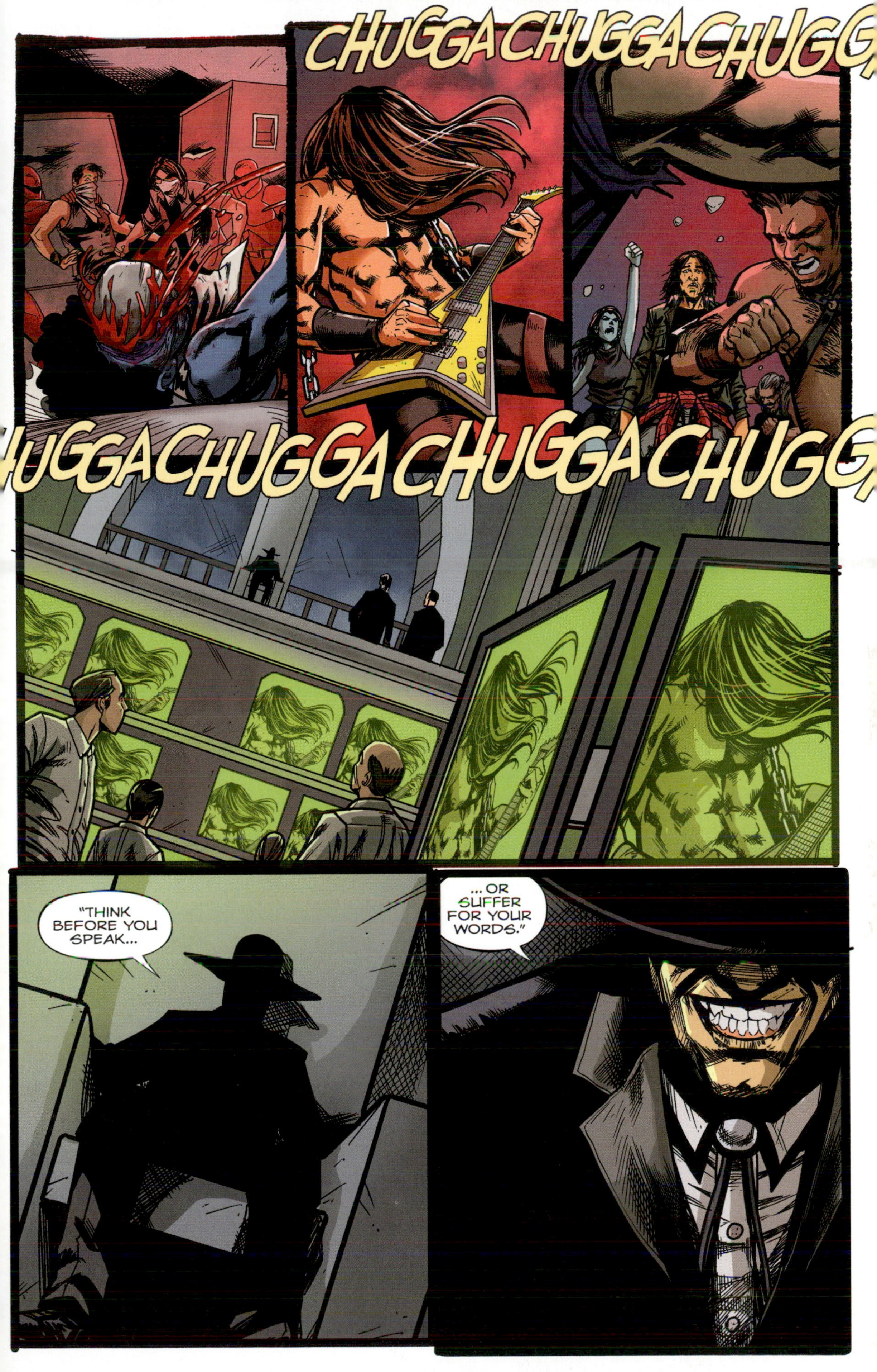
CHUGGACHUGGACHUGG
UGGACHUGGACHUGGACHUGG
"THINK BEFORE YOU SPEAK...
...OR SUFFER FOR YOUR WORDS."

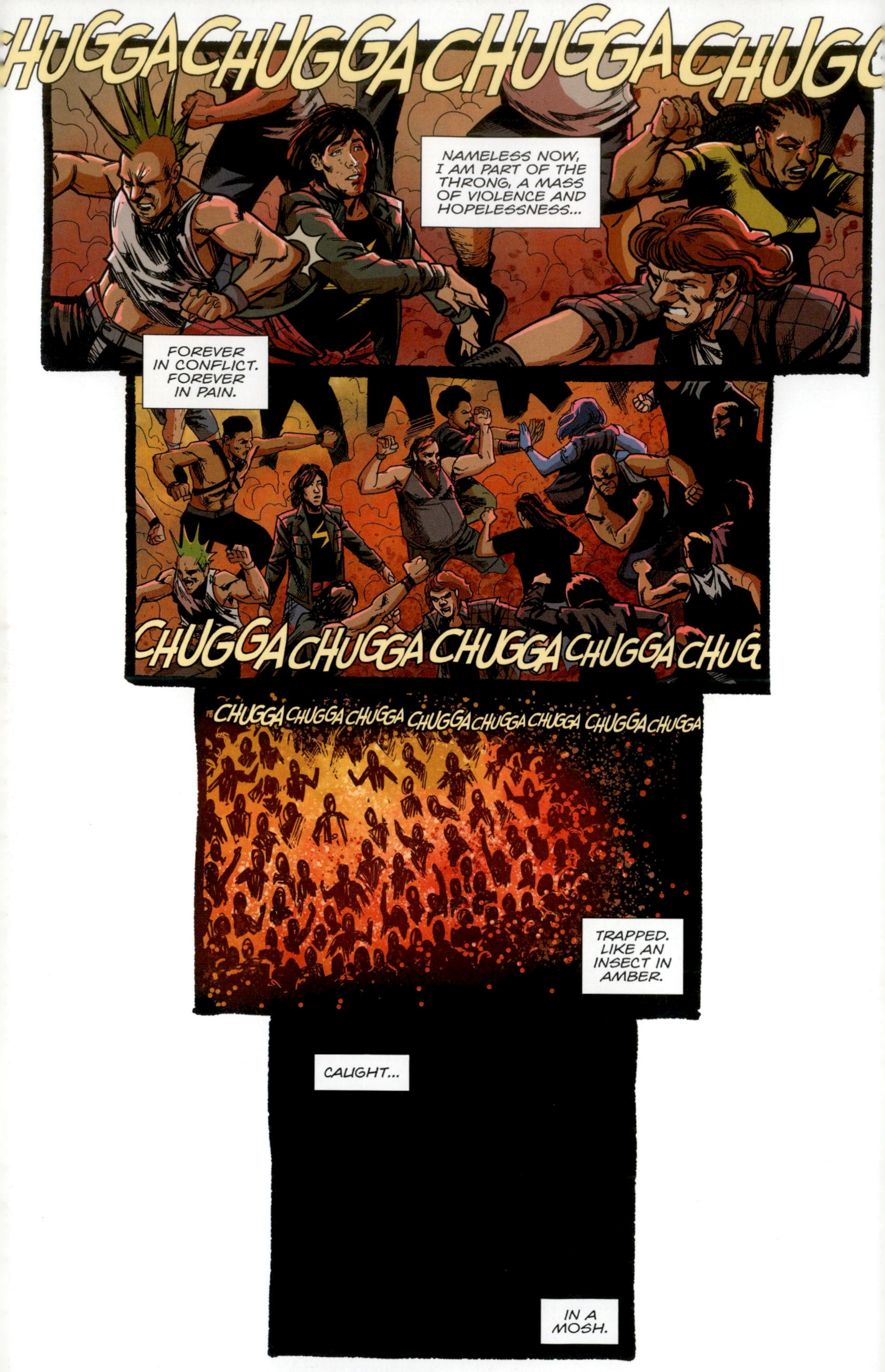
CHUGGA CHUGGA CHUGGA CHUGG
NAMELESS NOW, I AM PART OF THE THRONG, A MASS OF VIOLENCE AND HOPELESSNESS...
FOREVER IN CONFLICT. FOREVER IN PAIN.
CHUGGA CHUGGA CHUGGA CHUGGA CHUG
CHUGGA CHUGGA CHUGGA CHUGGA CHUGGA CHUGGA CHUGGA CHUGGA
TRAPPED. LIKE AN INSECT IN AMBER.
CAUGHT...
IN A MOSH.

TRACK THREE
I AM THE LAW

WRITTEN BY
SCOTT IAN

ILLUSTRATED BY
CHRIS WESTON

COLORED BY
ALADDIN COLLAR

"IF I'M SPREADING THE DISEASE
THEN JUDGE DREDD IS THE CURE!"

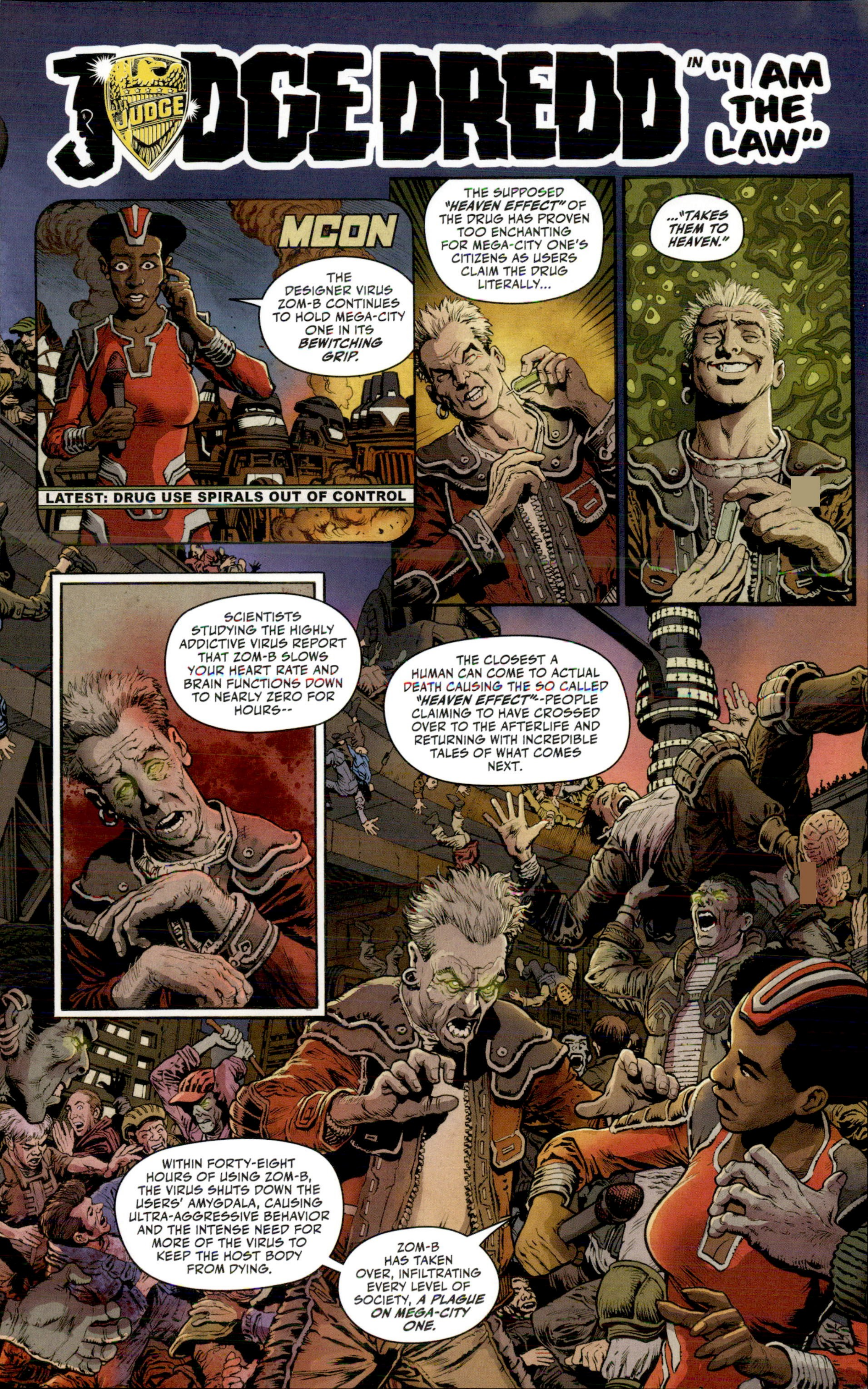
JUDGE DREDD IN "I AM THE LAW"
MCON
THE DESIGNER VIRUS ZOM-B CONTINUES TO HOLD MEGA-CITY ONE IN ITS BEWITCHING GRIP.
LATEST: DRUG USE SPIRALS OUT OF CONTROL
THE SUPPOSED "HEAVEN EFFECT" OF THE DRUG HAS PROVEN TOO ENCHANTING FOR MEGA-CITY ONE'S CITIZENS AS USERS CLAIM THE DRUG LITERALLY...
..."TAKES THEM TO HEAVEN."
SCIENTISTS STUDYING THE HIGHLY ADDICTIVE VIRUS REPORT THAT ZOM-B SLOWS YOUR HEART RATE AND BRAIN FUNCTIONS DOWN TO NEARLY ZERO FOR HOURS--
THE CLOSEST A HUMAN CAN COME TO ACTUAL DEATH CAUSING THE SO CALLED "HEAVEN EFFECT"--PEOPLE CLAIMING TO HAVE CROSSED OVER TO THE AFTERLIFE AND RETURNING WITH INCREDIBLE TALES OF WHAT COMES NEXT.
WITHIN FORTY-EIGHT HOURS OF USING ZOM-B, THE VIRUS SHUTS DOWN THE USERS' AMYGDALA, CAUSING ULTRA-AGGRESSIVE BEHAVIOR AND THE INTENSE NEED FOR MORE OF THE VIRUS TO KEEP THE HOST BODY FROM DYING.
ZOM-B HAS TAKEN OVER, INFILTRATING EVERY LEVEL OF SOCIETY, A PLAGUE ON MEGA-CITY ONE.

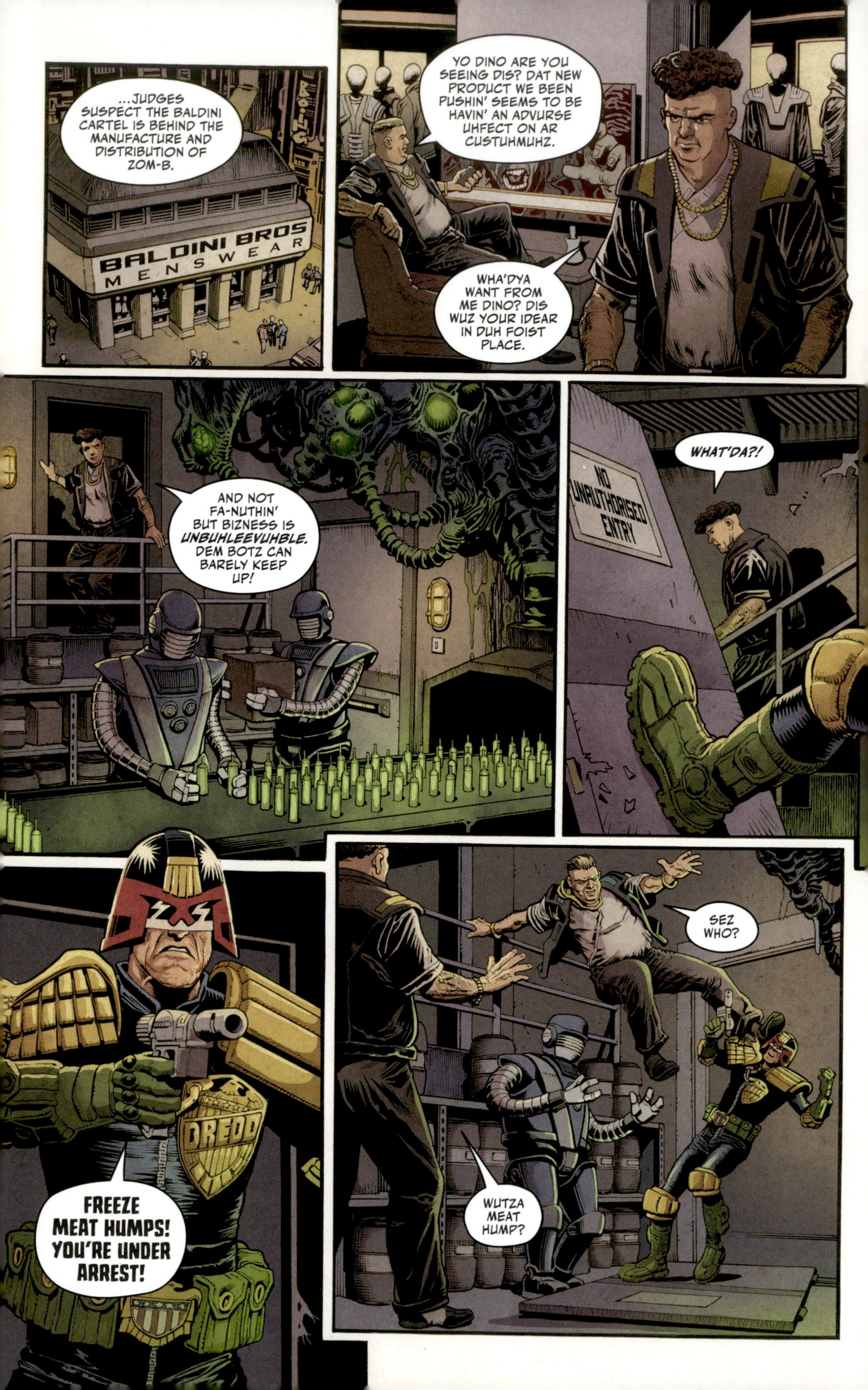
...JUDGES SUSPECT THE BALDINI CARTEL IS BEHIND THE MANUFACTURE AND DISTRIBUTION OF ZOM-B.
BALDINI BROS MENSWEAR
YO DINO ARE YOU SEEING DIS? DAT NEW PRODUCT WE BEEN PUSHIN' SEEMS TO BE HAVIN' AN ADVURSE UHFECT ON AR CUSTUHMUHZ.
WHA'DYA WANT FROM ME DINO? DIS WUZ YOUR IDEAR IN DUH FOIST PLACE.
AND NOT FA-NUTHIN' BUT BIZNESS IS UNBUHLEEVUHBLE. DEM BOTZ CAN BARELY KEEP UP!
NO UNAUTHORISED ENTRY
WHAT'DA?!
FREEZE MEAT HUMPS! YOU'RE UNDER ARREST!
DREDD
SEZ WHO?
WUTZA MEAT HUMP?

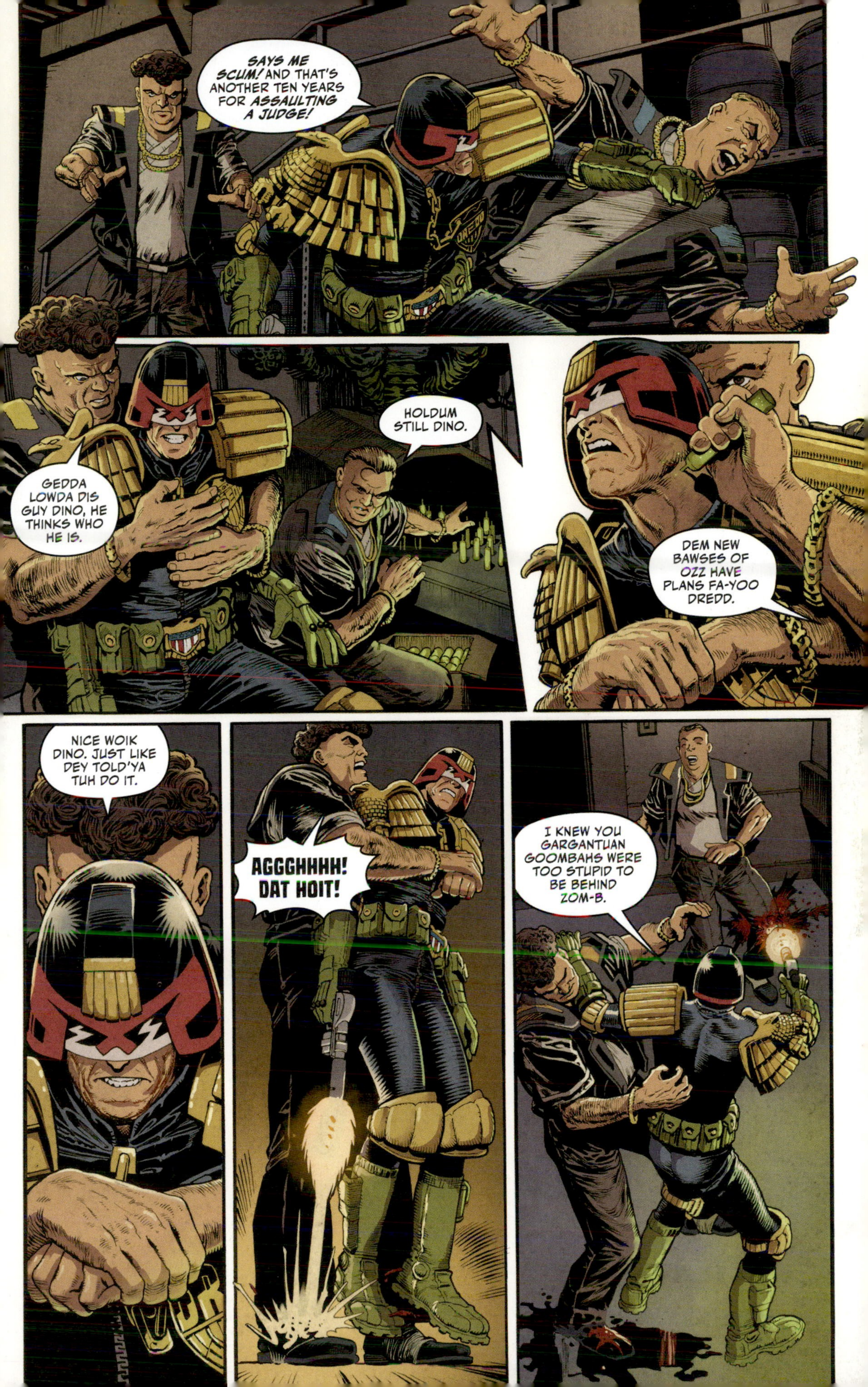
SAYS ME SCUM! AND THAT'S ANOTHER TEN YEARS FOR ASSAULTING A JUDGE!
GEDDA LOWDA DIS GUY DINO, HE THINKS WHO HE IS.
HOLDUM STILL DINO.
DEM NEW BAWSES OF OZZ HAVE PLANS FA-YOO DREDD.
NICE WOIK DINO. JUST LIKE DEY TOLD'YA TUH DO IT.
AGGGHHHH! DAT HOIT!
I KNEW YOU GARGANTUAN GOOMBAHS WERE TOO STUPID TO BE BEHIND ZOM-B.

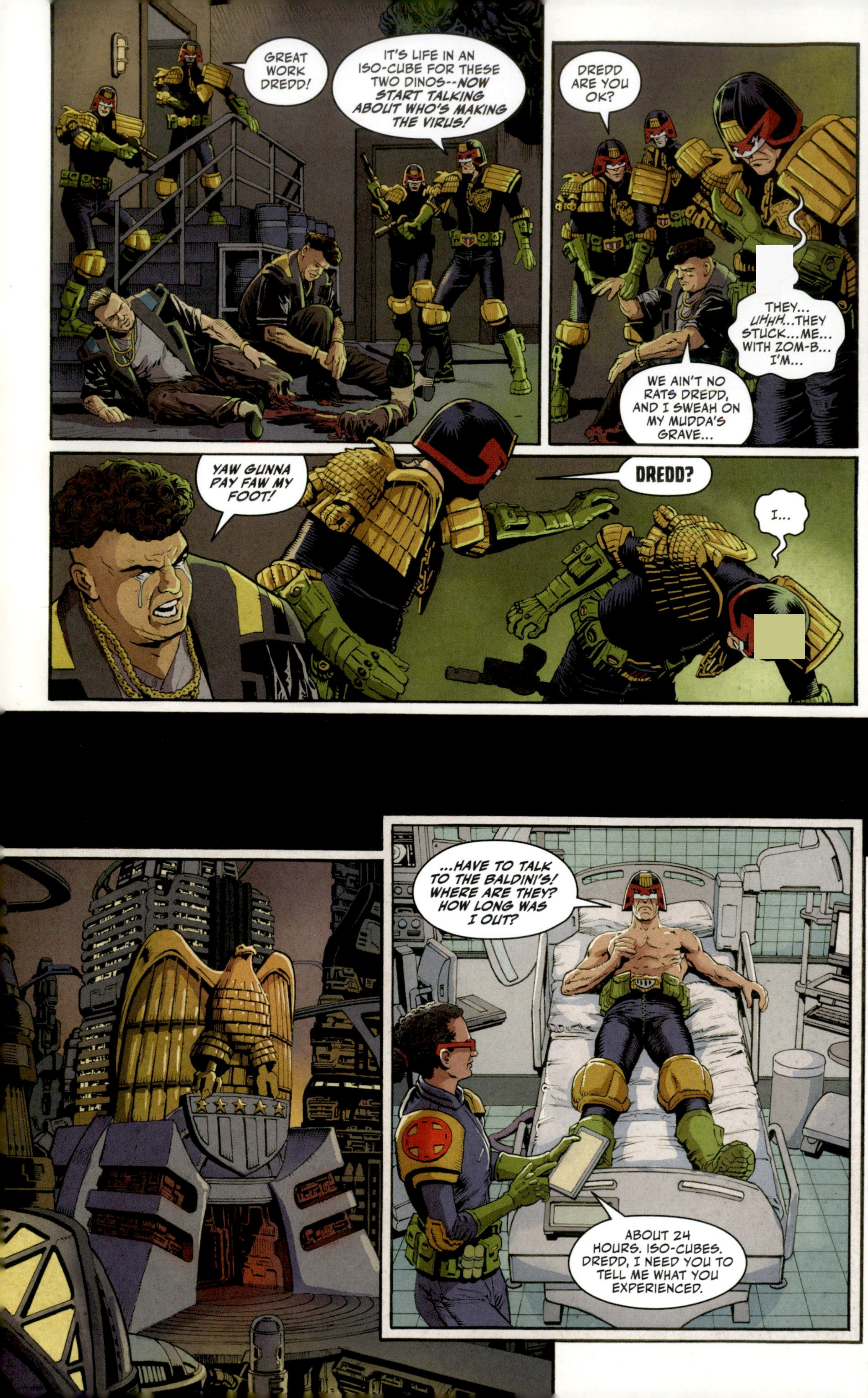
GREAT WORK DREDD!
IT'S LIFE IN AN ISO-CUBE FOR THESE TWO DINOS--NOW START TALKING ABOUT WHO'S MAKING THE VIRUS!
DREDD ARE YOU OK?
WE AIN'T NO RATS DREDD, AND I SWEAH ON MY MUDDA'S GRAVE...
THEY... UHHH...THEY STUCK...ME... WITH ZOM-B... I'M...
YAW GUNNA PAY FAW MY FOOT!
DREDD?
I...
...HAVE TO TALK TO THE BALDINI'S! WHERE ARE THEY? HOW LONG WAS I OUT?
ABOUT 24 HOURS. ISO-CUBES. DREDD, I NEED YOU TO TELL ME WHAT YOU EXPERIENCED.

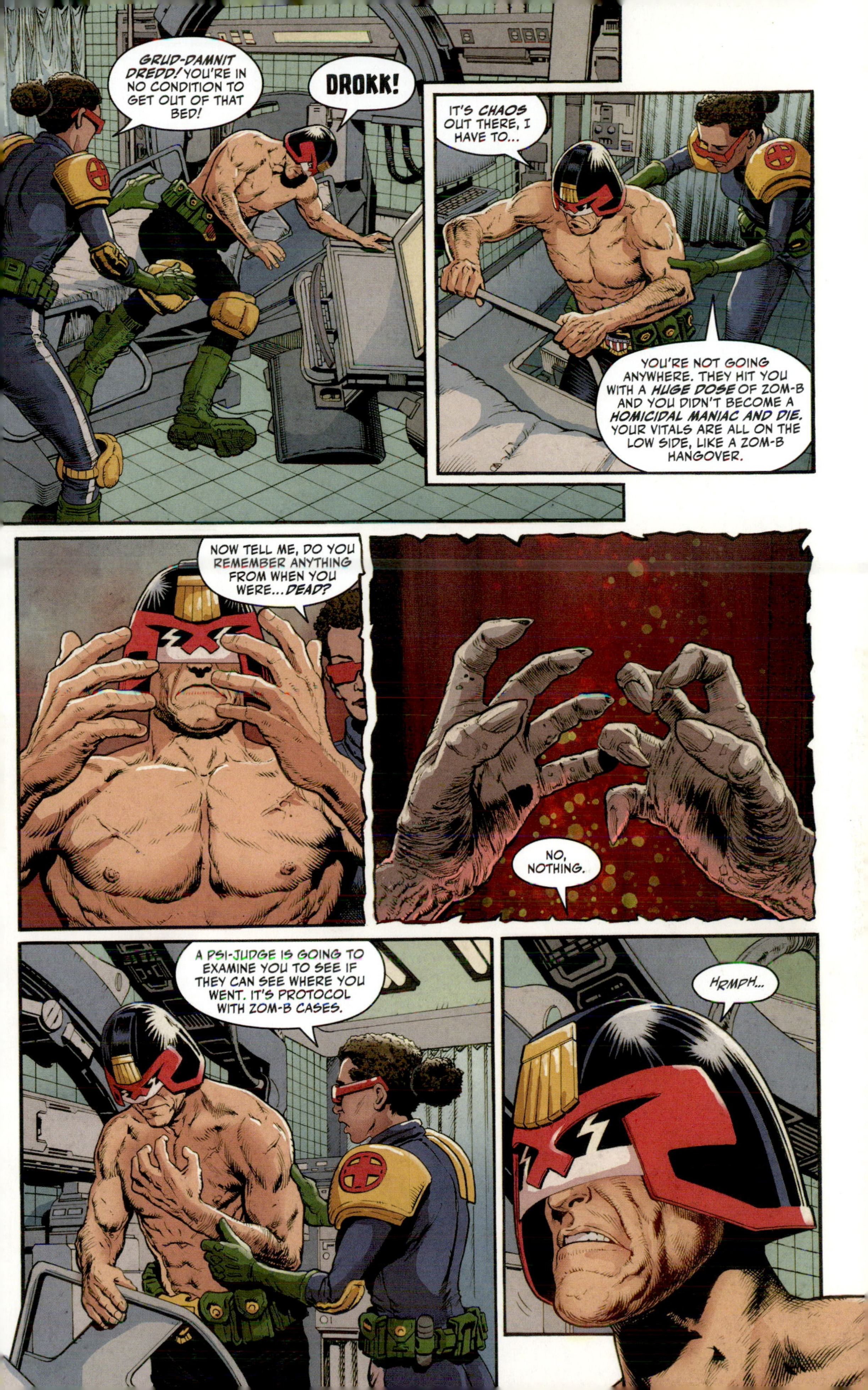
GRUD-DAMNIT DREDD! YOU'RE IN NO CONDITION TO GET OUT OF THAT BED!
DROKK!
IT'S CHAOS OUT THERE, I HAVE TO...
YOU'RE NOT GOING ANYWHERE. THEY HIT YOU WITH A HUGE DOSE OF ZOM-B AND YOU DIDN'T BECOME A HOMICIDAL MANIAC AND DIE. YOUR VITALS ARE ALL ON THE LOW SIDE, LIKE A ZOM-B HANGOVER.
NOW TELL ME, DO YOU REMEMBER ANYTHING FROM WHEN YOU WERE... DEAD?
NO, NOTHING.
A PSI-JUDGE IS GOING TO EXAMINE YOU TO SEE IF THEY CAN SEE WHERE YOU WENT. IT'S PROTOCOL WITH ZOM-B CASES.
HRMPH...

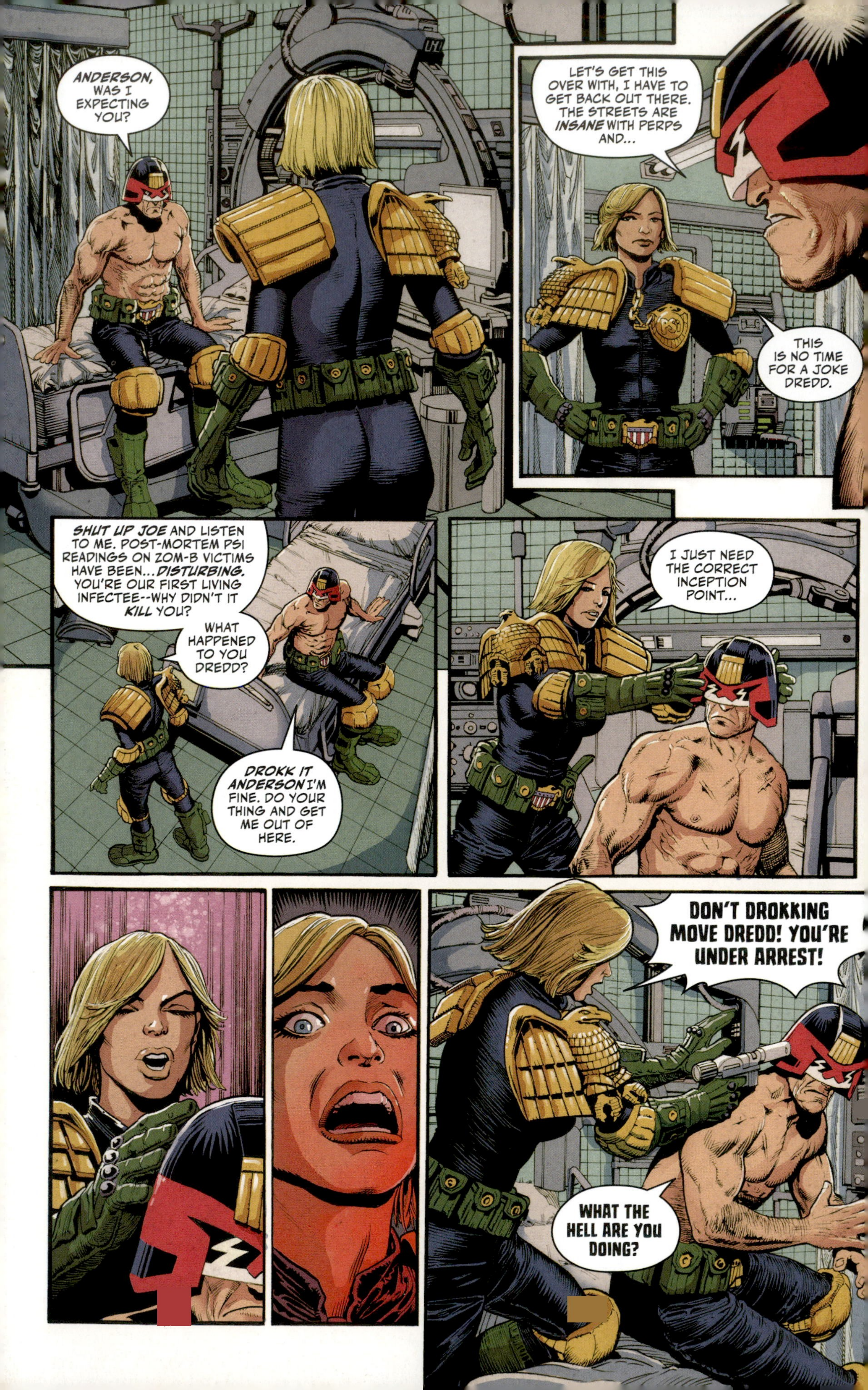
ANDERSON, WAS I EXPECTING YOU?
LET'S GET THIS OVER WITH, I HAVE TO GET BACK OUT THERE. THE STREETS ARE INSANE WITH PERPS AND...
THIS IS NO TIME FOR A JOKE DREDD.
SHUT UP JOE AND LISTEN TO ME. POST-MORTEM PSI READINGS ON ZOM-B VICTIMS HAVE BEEN...DISTURBING. YOU'RE OUR FIRST LIVING INFECTEE--WHY DIDN'T IT KILL YOU?
WHAT HAPPENED TO YOU DREDD?
DROKK IT ANDERSON I'M FINE. DO YOUR THING AND GET ME OUT OF HERE.
I JUST NEED THE CORRECT INCEPTION POINT...
DON'T DROKKING MOVE DREDD! YOU'RE UNDER ARREST!
WHAT THE HELL ARE YOU DOING?

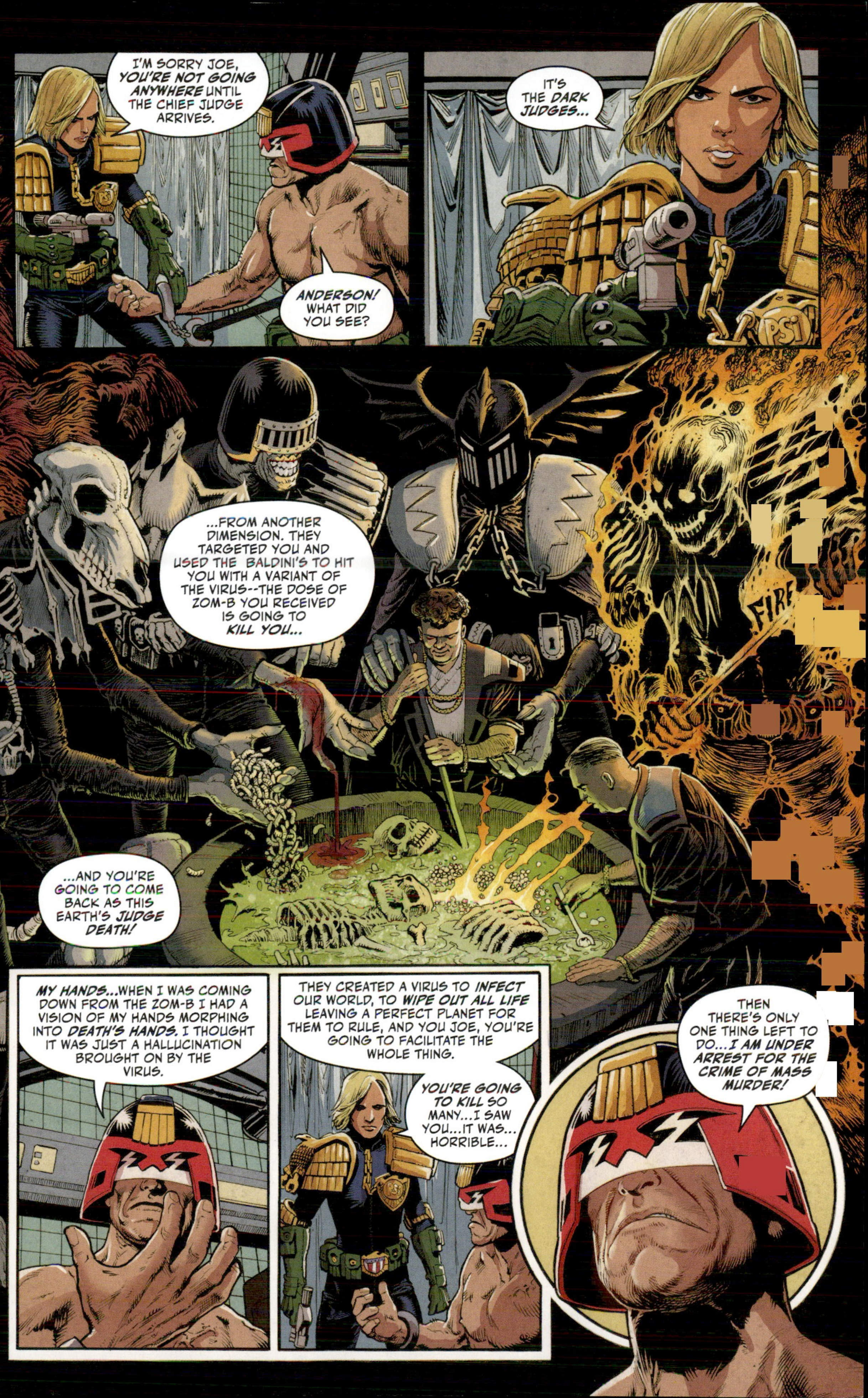
I'M SORRY JOE, *YOU'RE NOT GOING ANYWHERE* UNTIL THE CHIEF JUDGE ARRIVES.
ANDERSON! WHAT DID YOU SEE?
IT'S THE *DARK JUDGES...*
...FROM ANOTHER DIMENSION. THEY TARGETED YOU AND USED THE BALDINI'S TO HIT YOU WITH A VARIANT OF THE VIRUS--THE DOSE OF ZOM-B YOU RECEIVED IS GOING TO *KILL YOU...*
FIRE
...AND YOU'RE GOING TO COME BACK AS THIS EARTH'S *JUDGE DEATH!*
MY HANDS... WHEN I WAS COMING DOWN FROM THE ZOM-B I HAD A VISION OF MY HANDS MORPHING INTO *DEATH'S HANDS.* I THOUGHT IT WAS JUST A HALLUCINATION BROUGHT ON BY THE VIRUS.
THEY CREATED A VIRUS TO *INFECT* OUR WORLD, TO *WIPE OUT ALL LIFE* LEAVING A PERFECT PLANET FOR THEM TO RULE, AND YOU JOE, YOU'RE GOING TO FACILITATE THE WHOLE THING.
YOU'RE GOING TO KILL SO MANY...I SAW YOU...IT WAS... HORRIBLE...
THEN THERE'S ONLY ONE THING LEFT TO DO... *I AM UNDER ARREST FOR THE CRIME OF MASS MURDER!*

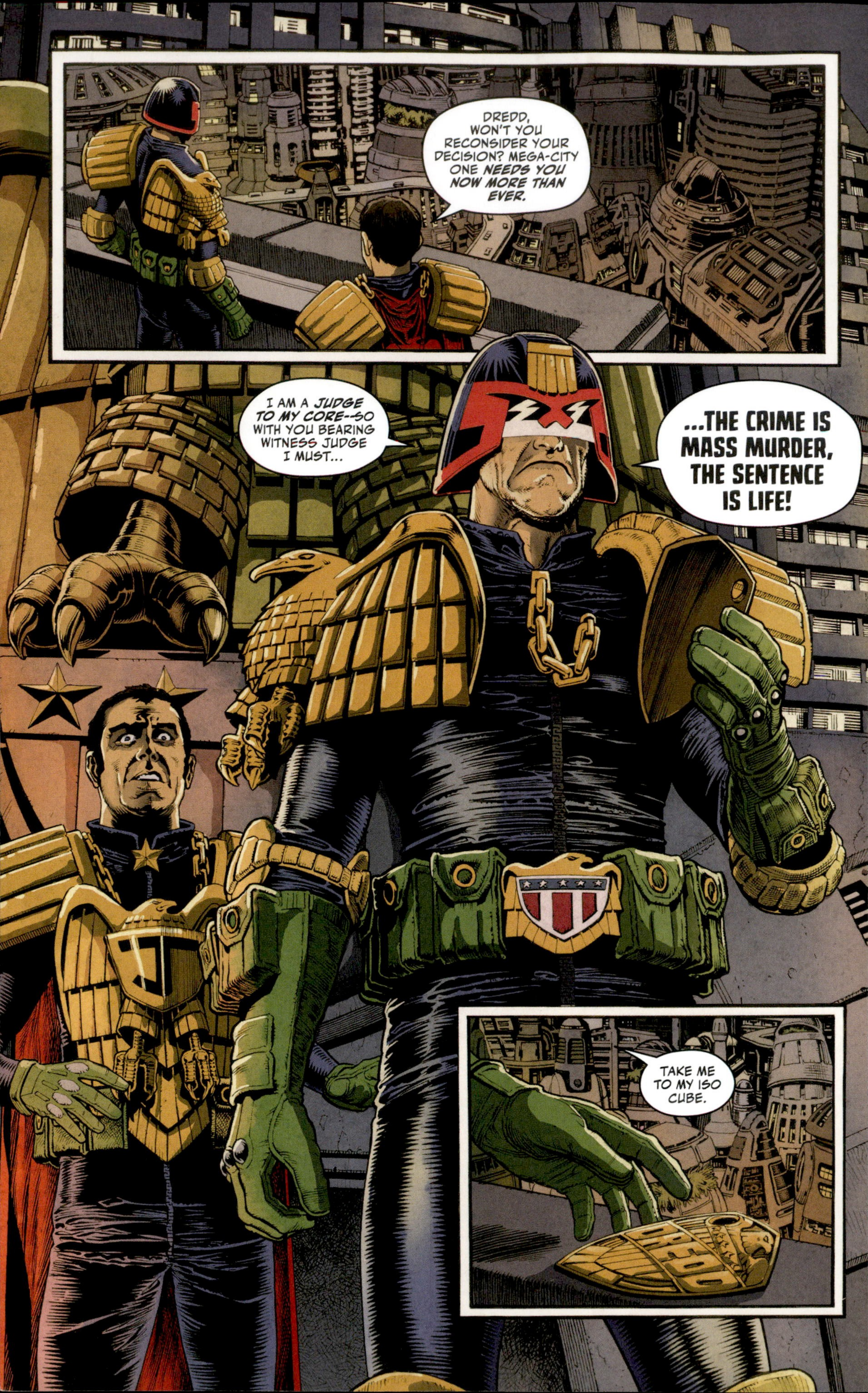
DREDD, WON'T YOU RECONSIDER YOUR DECISION? MEGA-CITY ONE NEEDS YOU NOW MORE THAN EVER.
I AM A JUDGE TO MY CORE--SO WITH YOU BEARING WITNESS JUDGE I MUST...
...THE CRIME IS MASS MURDER, THE SENTENCE IS LIFE!
TAKE ME TO MY ISO CUBE.
DREDD

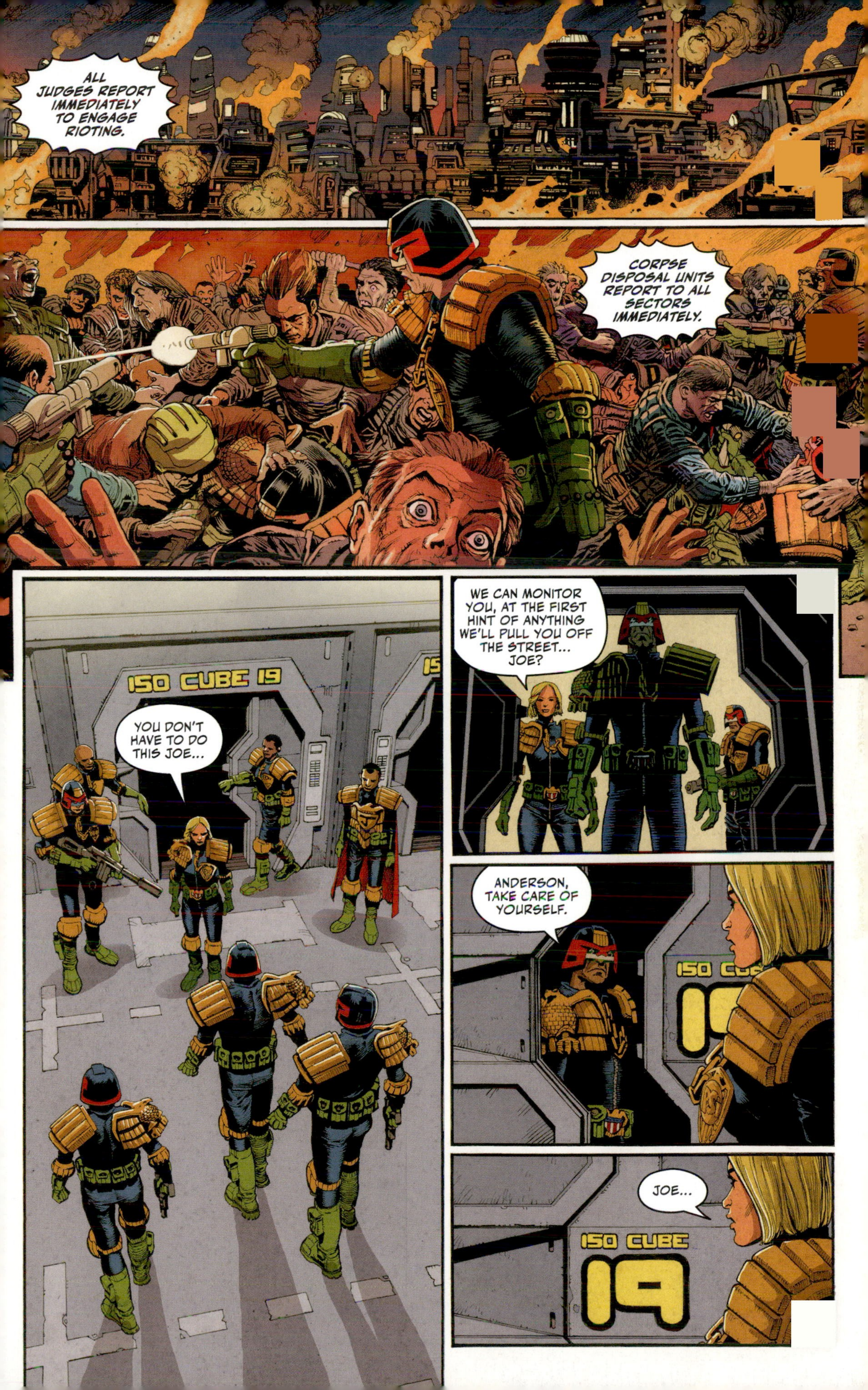
ALL JUDGES REPORT IMMEDIATELY TO ENGAGE RIOTING.
CORPSE DISPOSAL UNITS REPORT TO ALL SECTORS IMMEDIATELY.
ISO CUBE 19
YOU DON'T HAVE TO DO THIS JOE...
WE CAN MONITOR YOU, AT THE FIRST HINT OF ANYTHING WE'LL PULL YOU OFF THE STREET... JOE?
ANDERSON, TAKE CARE OF YOURSELF.
JOE...
ISO CUBE 19

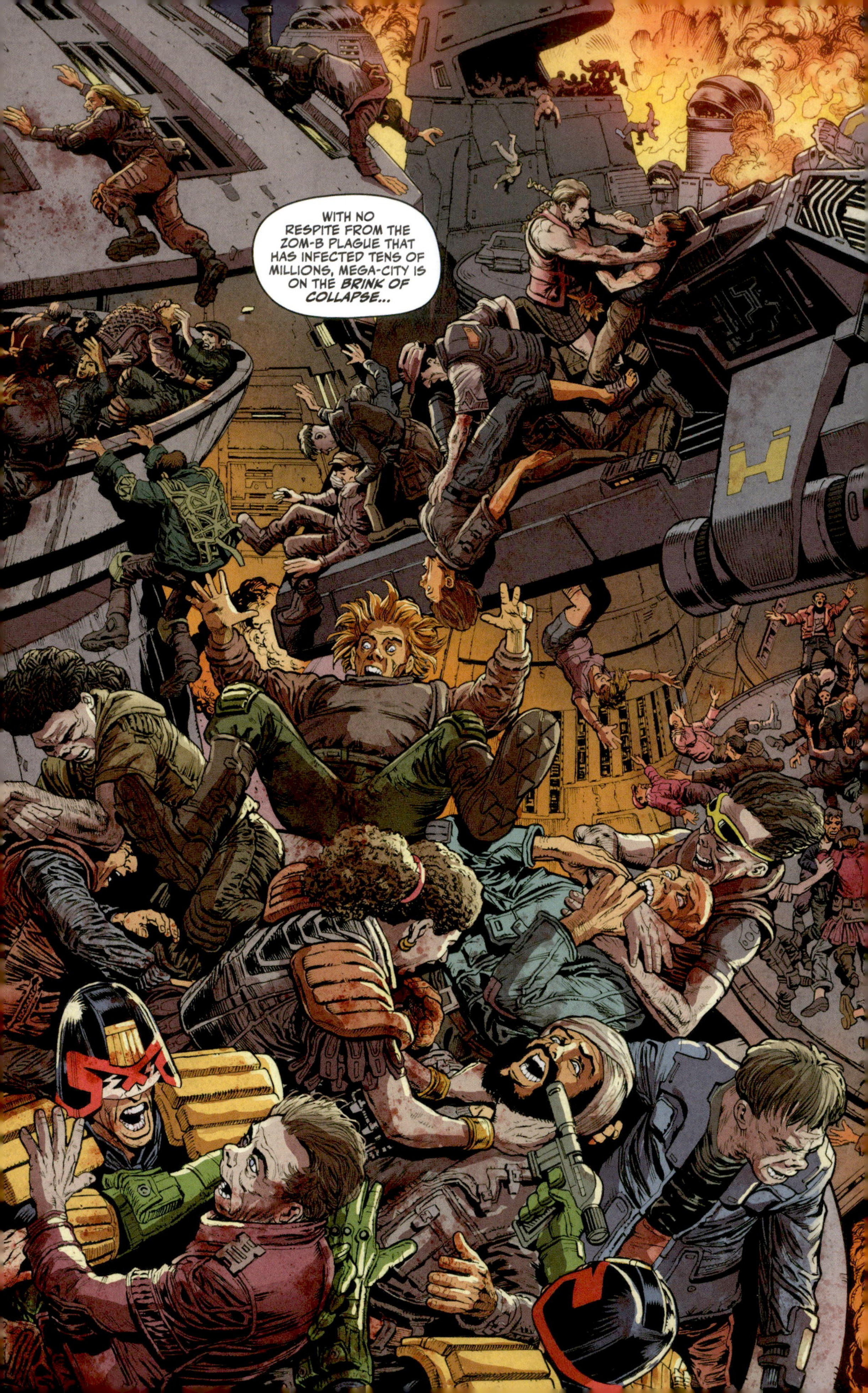
WITH NO RESPITE FROM THE ZOM-B PLAGUE THAT HAS INFECTED TENS OF MILLIONS, MEGA-CITY IS ON THE *BRINK OF COLLAPSE*...

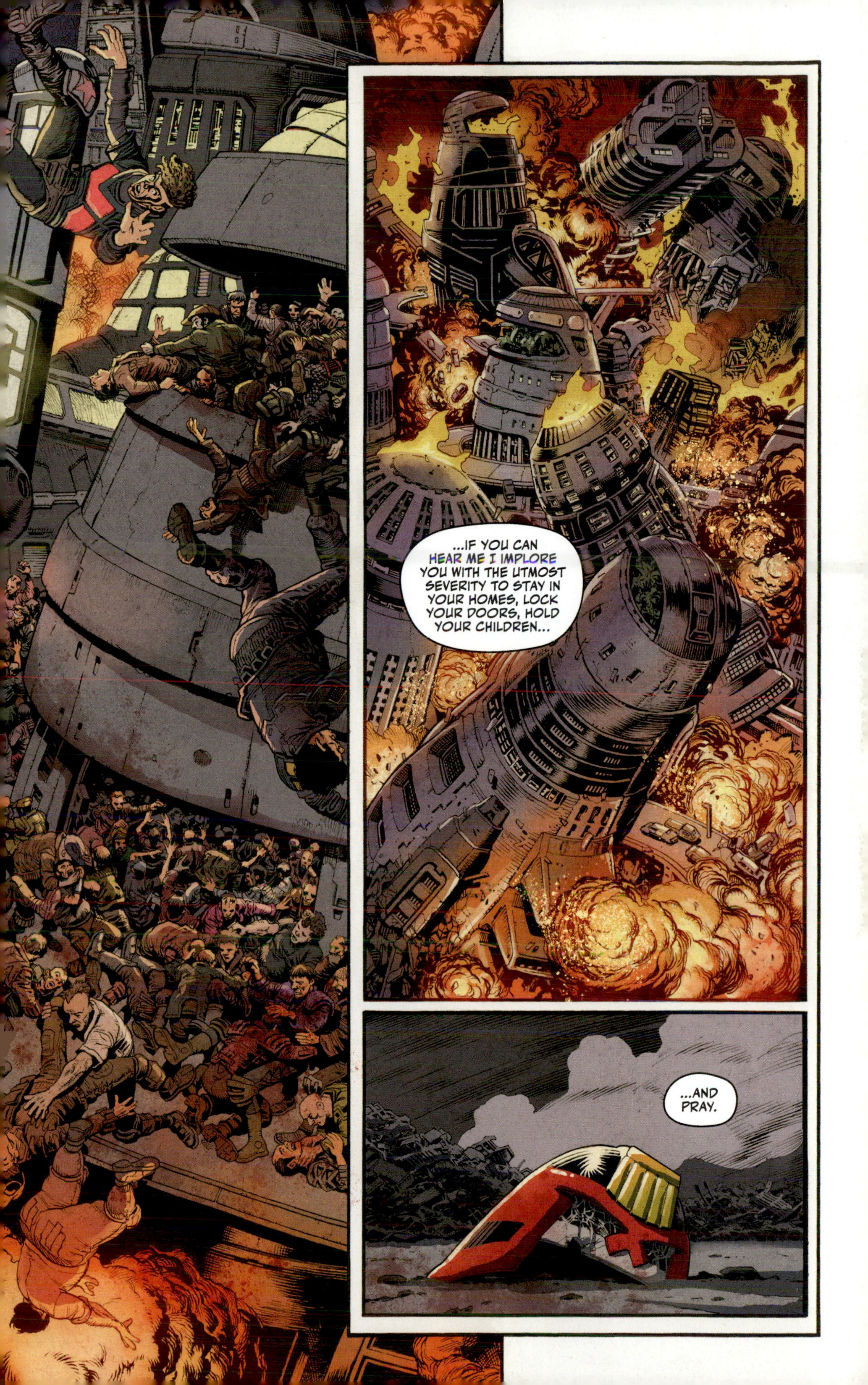
...IF YOU CAN HEAR ME I IMPLORE YOU WITH THE UTMOST SEVERITY TO STAY IN YOUR HOMES, LOCK YOUR DOORS, HOLD YOUR CHILDREN...
...AND PRAY.

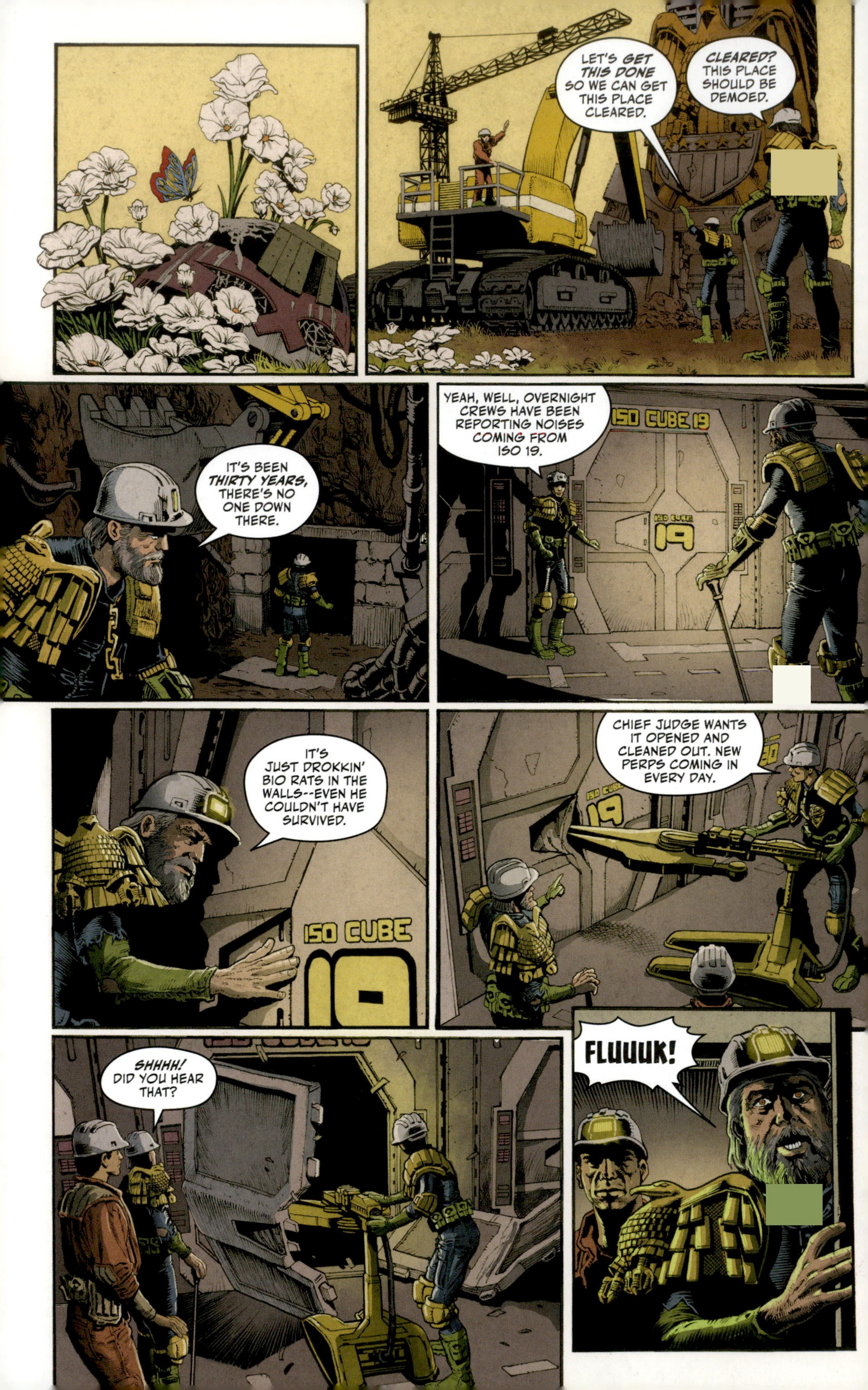

LET'S GET THIS DONE SO WE CAN GET THIS PLACE CLEARED.
CLEARED? THIS PLACE SHOULD BE DEMOED.
IT'S BEEN THIRTY YEARS, THERE'S NO ONE DOWN THERE.
YEAH, WELL, OVERNIGHT CREWS HAVE BEEN REPORTING NOISES COMING FROM ISO 19.
ISO CUBE 19
IT'S JUST DROKKIN' BIO RATS IN THE WALLS--EVEN HE COULDN'T HAVE SURVIVED.
ISO CUBE 19
CHIEF JUDGE WANTS IT OPENED AND CLEANED OUT. NEW PERPS COMING IN EVERY DAY.
SHHHH! DID YOU HEAR THAT?
FLUUUK!

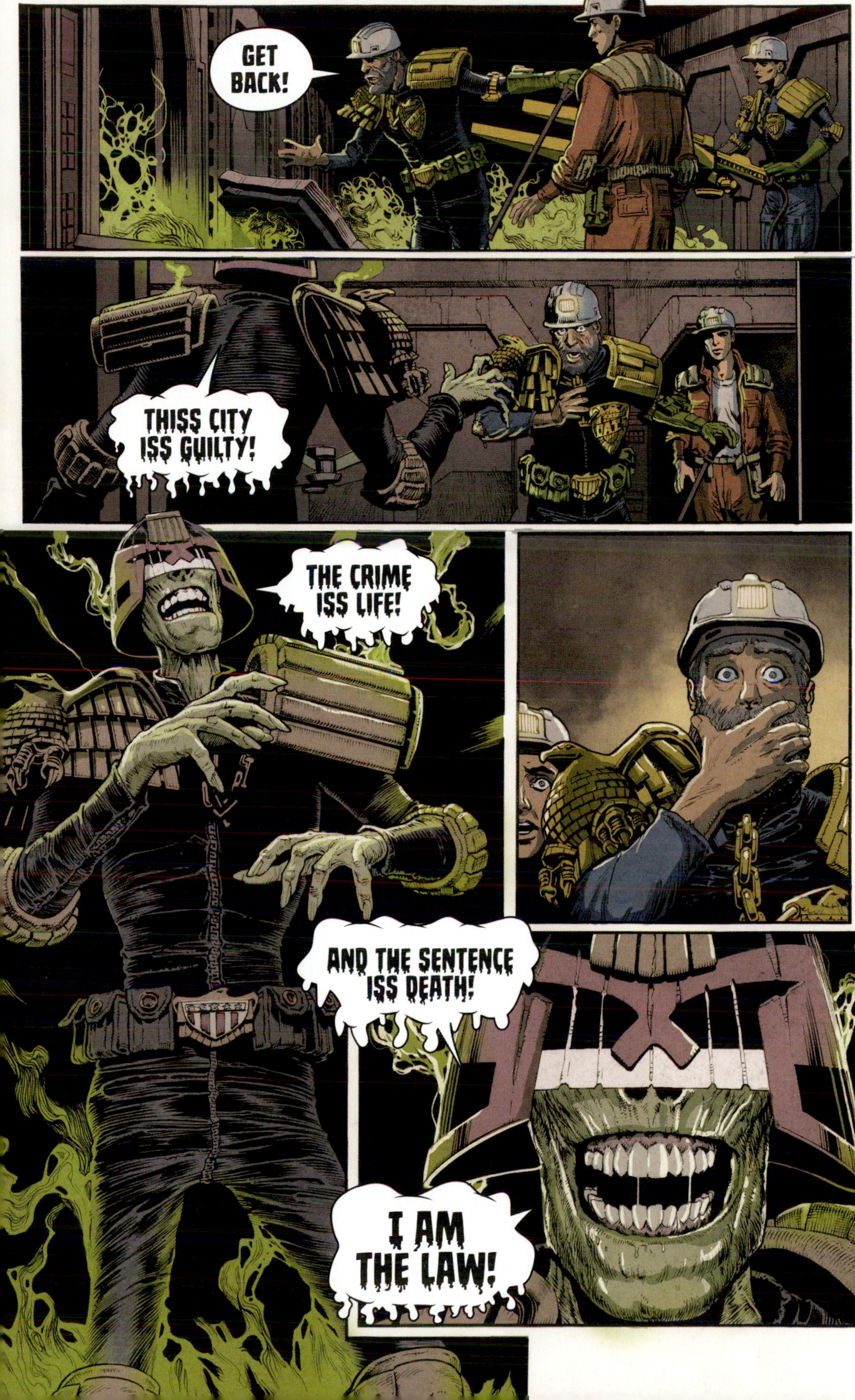
GET BACK!
THISS CITY ISS GUILTY!
THE CRIME ISS LIFE!
AND THE SENTENCE ISS DEATH!
I AM THE LAW!

TRACK FOUR
EFILNIKUFESIN (N.F.L.)

WRITTEN BY
RICK REMENDER
&
JOE TROHMAN

ILLUSTRATED BY
ROLAND BOSCHI

COLORED BY
DAN BROWN

"I'M FREAKING DYING UP HERE!
IS THIS MICROPHONE ON?"

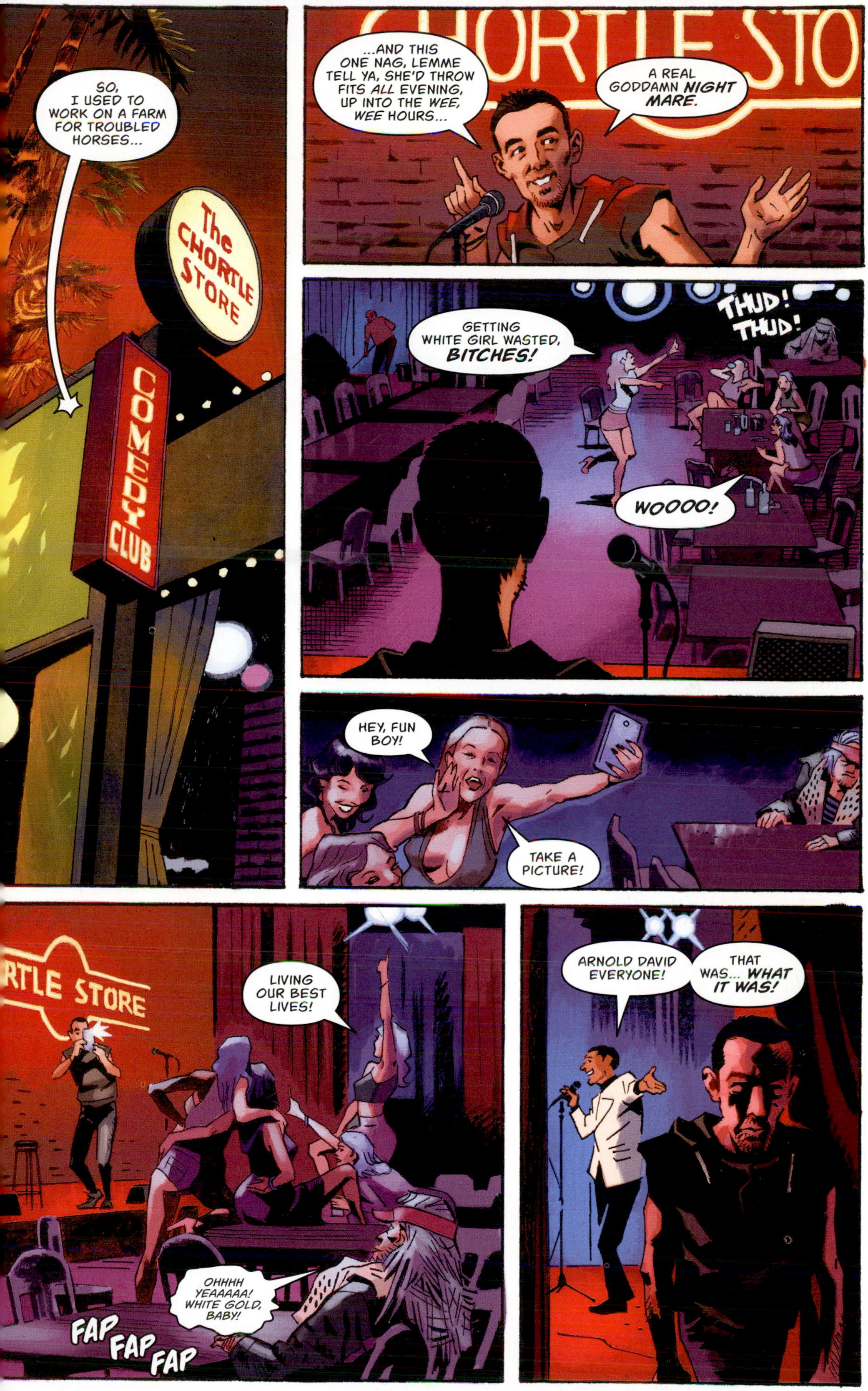

SO, I USED TO WORK ON A FARM FOR TROUBLED HORSES...
The CHORTLE STORE
COMEDY CLUB
CHORTLE STO
...AND THIS ONE NAG, LEMME TELL YA, SHE'D THROW FITS ALL EVENING, UP INTO THE WEE, WEE HOURS...
A REAL GODDAMN NIGHT MARE.
GETTING WHITE GIRL WASTED, BITCHES!
THUD! THUD!
WOOOO!
HEY, FUN BOY!
TAKE A PICTURE!
RTLE STORE
LIVING OUR BEST LIVES!
OHHHH YEAAAAA! WHITE GOLD, BABY!
FAP FAP FAP
ARNOLD DAVID EVERYONE!
THAT WAS... WHAT IT WAS!

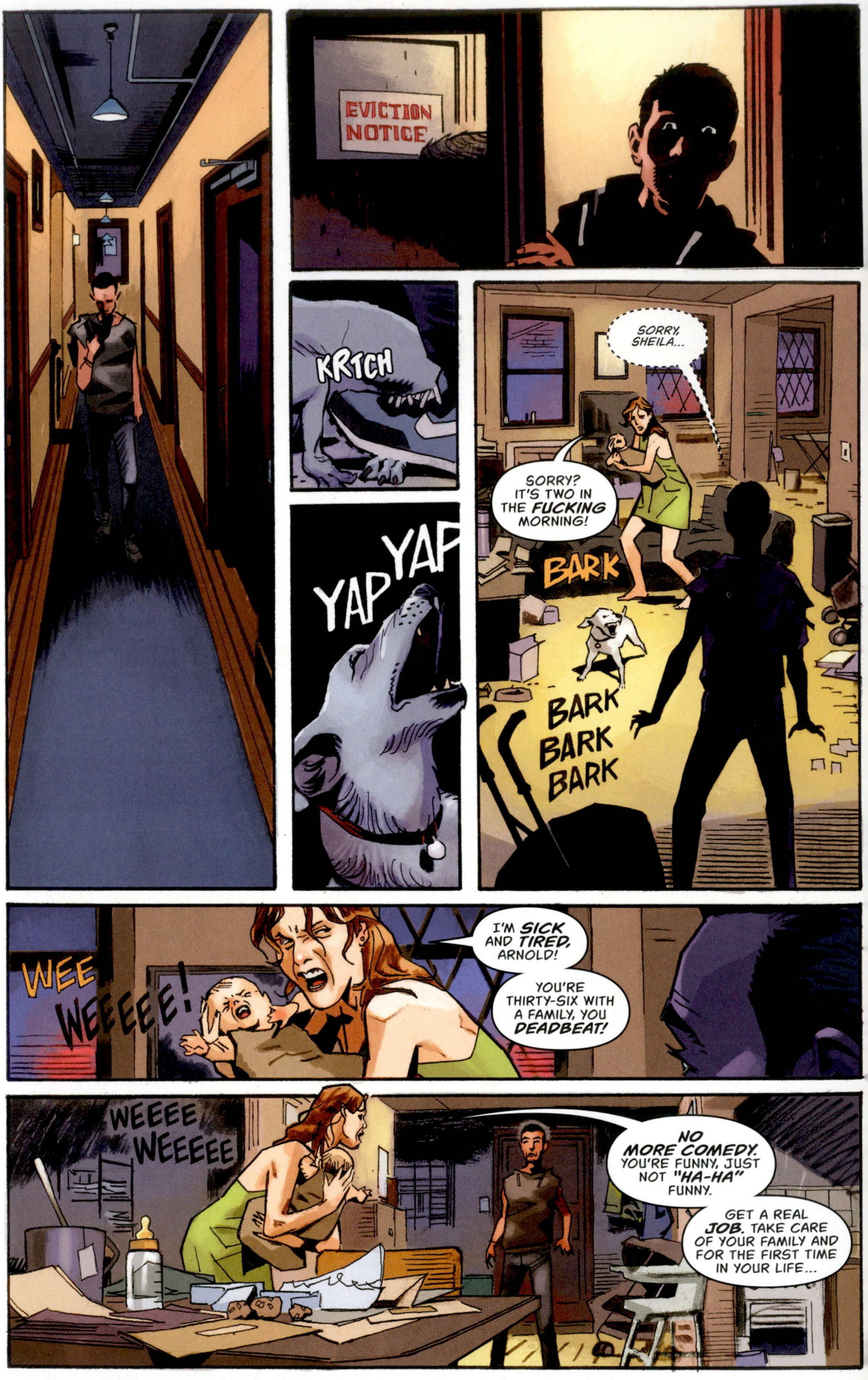
EVICTION NOTICE
KRTCH
YAP YAP
SORRY, SHEILA...
SORRY? IT'S TWO IN THE FUCKING MORNING!
BARK
BARK BARK BARK
WEE WEEEEE!
I'M SICK AND TIRED, ARNOLD!
YOU'RE THIRTY-SIX WITH A FAMILY, YOU DEADBEAT!
WEEEE WEEEEEE
NO MORE COMEDY. YOU'RE FUNNY, JUST NOT "HA-HA" FUNNY.
GET A REAL JOB. TAKE CARE OF YOUR FAMILY AND FOR THE FIRST TIME IN YOUR LIFE...

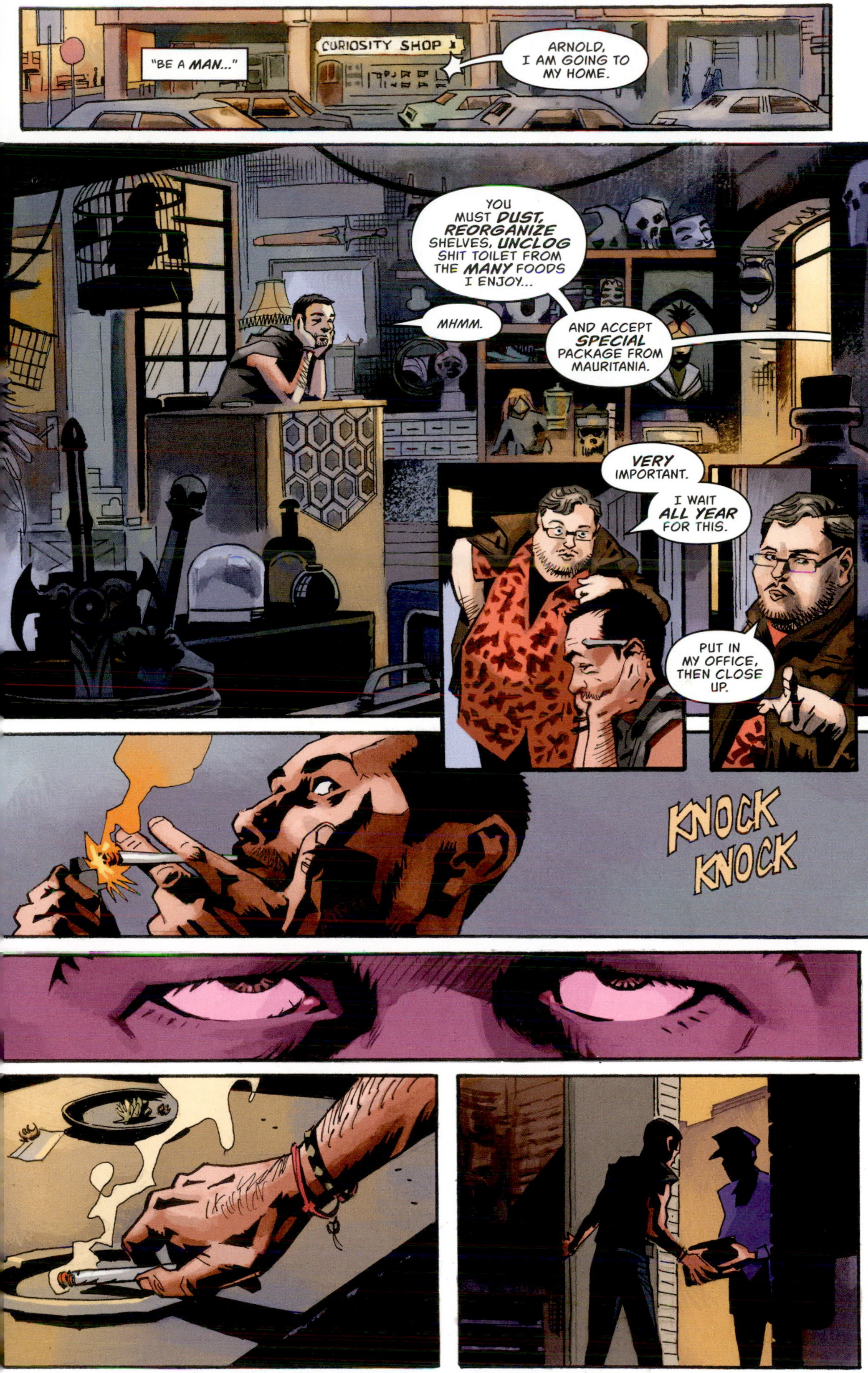

CURIOSITY SHOP
"BE A *MAN*..."
ARNOLD, I AM GOING TO MY HOME.
YOU MUST **DUST**, **REORGANIZE** SHELVES, **UNCLOG** SHIT TOILET FROM THE **MANY** FOODS I ENJOY...
MHMM.
AND ACCEPT **SPECIAL** PACKAGE FROM MAURITANIA.
VERY IMPORTANT.
I WAIT **ALL YEAR** FOR THIS.
PUT IN MY OFFICE, THEN CLOSE UP.
KNOCK KNOCK

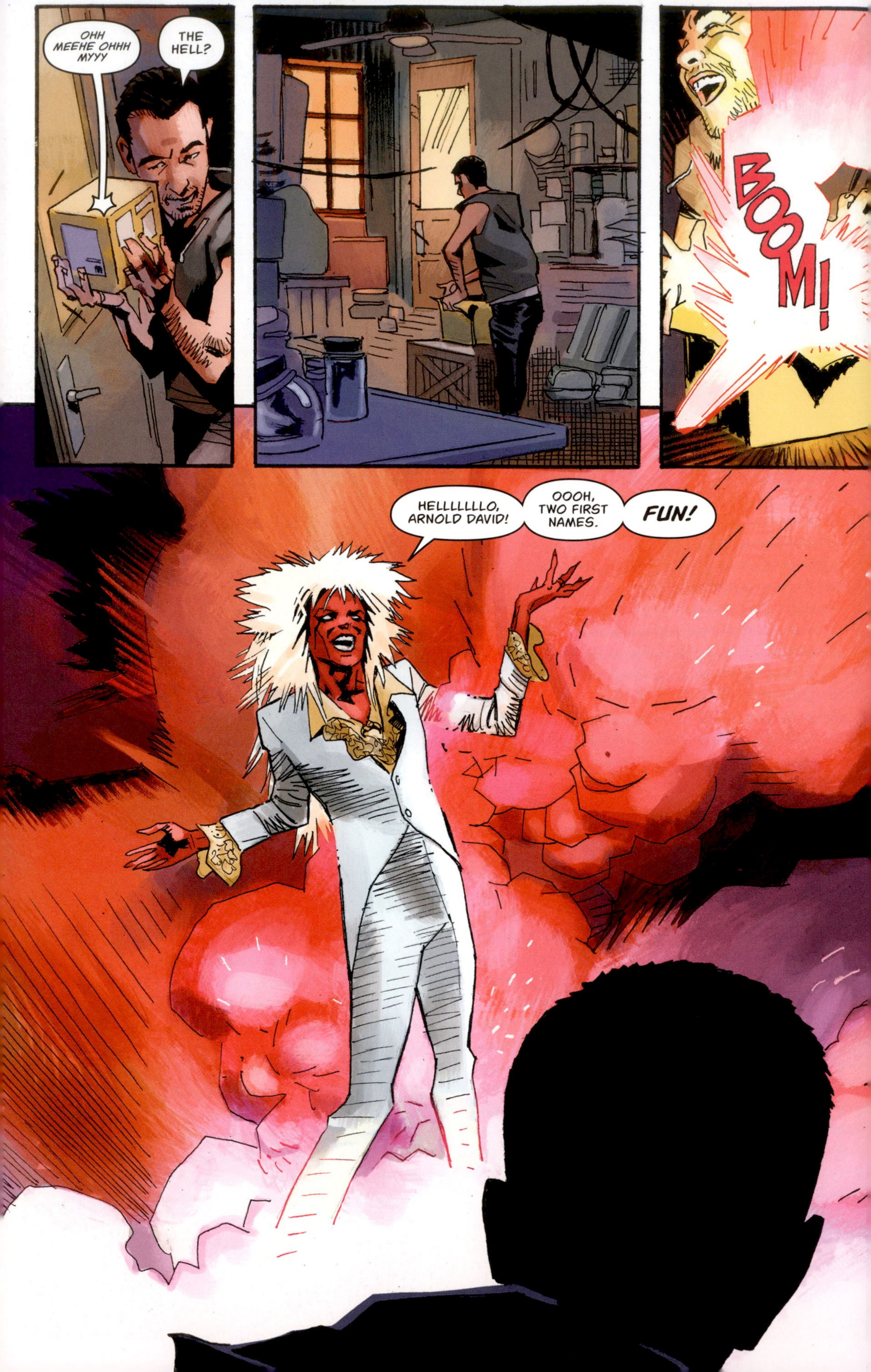
OHH MEEHE OHHH MYYY
THE HELL?
BOOM!
HELLLLLLLO, ARNOLD DAVID!
OOOH, TWO FIRST NAMES.
FUN!

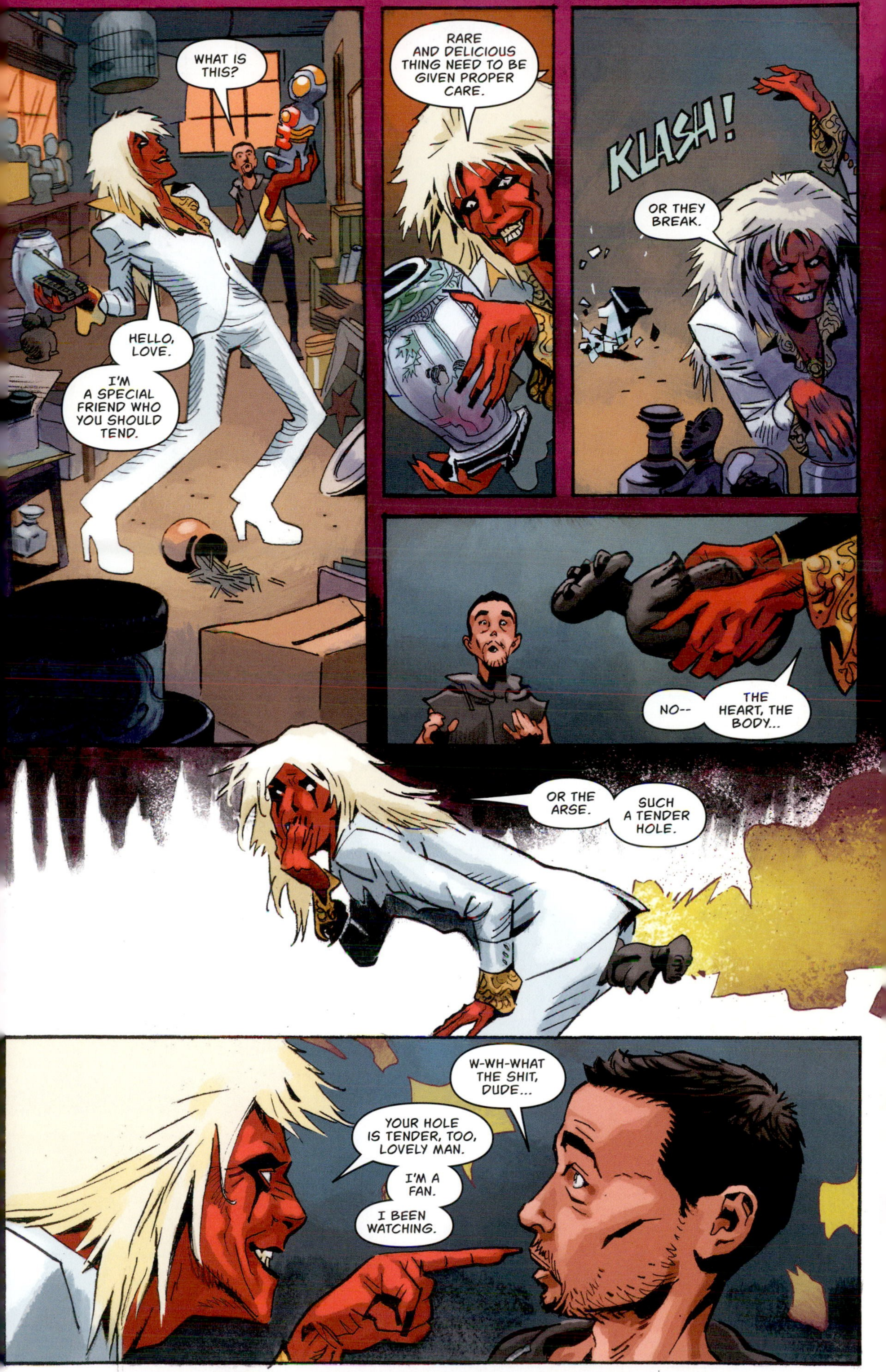
WHAT IS THIS?
HELLO, LOVE.
I'M A SPECIAL FRIEND WHO YOU SHOULD TEND.
RARE AND DELICIOUS THING NEED TO BE GIVEN PROPER CARE.
KLASH!
OR THEY BREAK.
NO--
THE HEART, THE BODY...
OR THE ARSE.
SUCH A TENDER HOLE.
W-WH-WHAT THE SHIT, DUDE...
YOUR HOLE IS TENDER, TOO, LOVELY MAN.
I'M A FAN.
I BEEN WATCHING.

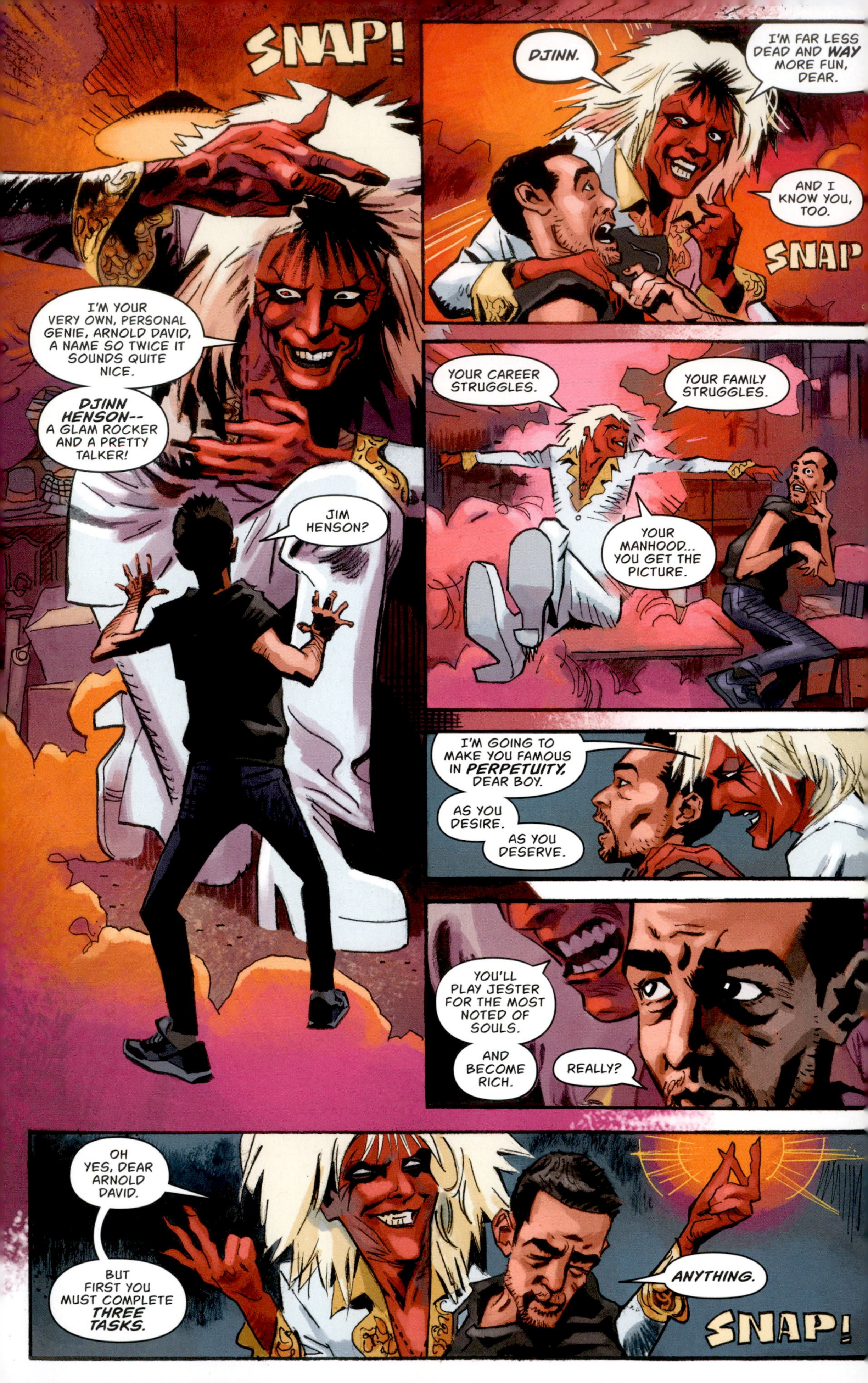
SNAP!
I'M YOUR VERY OWN, PERSONAL GENIE, ARNOLD DAVID, A NAME SO TWICE IT SOUNDS QUITE NICE.
DJINN HENSON-- A GLAM ROCKER AND A PRETTY TALKER!
JIM HENSON?
DJINN.
I'M FAR LESS DEAD AND WAY MORE FUN, DEAR.
AND I KNOW YOU, TOO.
SNAP
YOUR CAREER STRUGGLES.
YOUR FAMILY STRUGGLES.
YOUR MANHOOD... YOU GET THE PICTURE.
I'M GOING TO MAKE YOU FAMOUS IN PERPETUITY, DEAR BOY.
AS YOU DESIRE.
AS YOU DESERVE.
YOU'LL PLAY JESTER FOR THE MOST NOTED OF SOULS.
AND BECOME RICH.
REALLY?
OH YES, DEAR ARNOLD DAVID.
BUT FIRST YOU MUST COMPLETE THREE TASKS.
ANYTHING.
SNAP!

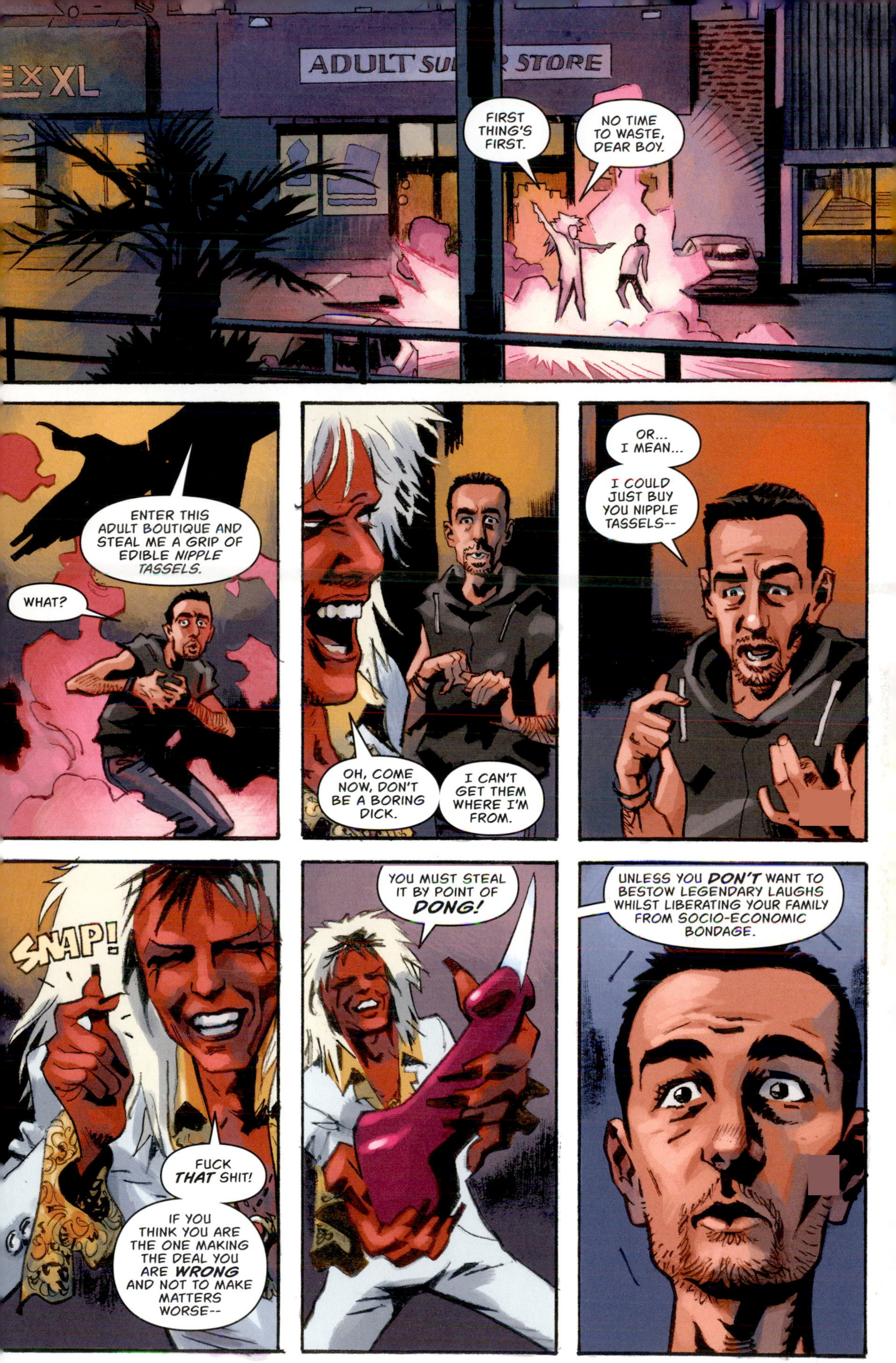
EXXL
ADULT SU R STORE
FIRST THING'S FIRST.
NO TIME TO WASTE, DEAR BOY.
ENTER THIS ADULT BOUTIQUE AND STEAL ME A GRIP OF EDIBLE *NIPPLE TASSELS.*
WHAT?
OH, COME NOW, DON'T BE A BORING DICK.
I CAN'T GET THEM WHERE I'M FROM.
OR... I MEAN...
I COULD JUST BUY YOU NIPPLE TASSELS--
SNAP!
FUCK **THAT** SHIT!
IF YOU THINK YOU ARE THE ONE MAKING THE DEAL YOU ARE **WRONG** AND NOT TO MAKE MATTERS WORSE--
YOU MUST STEAL IT BY POINT OF **DONG!**
UNLESS YOU **DON'T** WANT TO BESTOW LEGENDARY LAUGHS WHILST LIBERATING YOUR FAMILY FROM SOCIO-ECONOMIC BONDAGE.

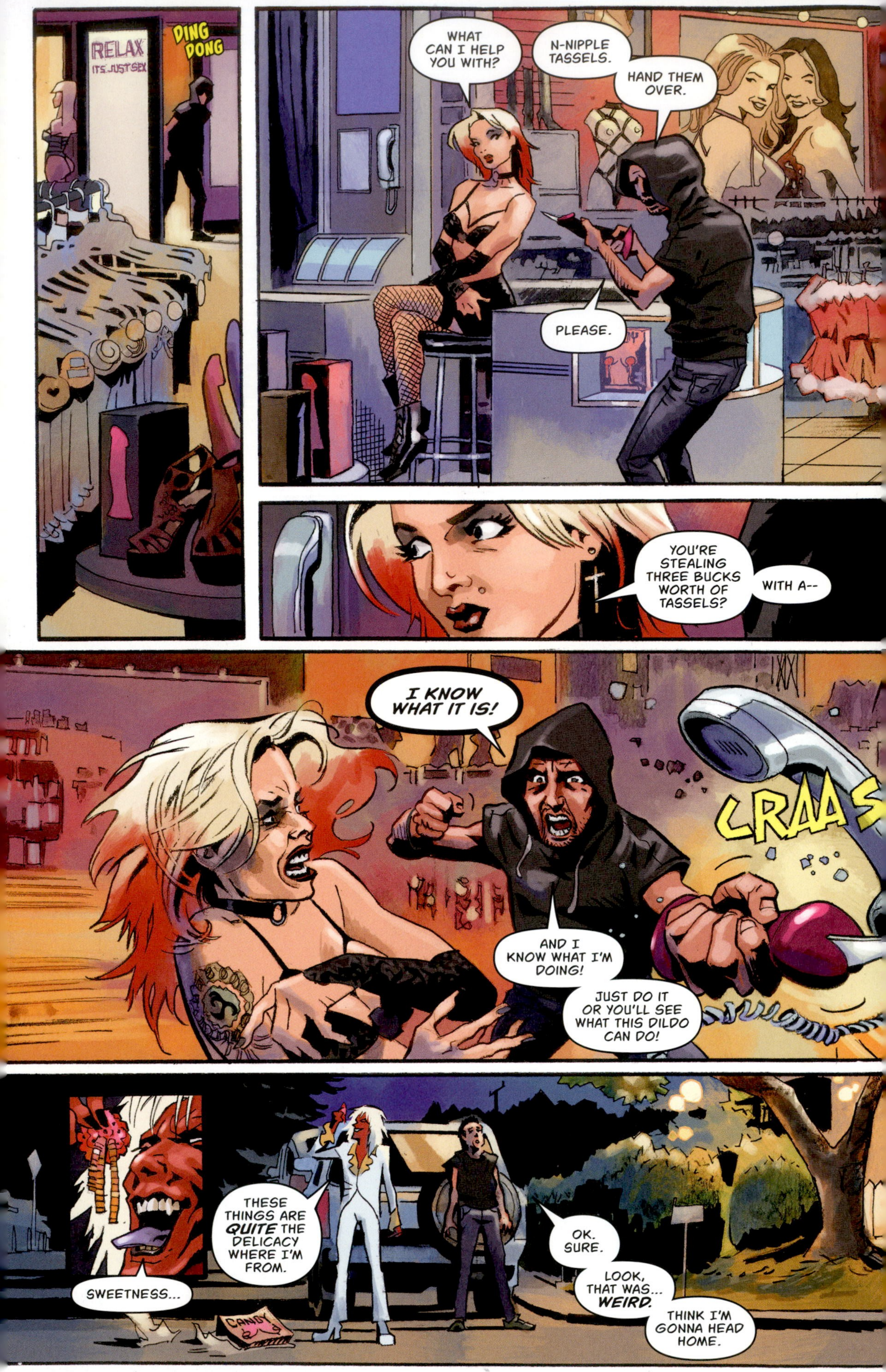
RELAX
IT'S JUST SEX
DING DONG
WHAT CAN I HELP YOU WITH?
N-NIPPLE TASSELS.
HAND THEM OVER.
PLEASE.
YOU'RE STEALING THREE BUCKS WORTH OF TASSELS?
WITH A--
I KNOW WHAT IT IS!
CRAAS
AND I KNOW WHAT I'M DOING!
JUST DO IT OR YOU'LL SEE WHAT THIS DILDO CAN DO!
SWEETNESS...
THESE THINGS ARE QUITE THE DELICACY WHERE I'M FROM.
CANDY
OK. SURE.
LOOK, THAT WAS... WEIRD.
THINK I'M GONNA HEAD HOME.

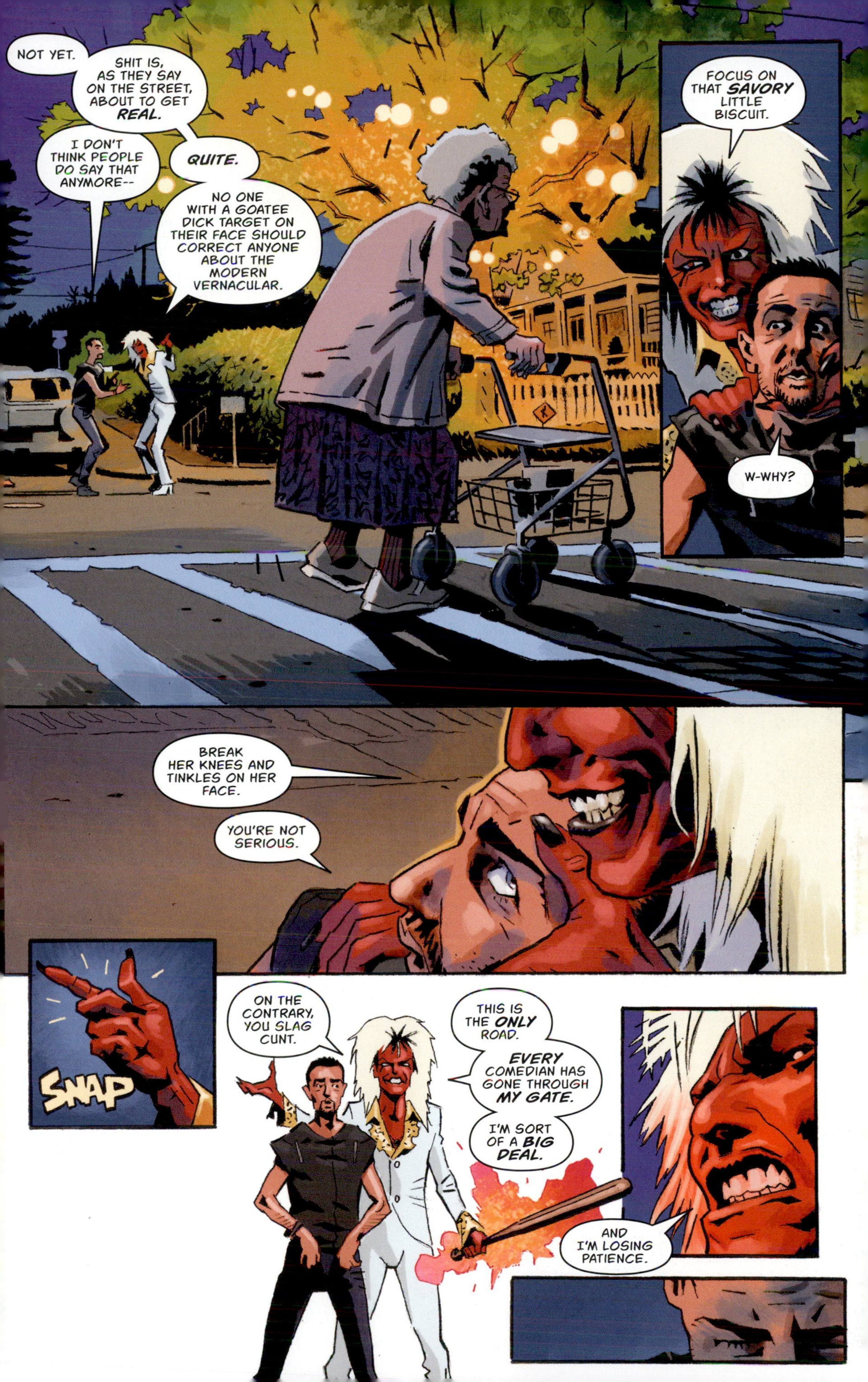
NOT YET.
SHIT IS, AS THEY SAY ON THE STREET, ABOUT TO GET REAL.
I DON'T THINK PEOPLE DO SAY THAT ANYMORE--
QUITE.
NO ONE WITH A GOATEE DICK TARGET ON THEIR FACE SHOULD CORRECT ANYONE ABOUT THE MODERN VERNACULAR.
FOCUS ON THAT SAVORY LITTLE BISCUIT.
W-WHY?
BREAK HER KNEES AND TINKLES ON HER FACE.
YOU'RE NOT SERIOUS.
SNAP
ON THE CONTRARY, YOU SLAG CUNT.
THIS IS THE ONLY ROAD.
EVERY COMEDIAN HAS GONE THROUGH MY GATE.
I'M SORT OF A BIG DEAL.
AND I'M LOSING PATIENCE.

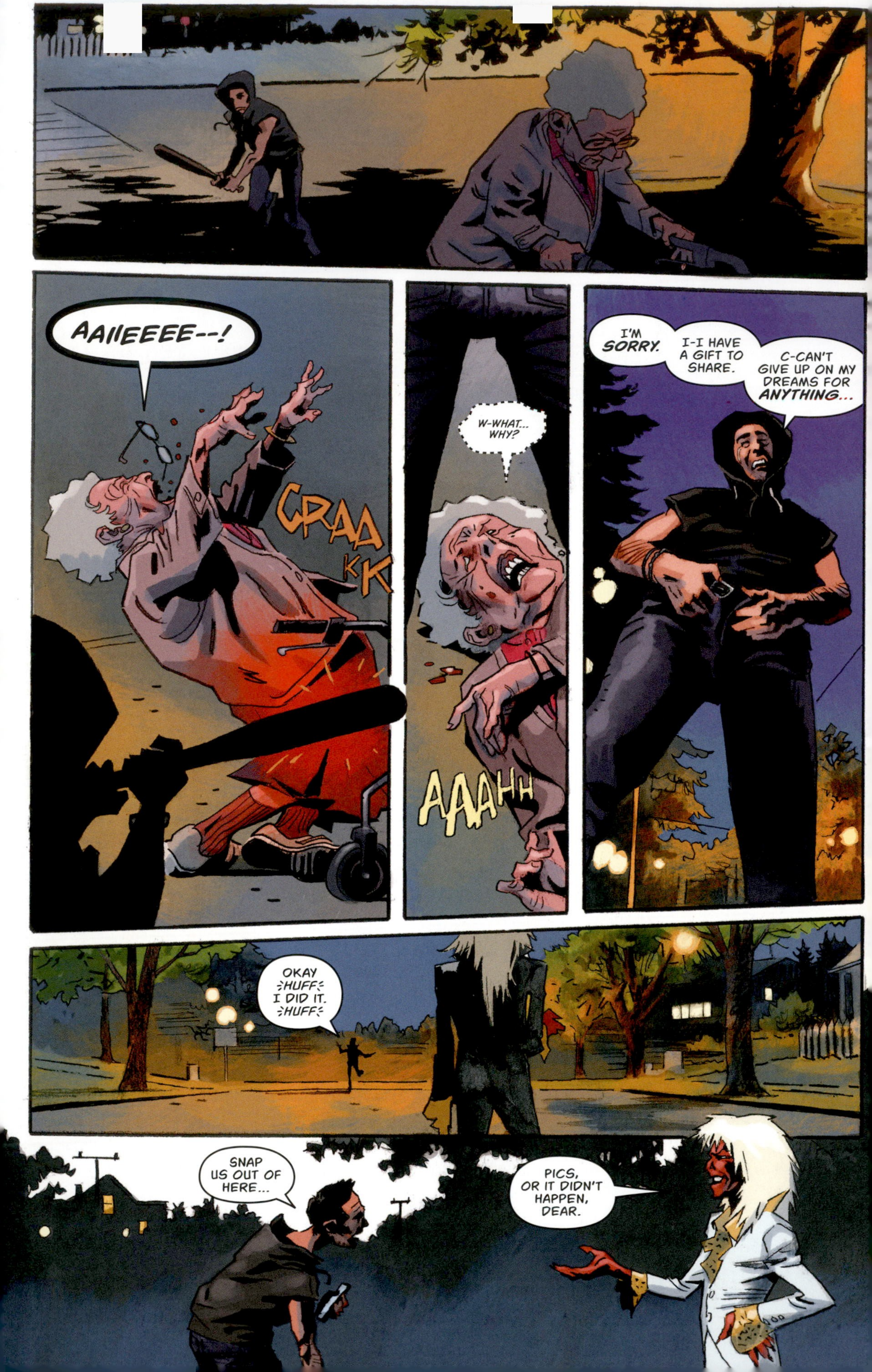
AAIIEEEE--!
GRAAKK
W-WHAT... WHY?
AAAHH
I'M SORRY.
I-I HAVE A GIFT TO SHARE.
C-CAN'T GIVE UP ON MY DREAMS FOR ANYTHING...
OKAY *HUFF* I DID IT. *HUFF*
SNAP US OUT OF HERE...
PICS, OR IT DIDN'T HAPPEN, DEAR.

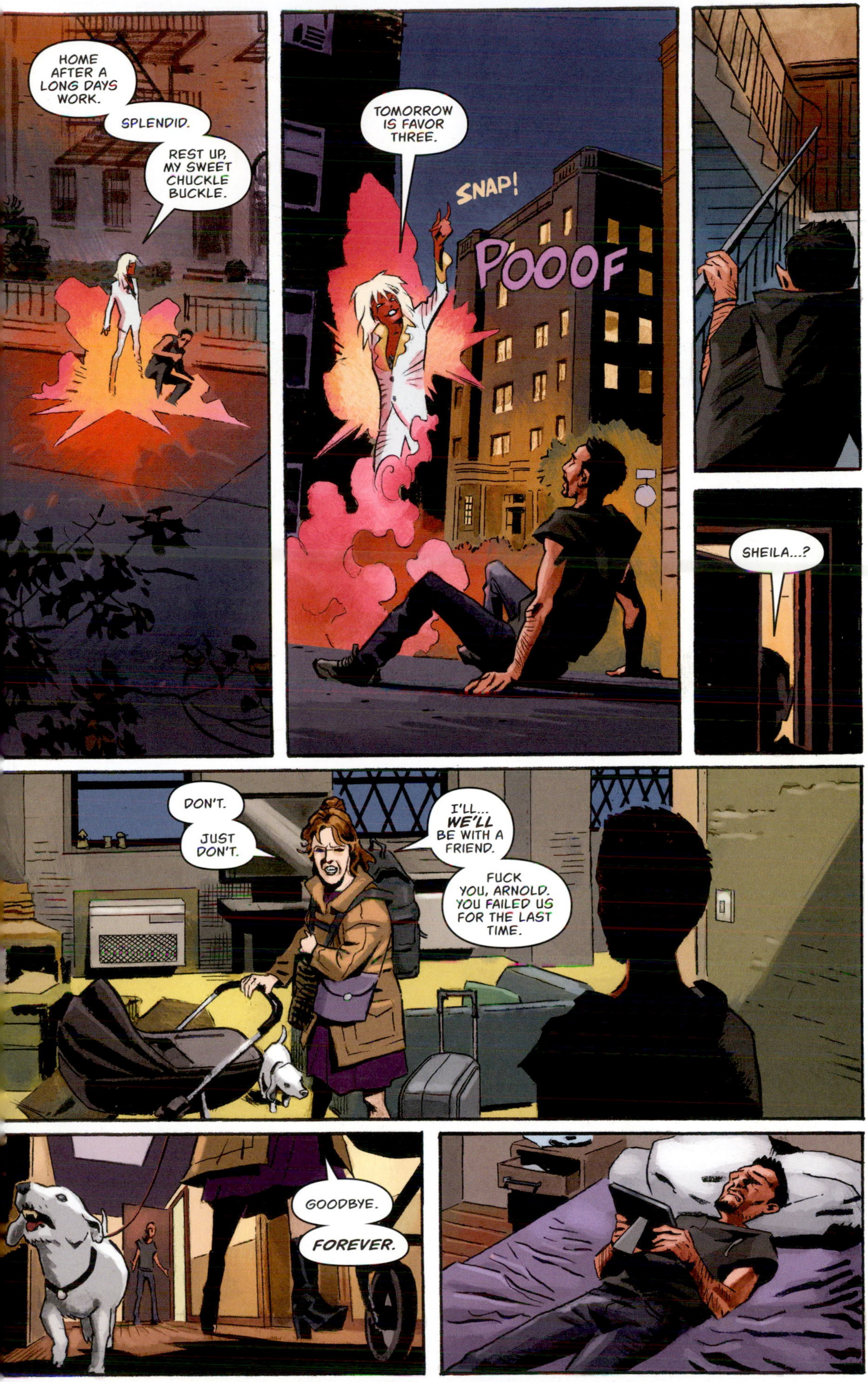
HOME AFTER A LONG DAYS WORK.
SPLENDID.
REST UP, MY SWEET CHUCKLE BUCKLE.
TOMORROW IS FAVOR THREE.
SNAP!
POOOF
SHEILA...?
DON'T.
JUST DON'T.
I'LL... WE'LL BE WITH A FRIEND.
FUCK YOU, ARNOLD. YOU FAILED US FOR THE LAST TIME.
GOODBYE.
FOREVER.

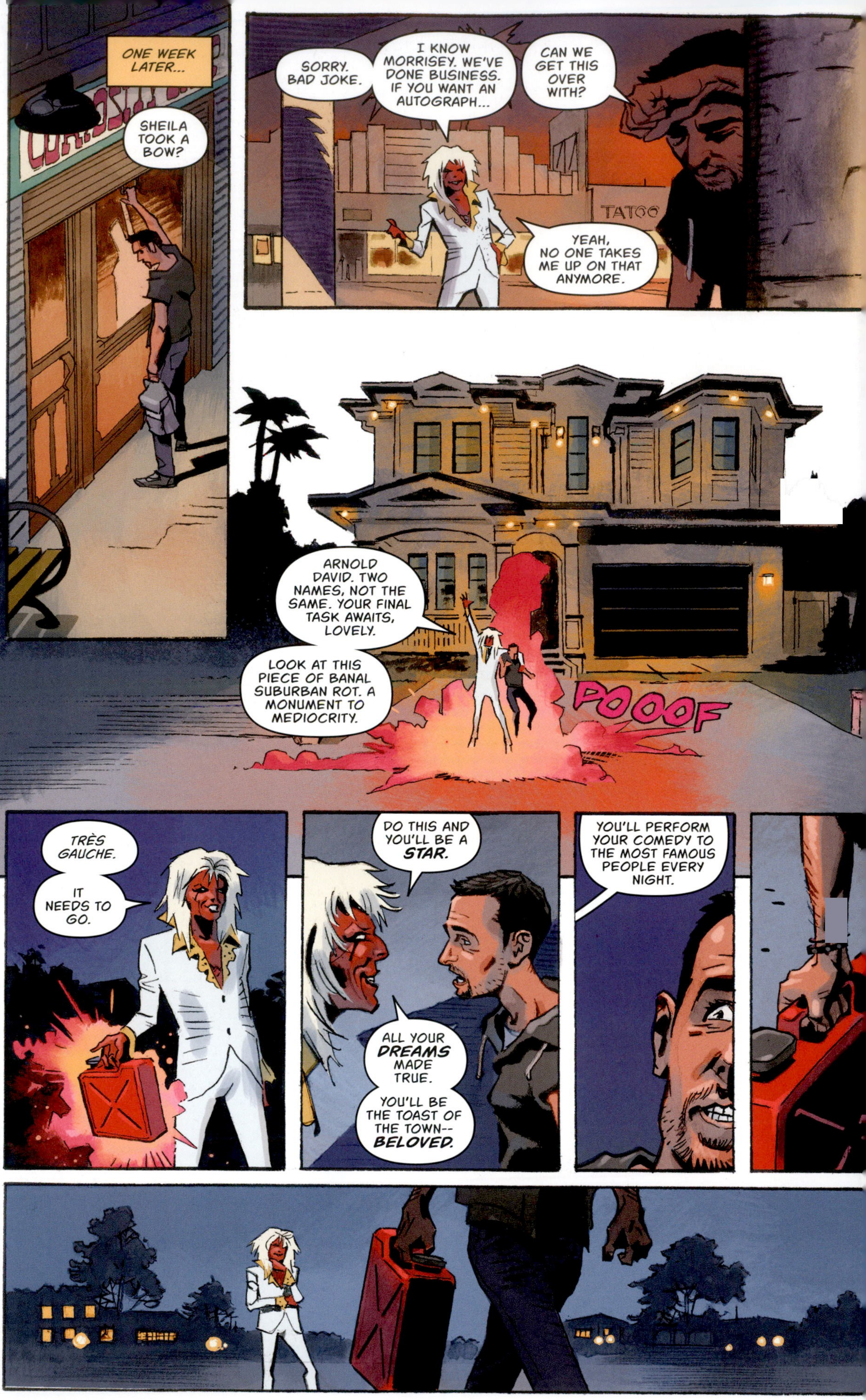
ONE WEEK LATER...
SHEILA TOOK A BOW?
SORRY. BAD JOKE.
I KNOW MORRISEY. WE'VE DONE BUSINESS. IF YOU WANT AN AUTOGRAPH...
CAN WE GET THIS OVER WITH?
YEAH, NO ONE TAKES ME UP ON THAT ANYMORE.
TATOO
ARNOLD DAVID. TWO NAMES, NOT THE SAME. YOUR FINAL TASK AWAITS, LOVELY.
LOOK AT THIS PIECE OF BANAL SUBURBAN ROT. A MONUMENT TO MEDIOCRITY.
POOOF
TRÈS GAUCHE.
IT NEEDS TO GO.
DO THIS AND YOU'LL BE A STAR.
ALL YOUR DREAMS MADE TRUE.
YOU'LL BE THE TOAST OF THE TOWN-- BELOVED.
YOU'LL PERFORM YOUR COMEDY TO THE MOST FAMOUS PEOPLE EVERY NIGHT.

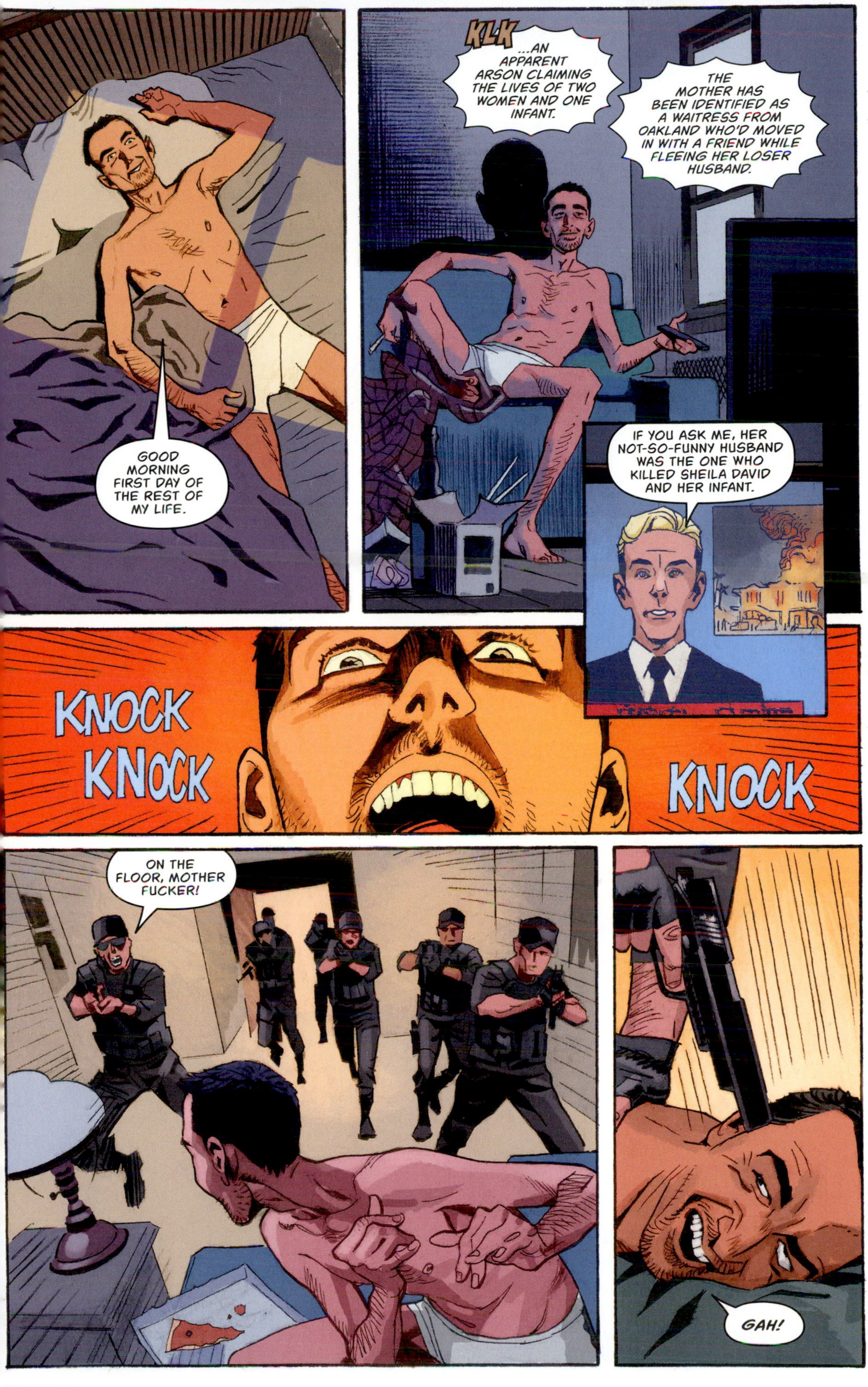
GOOD MORNING FIRST DAY OF THE REST OF MY LIFE.
KLK
...AN APPARENT ARSON CLAIMING THE LIVES OF TWO WOMEN AND ONE INFANT.
THE MOTHER HAS BEEN IDENTIFIED AS A WAITRESS FROM OAKLAND WHO'D MOVED IN WITH A FRIEND WHILE FLEEING HER LOSER HUSBAND.
IF YOU ASK ME, HER NOT-SO-FUNNY HUSBAND WAS THE ONE WHO KILLED SHEILA DAVID AND HER INFANT.
KNOCK
KNOCK
KNOCK
ON THE FLOOR, MOTHER FUCKER!
GAH!

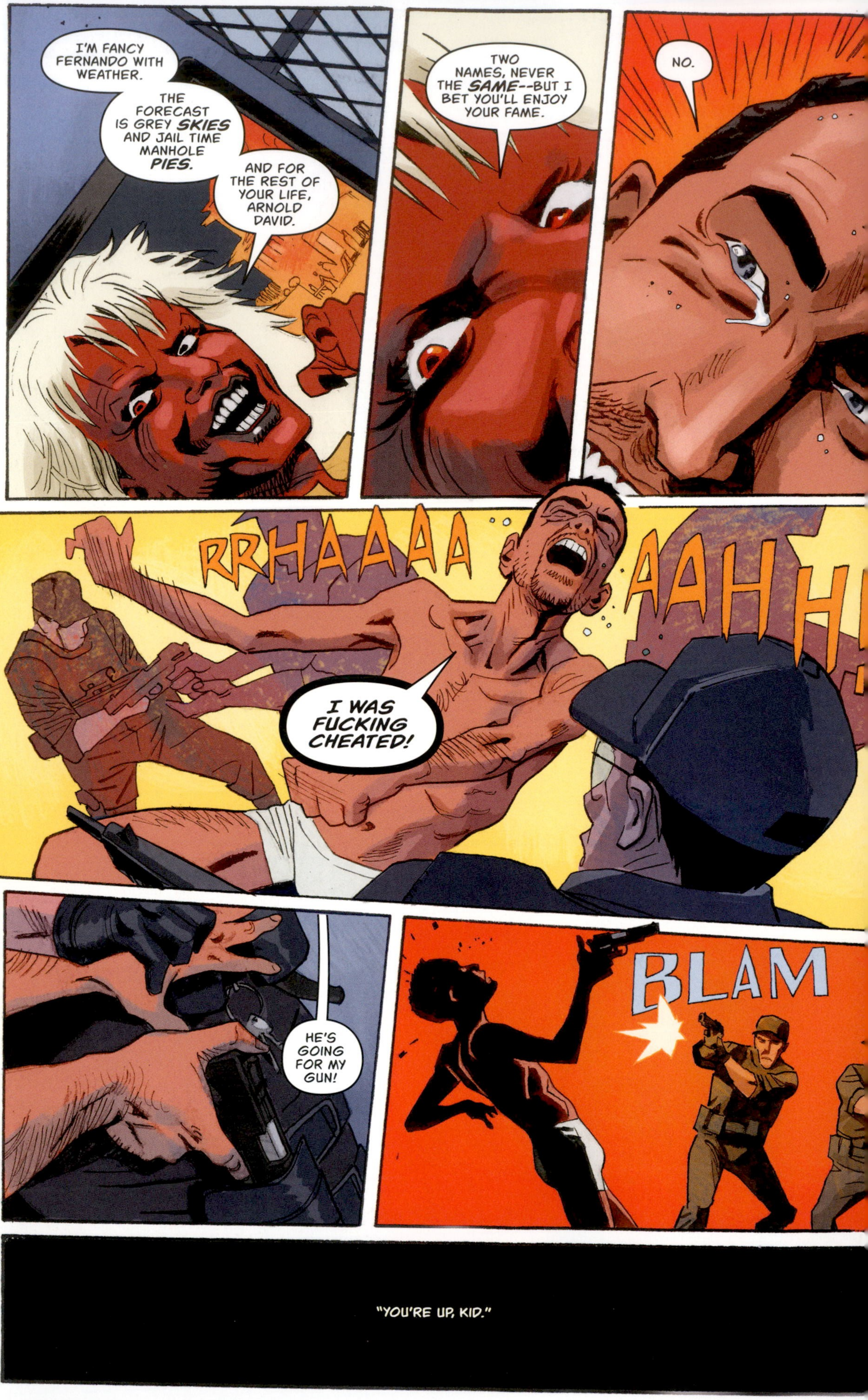
I'M FANCY FERNANDO WITH WEATHER.
THE FORECAST IS GREY SKIES AND JAIL TIME MANHOLE PIES.
AND FOR THE REST OF YOUR LIFE, ARNOLD DAVID.
TWO NAMES, NEVER THE SAME--BUT I BET YOU'LL ENJOY YOUR FAME.
NO.
RRHAAAAAAHH!
I WAS FUCKING CHEATED!
HE'S GOING FOR MY GUN!
BLAM
"YOU'RE UP, KID."

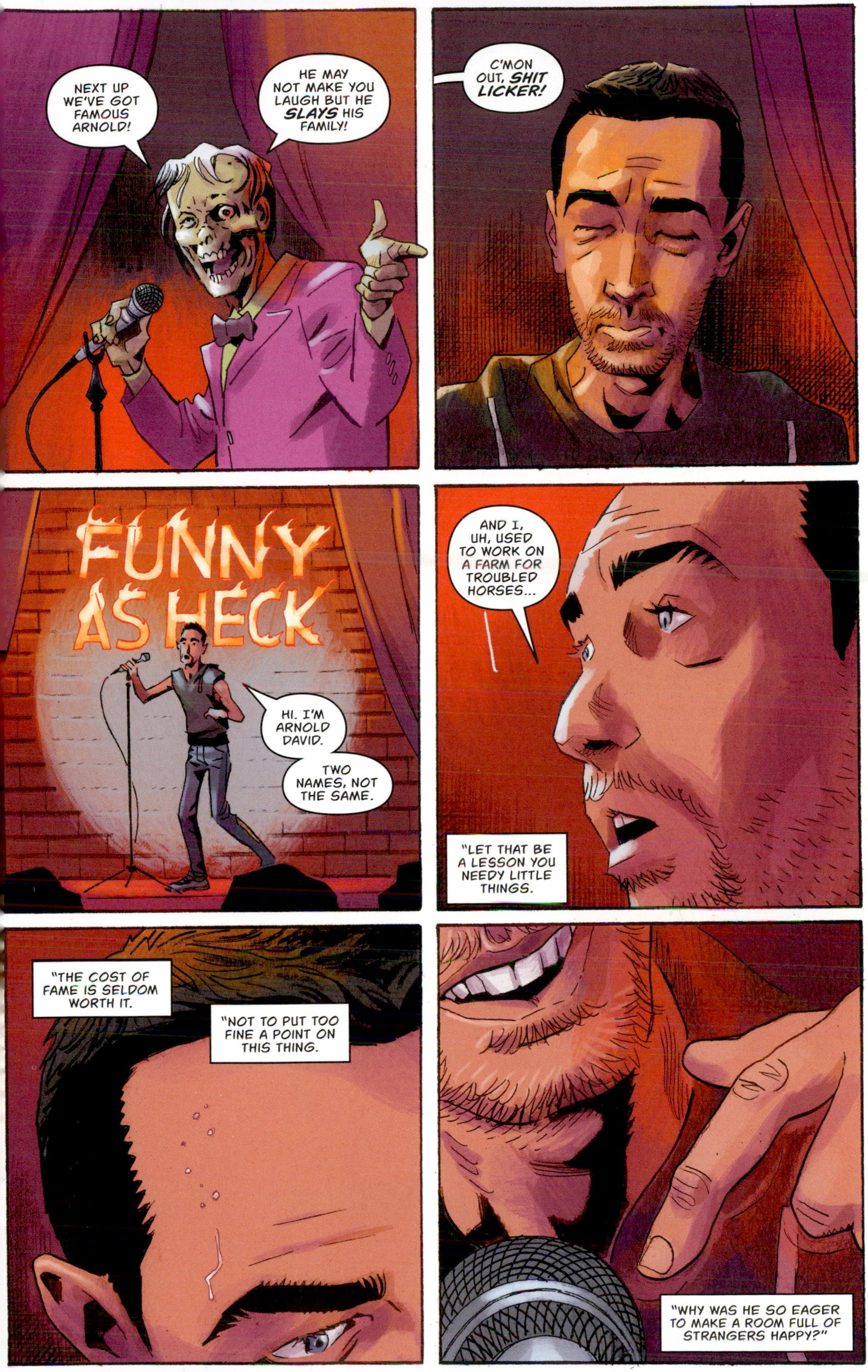

NEXT UP WE'VE GOT FAMOUS ARNOLD!
HE MAY NOT MAKE YOU LAUGH BUT HE SLAYS HIS FAMILY!
C'MON OUT, SHIT LICKER!
FUNNY AS HECK
HI. I'M ARNOLD DAVID.
TWO NAMES, NOT THE SAME.
AND I, UH, USED TO WORK ON A FARM FOR TROUBLED HORSES...
"LET THAT BE A LESSON YOU NEEDY LITTLE THINGS.
"THE COST OF FAME IS SELDOM WORTH IT.
"NOT TO PUT TOO FINE A POINT ON THIS THING.
"WHY WAS HE SO EAGER TO MAKE A ROOM FULL OF STRANGERS HAPPY?"

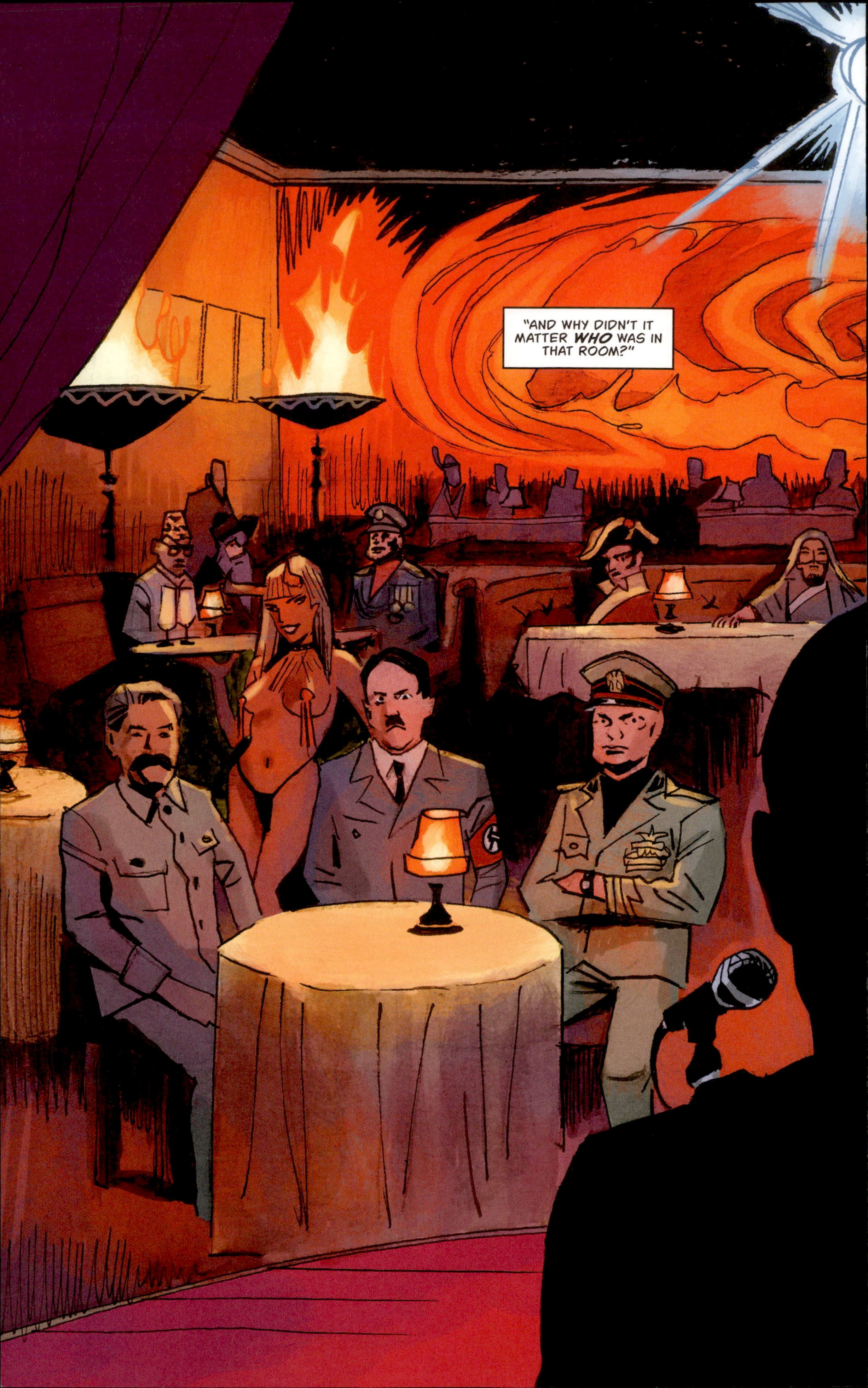
"AND WHY DIDN'T IT MATTER **WHO** WAS IN THAT ROOM?"

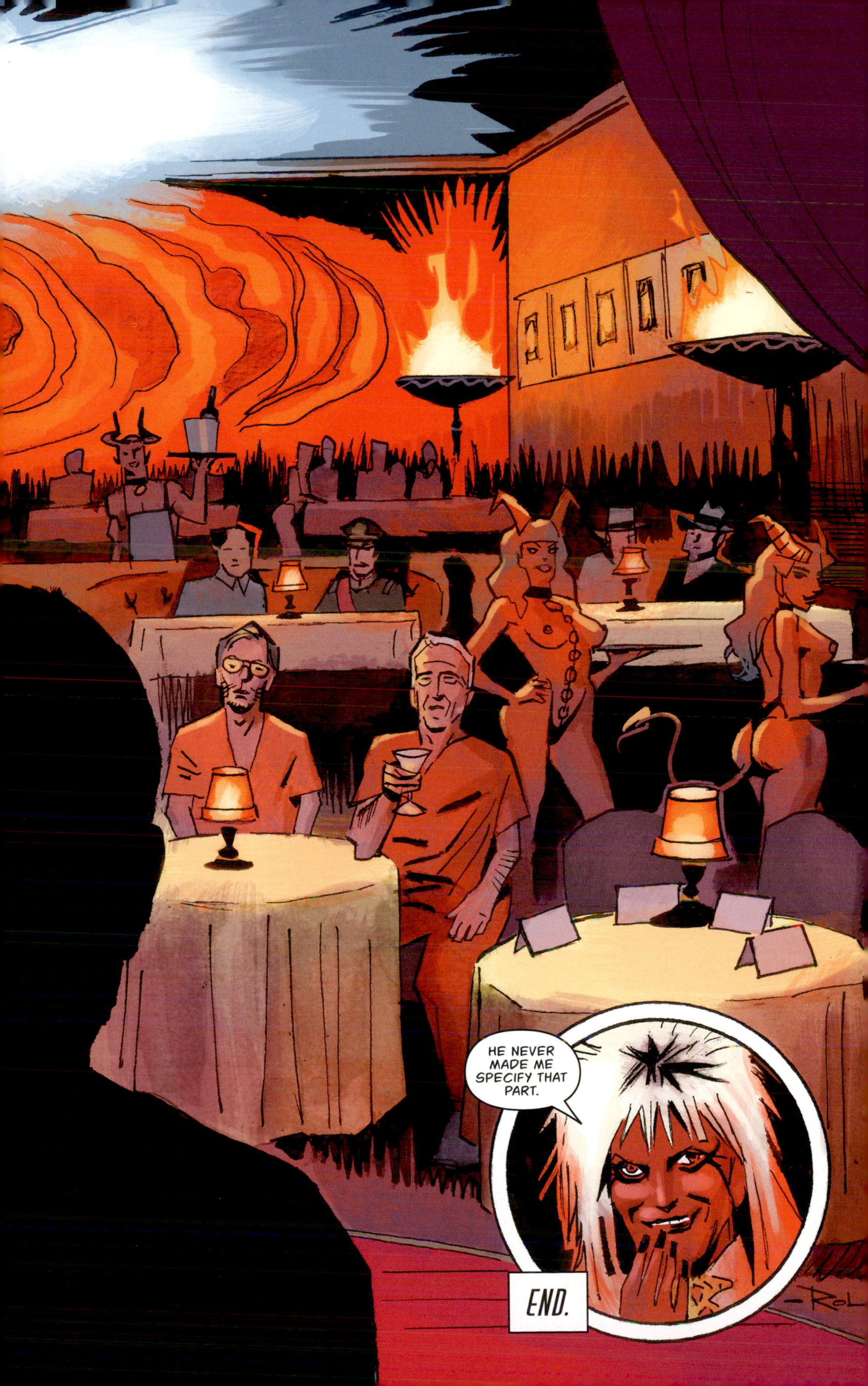
HE NEVER MADE ME SPECIFY THAT PART.
END.

TRACK FIVE
A SKELETON IN THE CLOSET

WRITTEN BY
**COREY
TAYLOR**

ILLUSTRATED BY
**MAAN
HOUSE**

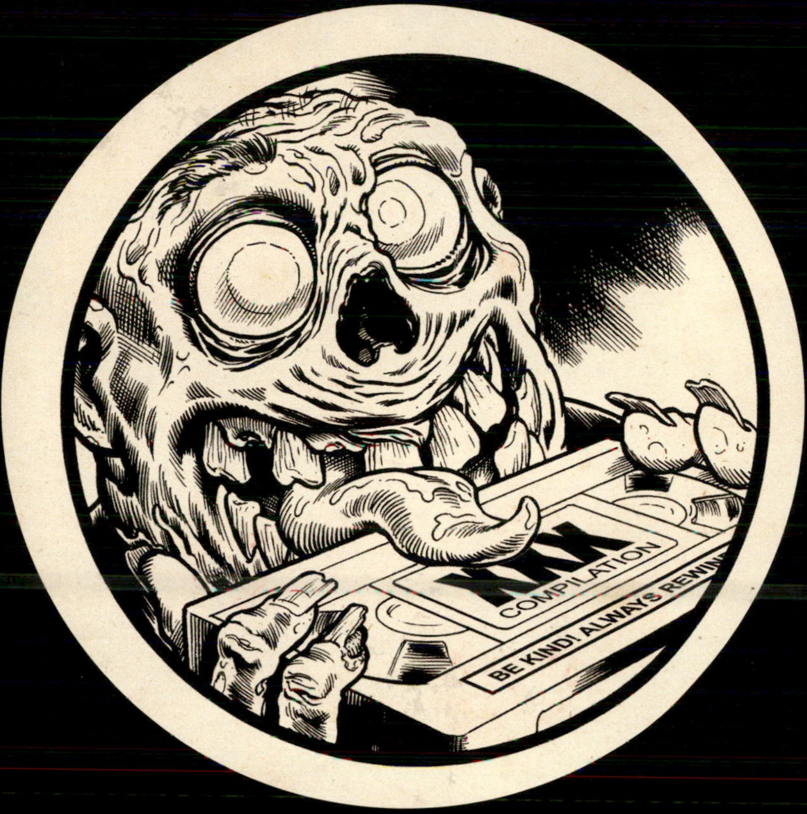
COMPILATION
BE KIND! ALWAYS REWIN

"I BET THIS GUY WAS OUT RETURNING VIDEO TAPES BEFORE THIS STORY STARTED!"

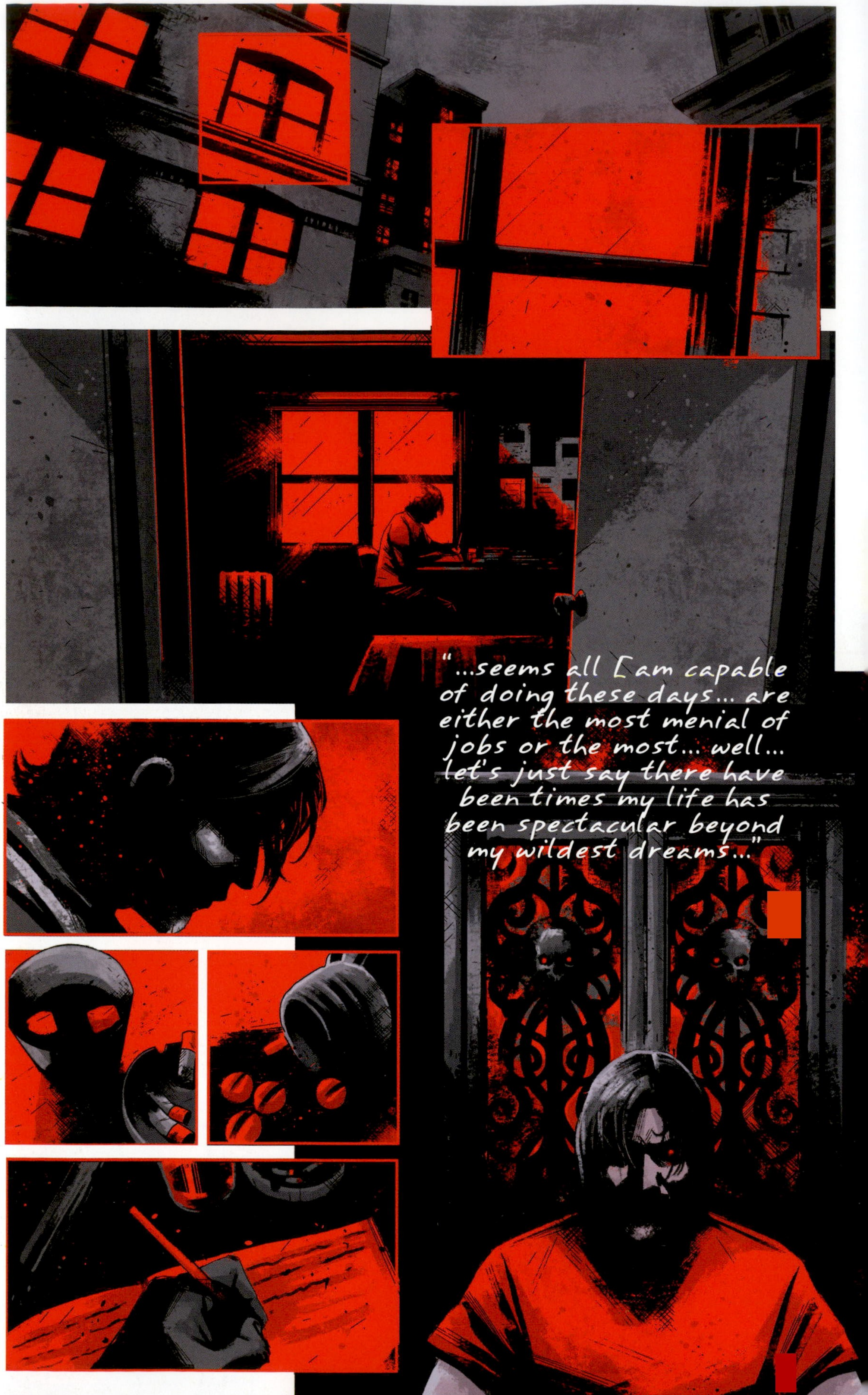
"...seems all I am capable of doing these days... are either the most menial of jobs or the most... well... let's just say there have been times my life has been spectacular beyond my wildest dreams..."

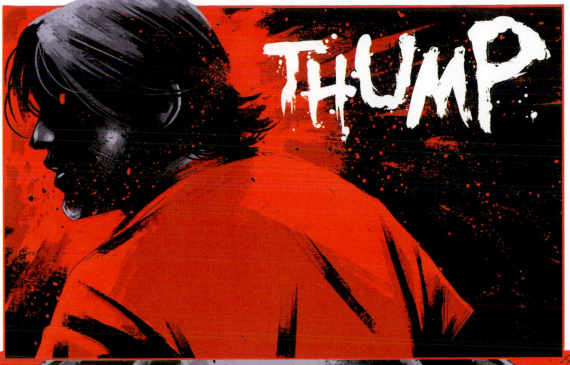

THUMP

"...and indeed my worst nightmares. It's getting a bit cramped here. We'll have to be moving on soon. Perhaps a little... parting gift tonight...?"

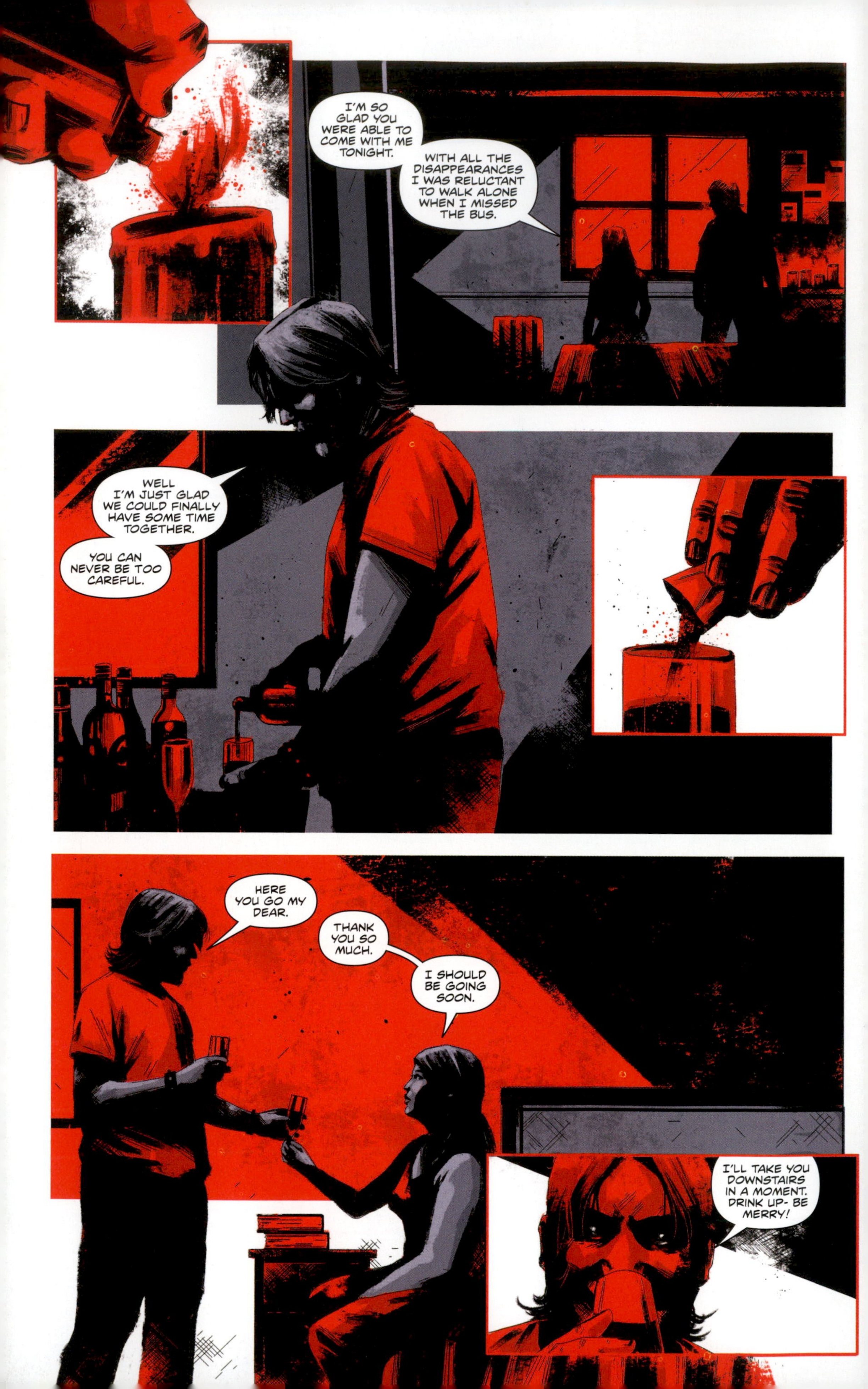
I'M SO GLAD YOU WERE ABLE TO COME WITH ME TONIGHT.
WITH ALL THE DISAPPEARANCES I WAS RELUCTANT TO WALK ALONE WHEN I MISSED THE BUS.
WELL I'M JUST GLAD WE COULD FINALLY HAVE SOME TIME TOGETHER.
YOU CAN NEVER BE TOO CAREFUL.
HERE YOU GO MY DEAR.
THANK YOU SO MUCH.
I SHOULD BE GOING SOON.
I'LL TAKE YOU DOWNSTAIRS IN A MOMENT. DRINK UP- BE MERRY!

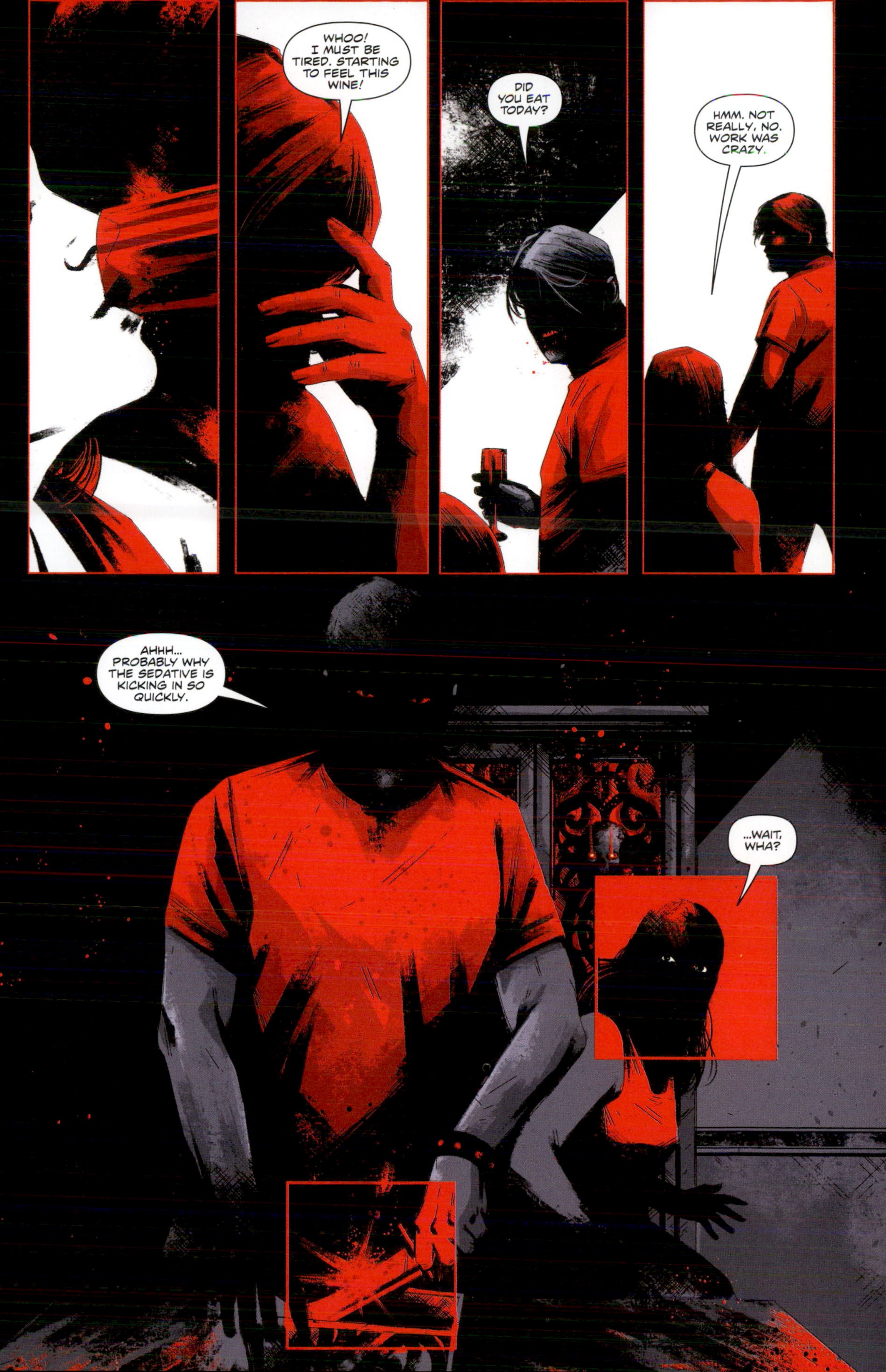
WHOO! I MUST BE TIRED. STARTING TO FEEL THIS WINE!
DID YOU EAT TODAY?
HMM. NOT REALLY, NO. WORK WAS CRAZY.
AHHH... PROBABLY WHY THE SEDATIVE IS KICKING IN SO QUICKLY.
...WAIT, WHA?

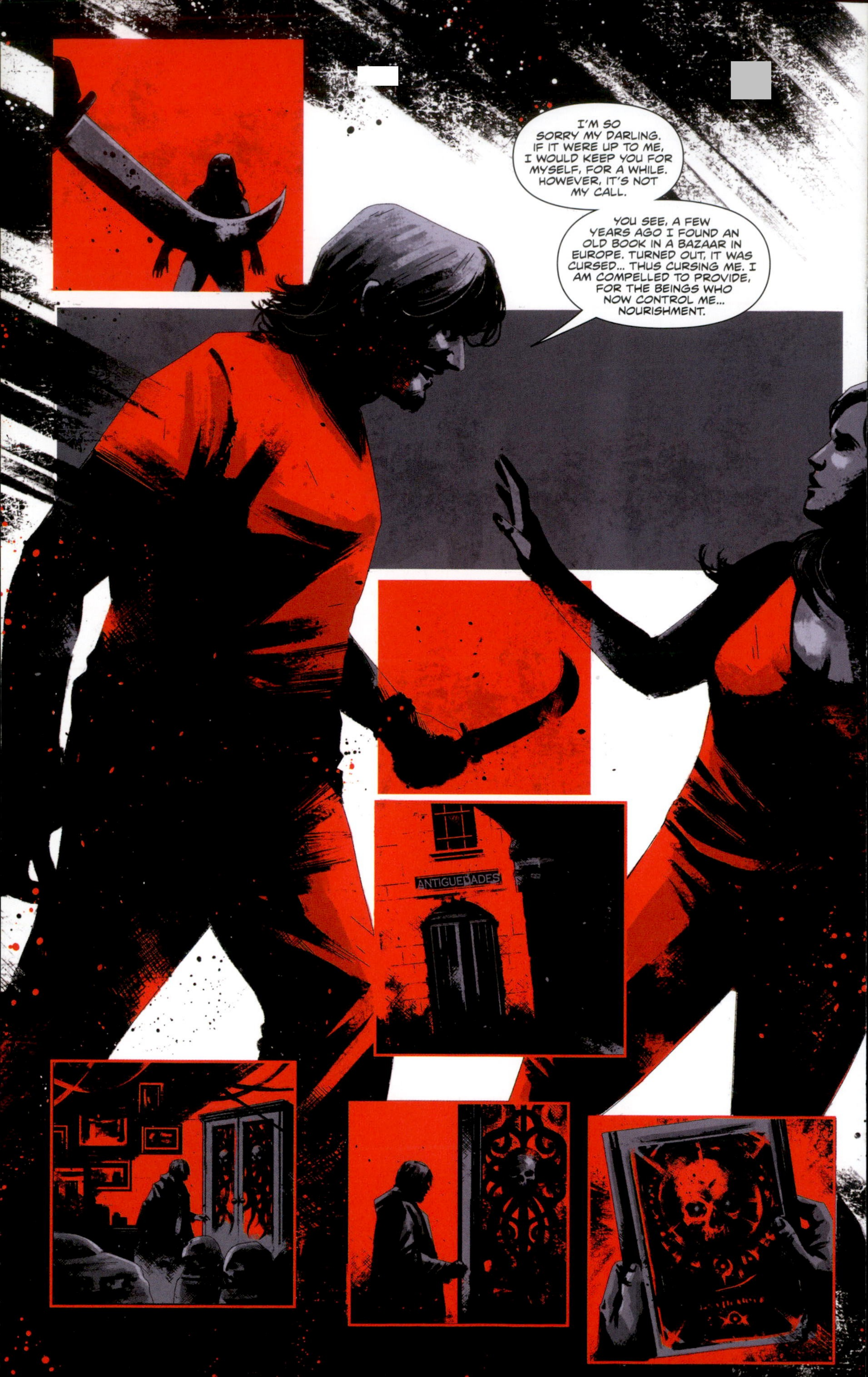
I'M SO SORRY MY DARLING. IF IT WERE UP TO ME, I WOULD KEEP YOU FOR MYSELF, FOR A WHILE. HOWEVER, IT'S NOT MY CALL.
YOU SEE, A FEW YEARS AGO I FOUND AN OLD BOOK IN A BAZAAR IN EUROPE. TURNED OUT, IT WAS CURSED... THUS CURSING ME. I AM COMPELLED TO PROVIDE, FOR THE BEINGS WHO NOW CONTROL ME... NOURISHMENT.
ANTIGUEDADES

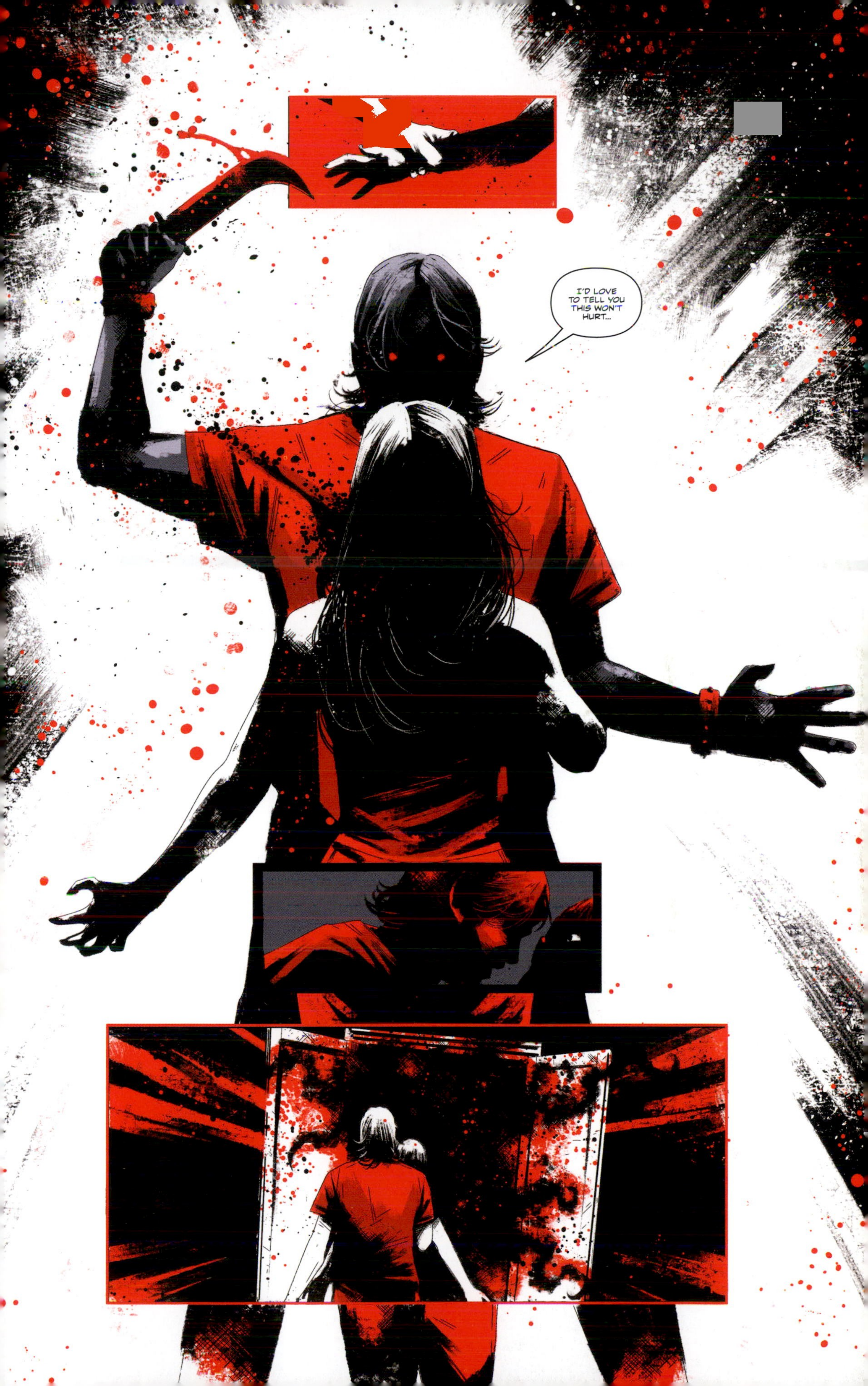
I'D LOVE TO TELL YOU THIS WON'T HURT...

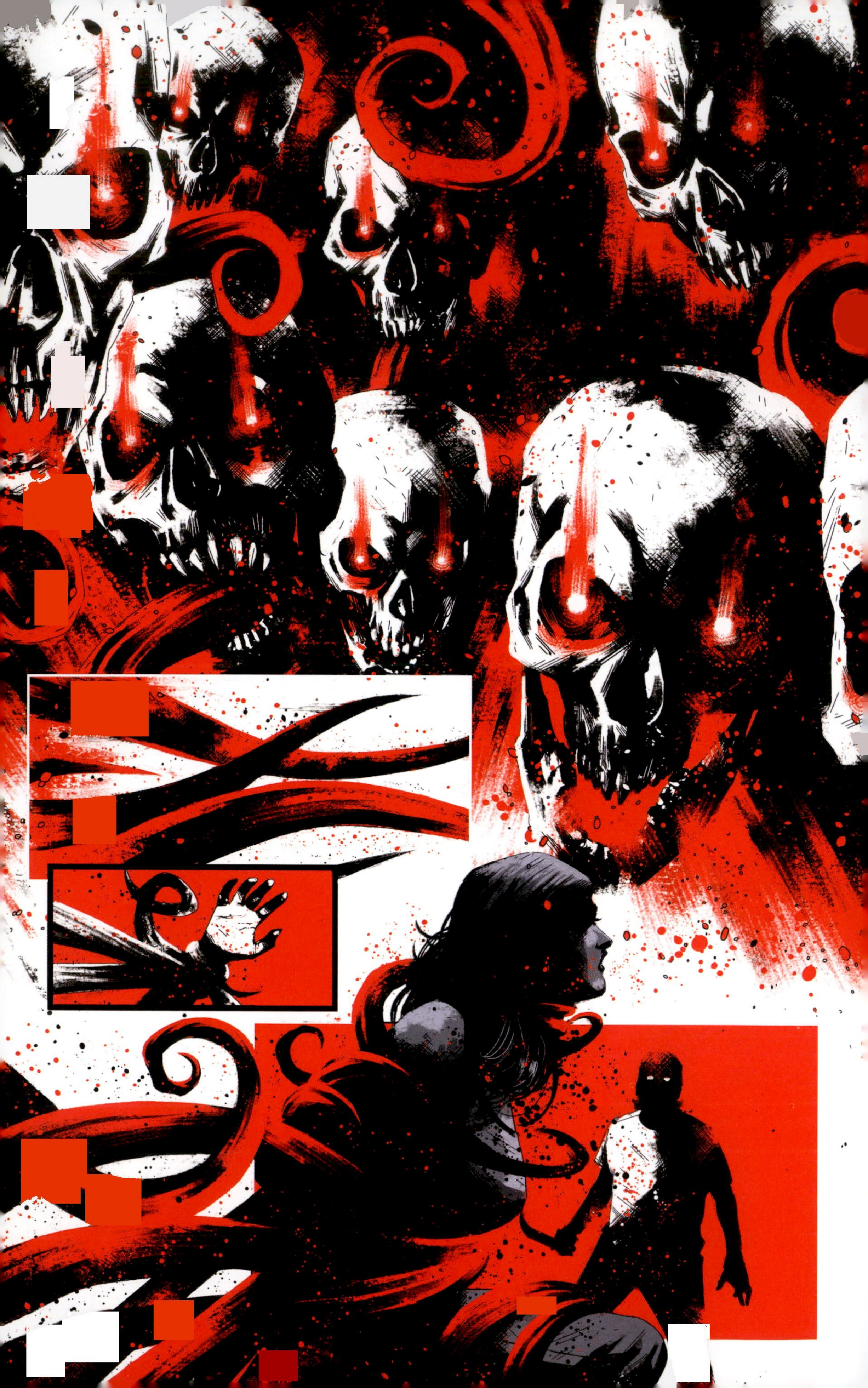

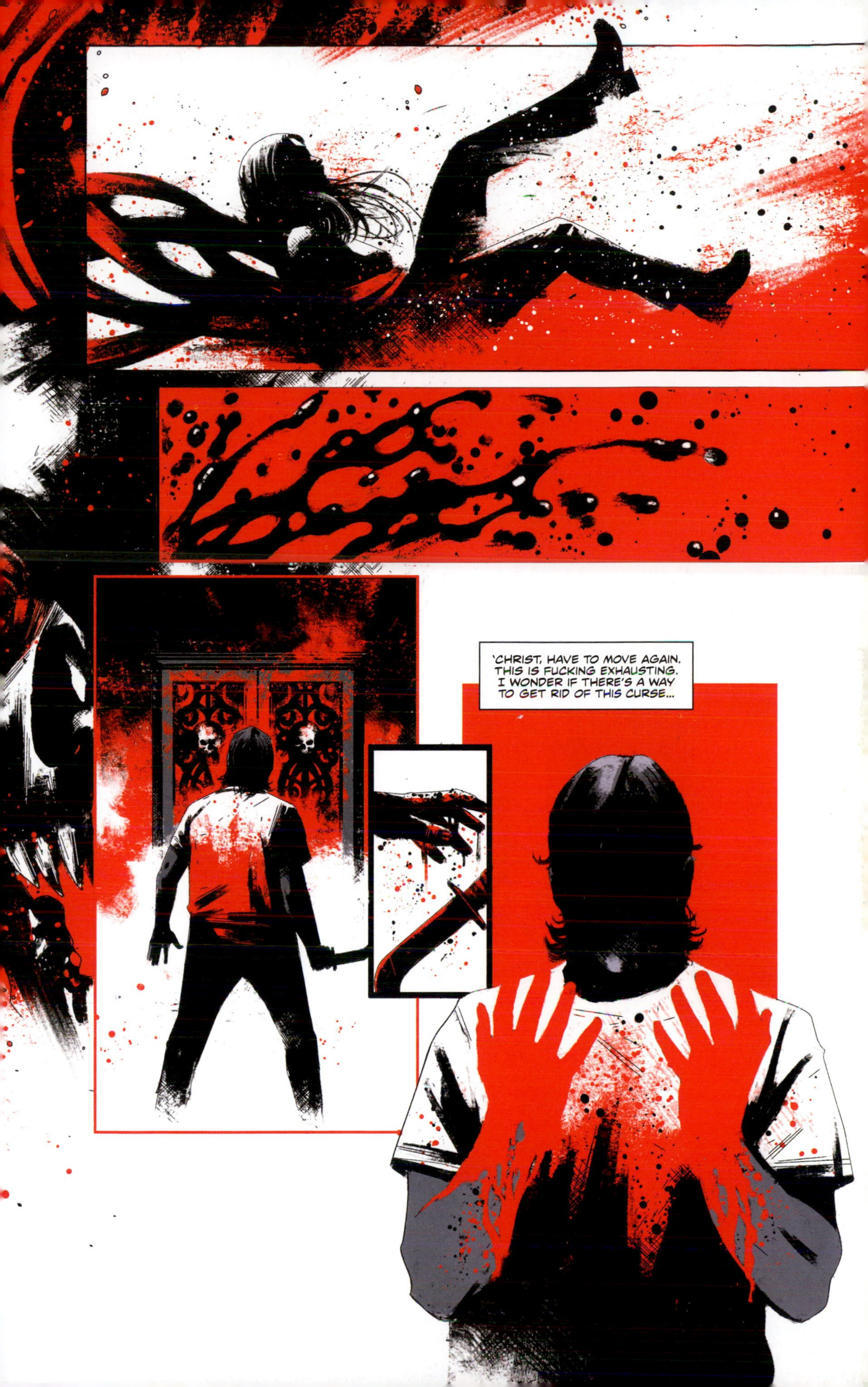
'CHRIST, HAVE TO MOVE AGAIN. THIS IS FUCKING EXHAUSTING. I WONDER IF THERE'S A WAY TO GET RID OF THIS CURSE...

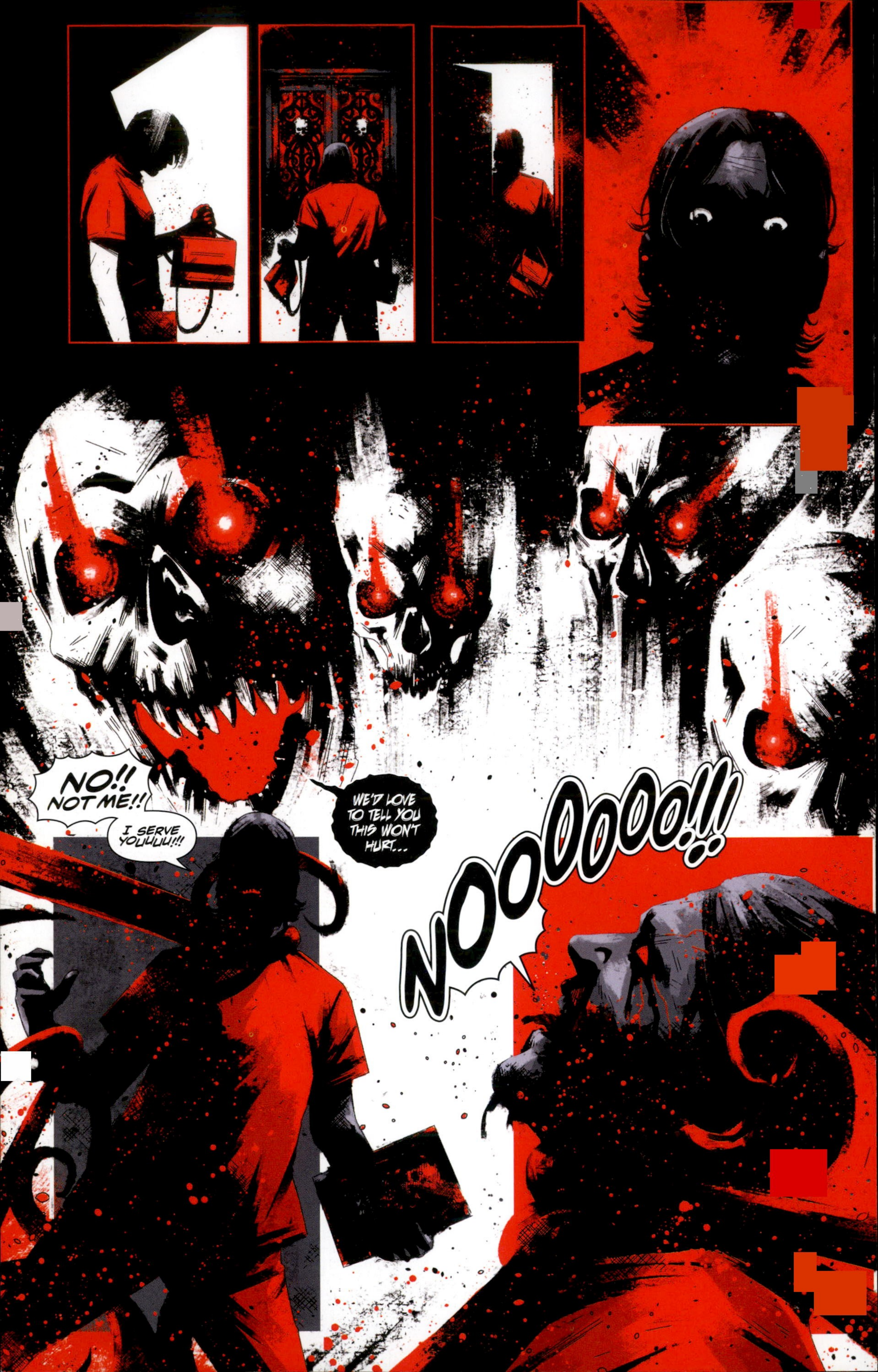
NO!! NOT ME!!
I SERVE YOUUUU!!!
WE'D LOVE TO TELL YOU THIS WON'T HURT...
NOOOOOOO!!!

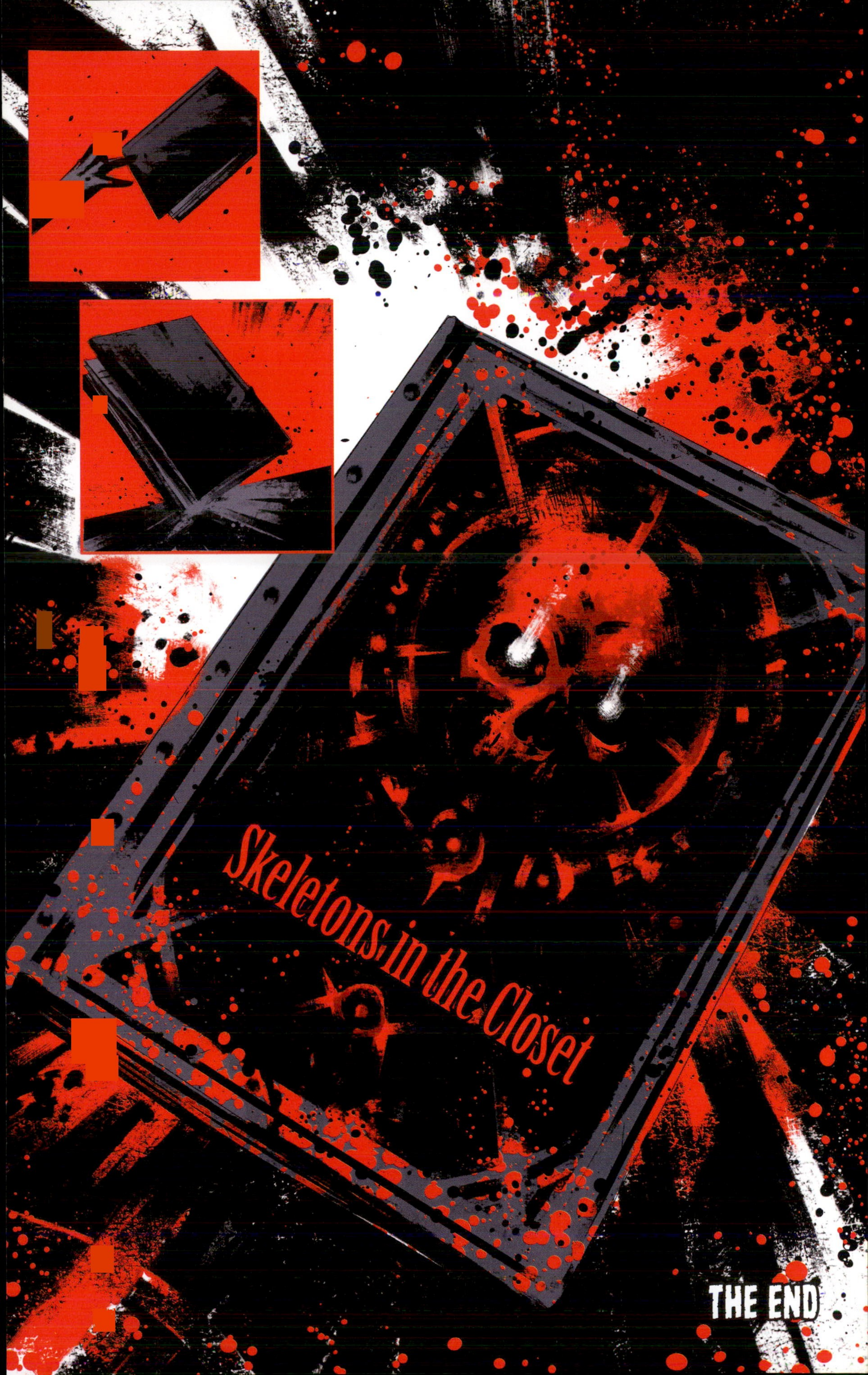
Skeletons in the Closet
THE END

TRACK SIX
INDIANS

WRITTEN BY
GRANT MORRISON

ILLUSTRATED BY
FREDDIE WILLIAMS II

COLORED BY
ANDREW DALHOUSE

"ON THIS EARTH THERE WAS A PANDEMIC NAMED
AFTER A BEER! WHAT COULD GO WRONG?"

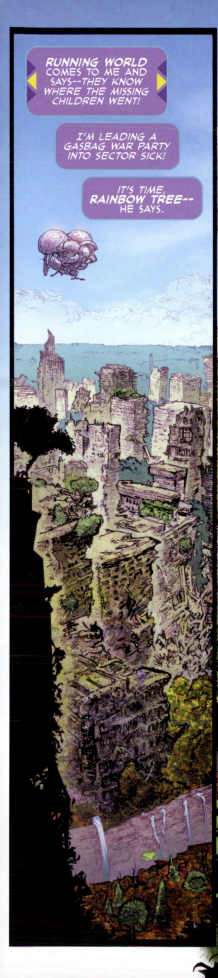

RUNNING WORLD COMES TO ME AND SAYS--THEY KNOW WHERE THE MISSING CHILDREN WENT!

I'M LEADING A GASBAG WAR PARTY INTO SECTOR SICK!

IT'S TIME, RAINBOW TREE-- HE SAYS.

THIS IS THE PLACE WE KNOW AS VANISHED HILLS, AND DO OUR VERY BEST TO AVOID, BUT I CAN'T SAY NO--

AS MEDICINE BROTHER OF THE PAINTED PEOPLE, I HAVE NO CHOICE.

THERE'S NO POINT IN CRYING ABOUT IT.

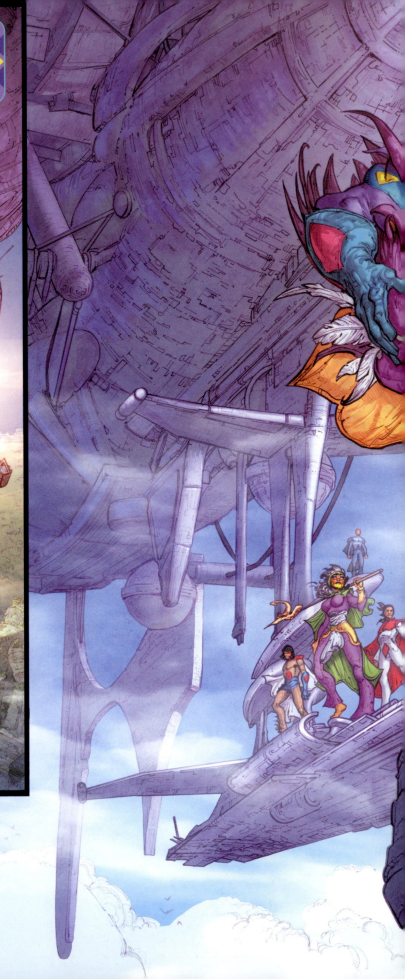

WHY WOULD THESE DISEASED DWARVES PROVOKE US?-- SAYS RUNNING WORLD. I DON'T CARE HOW BIG THEIR ROTTEN MONUMENTS ARE.

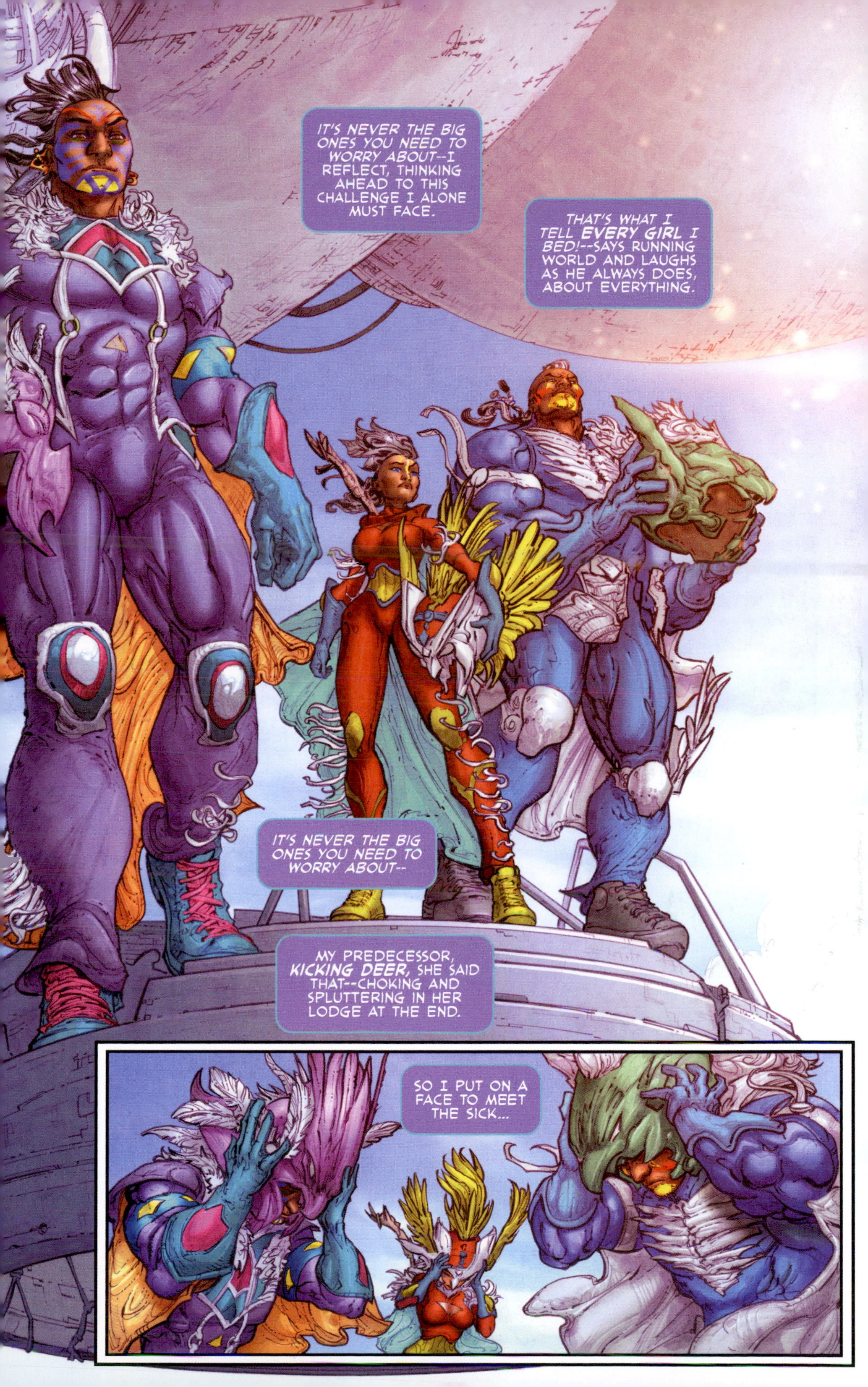
IT'S NEVER THE BIG ONES YOU NEED TO WORRY ABOUT--I REFLECT, THINKING AHEAD TO THIS CHALLENGE I ALONE MUST FACE.
THAT'S WHAT I TELL EVERY GIRL I BED!--SAYS RUNNING WORLD AND LAUGHS AS HE ALWAYS DOES, ABOUT EVERYTHING.
IT'S NEVER THE BIG ONES YOU NEED TO WORRY ABOUT--
MY PREDECESSOR, KICKING DEER, SHE SAID THAT--CHOKING AND SPLUTTERING IN HER LODGE AT THE END.
SO I PUT ON A FACE TO MEET THE SICK...

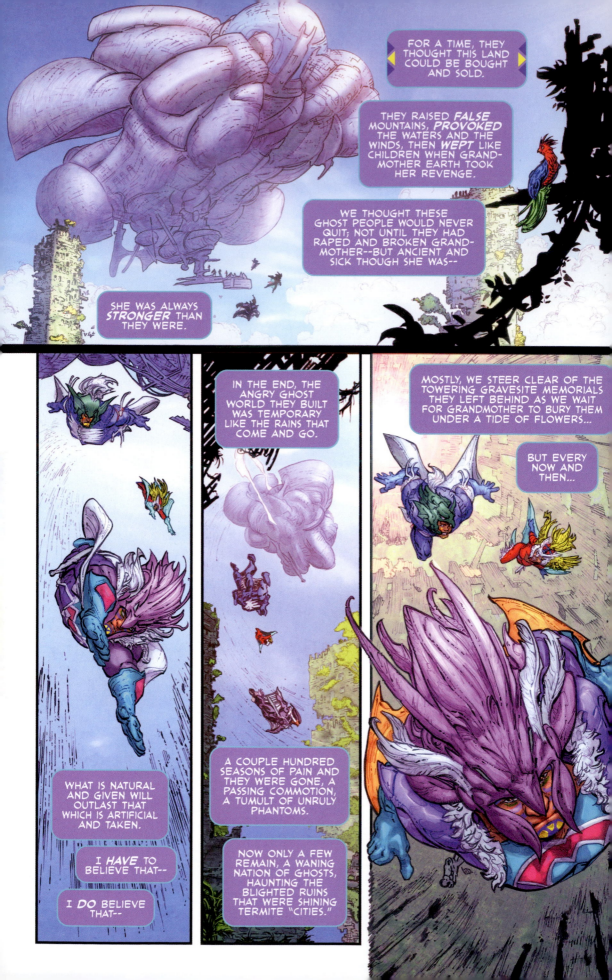

FOR A TIME, THEY THOUGHT THIS LAND COULD BE BOUGHT AND SOLD.

THEY RAISED *FALSE* MOUNTAINS, *PROVOKED* THE WATERS AND THE WINDS, THEN *WEPT* LIKE CHILDREN WHEN GRANDMOTHER EARTH TOOK HER REVENGE.

WE THOUGHT THESE GHOST PEOPLE WOULD NEVER QUIT; NOT UNTIL THEY HAD RAPED AND BROKEN GRANDMOTHER--BUT ANCIENT AND SICK THOUGH SHE WAS--

SHE WAS ALWAYS *STRONGER* THAN THEY WERE.

IN THE END, THE ANGRY GHOST WORLD THEY BUILT WAS TEMPORARY LIKE THE RAINS THAT COME AND GO.

MOSTLY, WE STEER CLEAR OF THE TOWERING GRAVESITE MEMORIALS THEY LEFT BEHIND AS WE WAIT FOR GRANDMOTHER TO BURY THEM UNDER A TIDE OF FLOWERS...

BUT EVERY NOW AND THEN...

WHAT IS NATURAL AND GIVEN WILL OUTLAST THAT WHICH IS ARTIFICIAL AND TAKEN.

I *HAVE* TO BELIEVE THAT--

I *DO* BELIEVE THAT--

A COUPLE HUNDRED SEASONS OF PAIN AND THEY WERE GONE, A PASSING COMMOTION, A TUMULT OF UNRULY PHANTOMS.

NOW ONLY A FEW REMAIN, A WANING NATION OF GHOSTS, HAUNTING THE BLIGHTED RUINS THAT WERE SHINING TERMITE "CITIES."

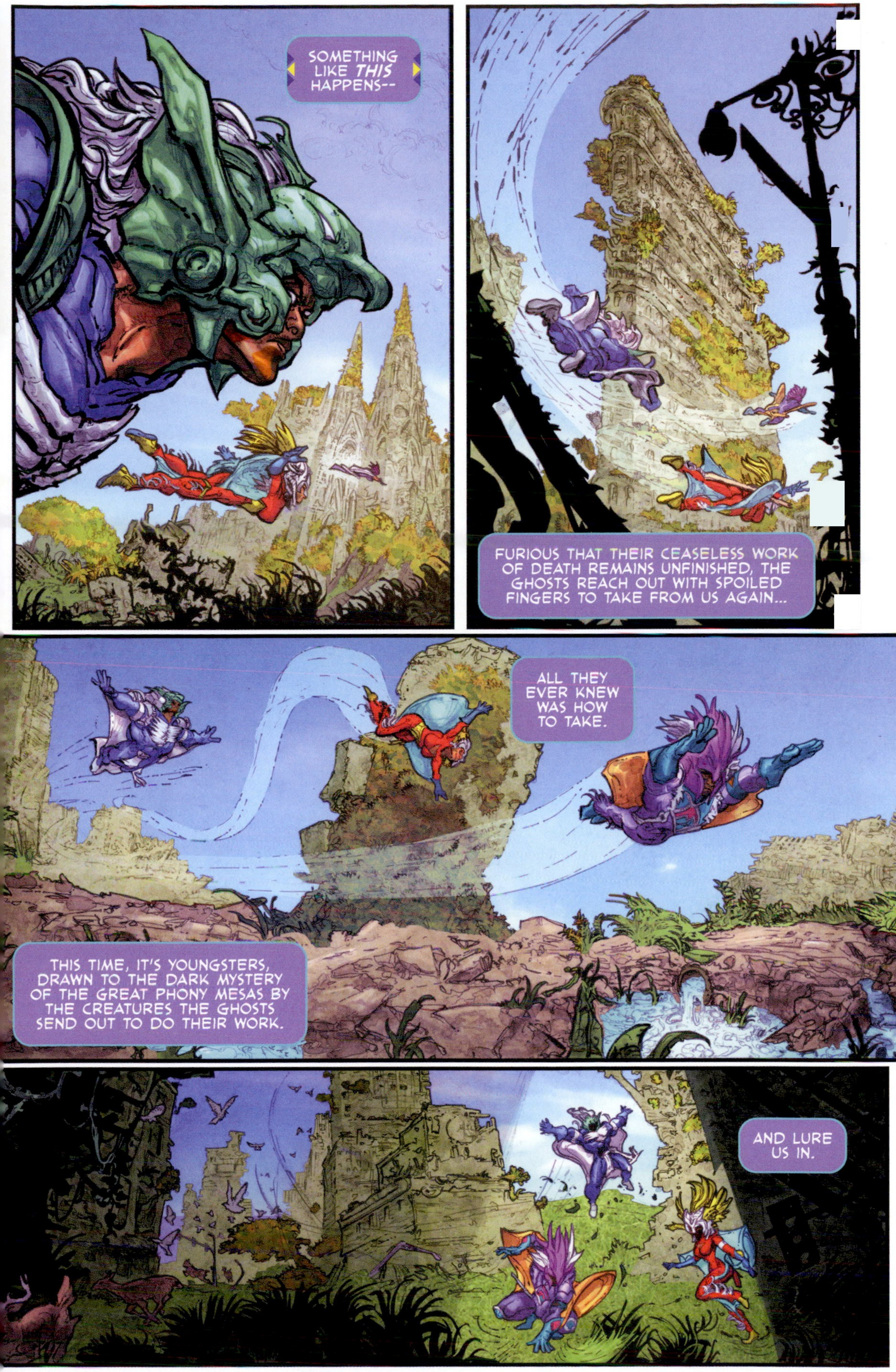
SOMETHING LIKE *THIS* HAPPENS--
FURIOUS THAT THEIR CEASELESS WORK OF DEATH REMAINS UNFINISHED, THE GHOSTS REACH OUT WITH SPOILED FINGERS TO TAKE FROM US AGAIN...
ALL THEY EVER KNEW WAS HOW TO TAKE.
THIS TIME, IT'S YOUNGSTERS, DRAWN TO THE DARK MYSTERY OF THE GREAT PHONY MESAS BY THE CREATURES THE GHOSTS SEND OUT TO DO THEIR WORK.
AND LURE US IN.

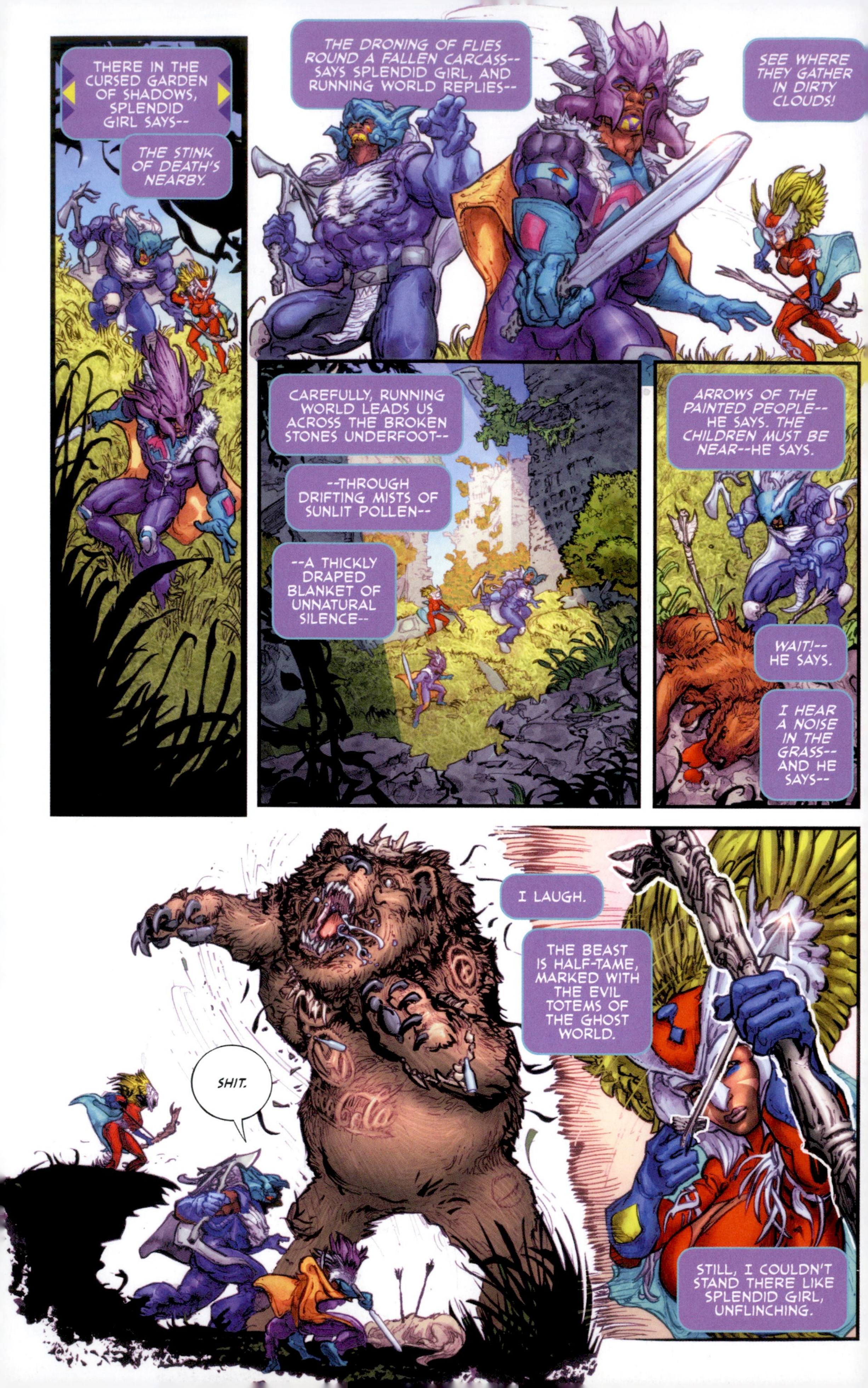
THERE IN THE CURSED GARDEN OF SHADOWS, SPLENDID GIRL SAYS--
THE STINK OF DEATH'S NEARBY.
THE DRONING OF FLIES ROUND A FALLEN CARCASS-- SAYS SPLENDID GIRL, AND RUNNING WORLD REPLIES--
SEE WHERE THEY GATHER IN DIRTY CLOUDS!
CAREFULLY, RUNNING WORLD LEADS US ACROSS THE BROKEN STONES UNDERFOOT--
--THROUGH DRIFTING MISTS OF SUNLIT POLLEN--
--A THICKLY DRAPED BLANKET OF UNNATURAL SILENCE--
ARROWS OF THE PAINTED PEOPLE-- HE SAYS. THE CHILDREN MUST BE NEAR--HE SAYS.
WAIT!-- HE SAYS.
I HEAR A NOISE IN THE GRASS-- AND HE SAYS--
I LAUGH.
THE BEAST IS HALF-TAME, MARKED WITH THE EVIL TOTEMS OF THE GHOST WORLD.
SHIT.
STILL, I COULDN'T STAND THERE LIKE SPLENDID GIRL, UNFLINCHING.

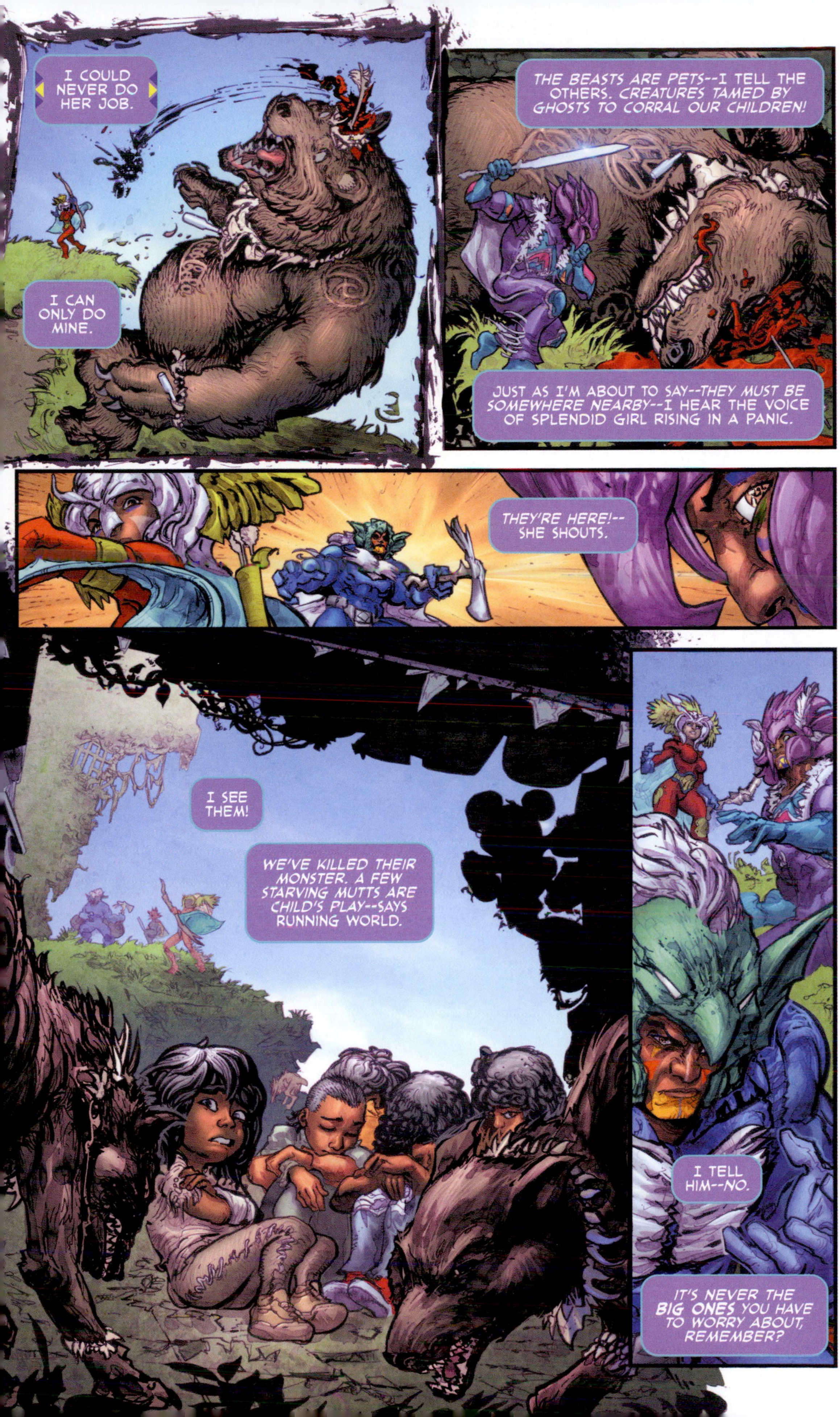

I COULD NEVER DO HER JOB.
I CAN ONLY DO MINE.
THE BEASTS ARE PETS--I TELL THE OTHERS. CREATURES TAMED BY GHOSTS TO CORRAL OUR CHILDREN!
JUST AS I'M ABOUT TO SAY--THEY MUST BE SOMEWHERE NEARBY--I HEAR THE VOICE OF SPLENDID GIRL RISING IN A PANIC.
THEY'RE HERE!--SHE SHOUTS.
I SEE THEM!
WE'VE KILLED THEIR MONSTER. A FEW STARVING MUTTS ARE CHILD'S PLAY--SAYS RUNNING WORLD.
I TELL HIM--NO.
IT'S NEVER THE BIG ONES YOU HAVE TO WORRY ABOUT, REMEMBER?

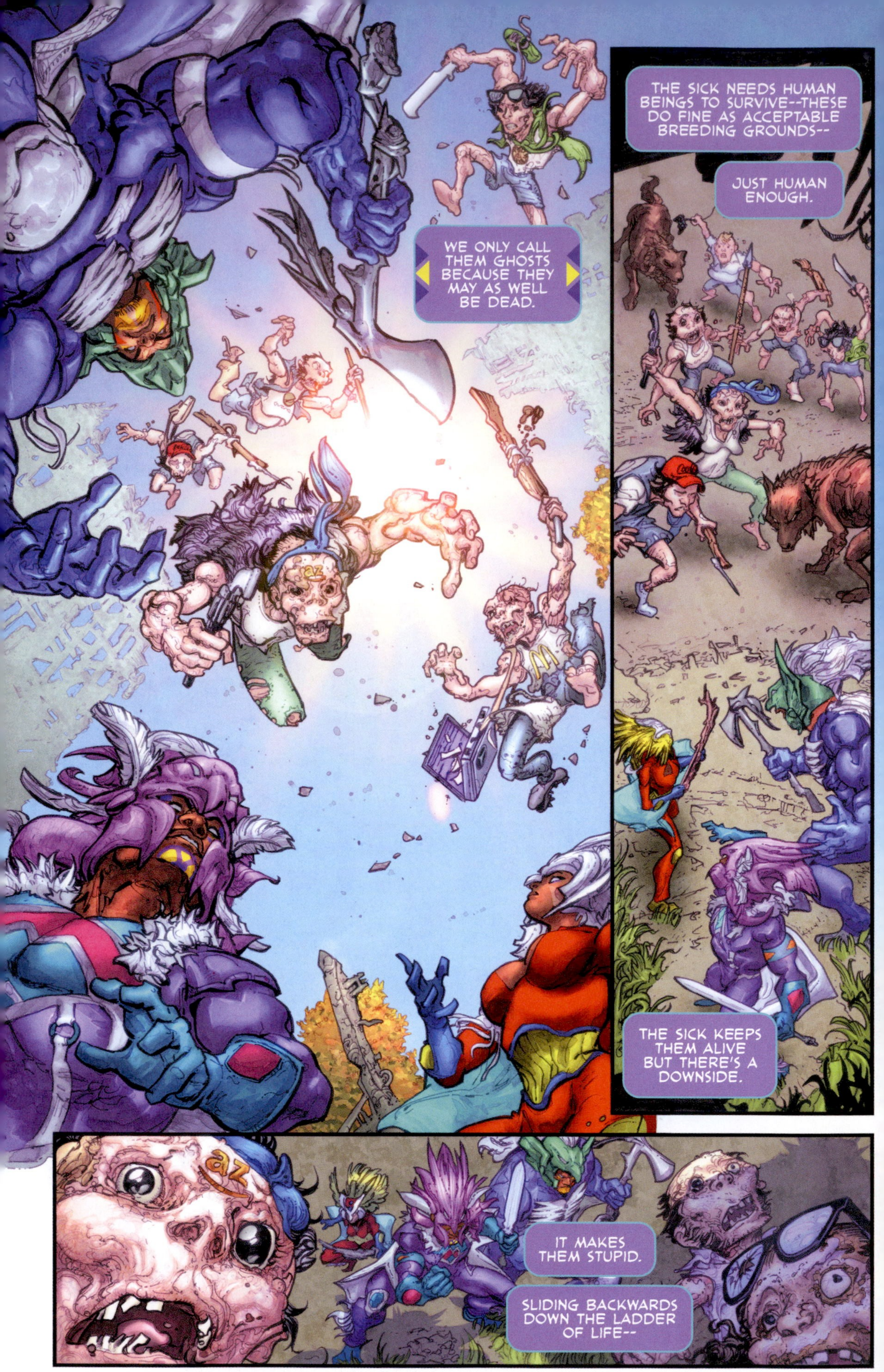
WE ONLY CALL THEM GHOSTS BECAUSE THEY MAY AS WELL BE DEAD.
THE SICK NEEDS HUMAN BEINGS TO SURVIVE--THESE DO FINE AS ACCEPTABLE BREEDING GROUNDS--
JUST HUMAN ENOUGH.
THE SICK KEEPS THEM ALIVE BUT THERE'S A DOWNSIDE.
IT MAKES THEM STUPID.
SLIDING BACKWARDS DOWN THE LADDER OF LIFE--

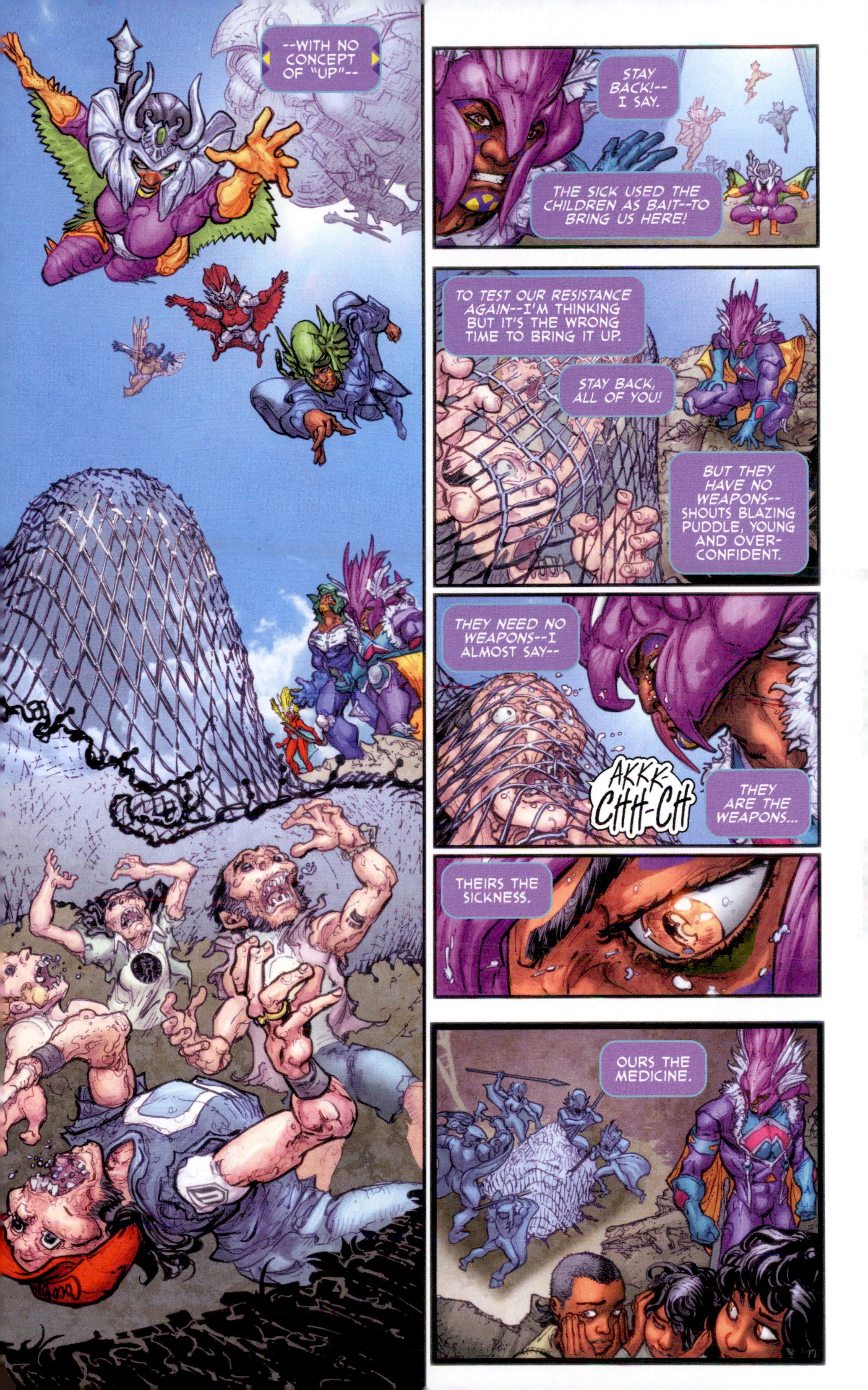
--WITH NO CONCEPT OF "UP"--
STAY BACK!--I SAY.
THE SICK USED THE CHILDREN AS BAIT--TO BRING US HERE!
TO TEST OUR RESISTANCE AGAIN--I'M THINKING BUT IT'S THE WRONG TIME TO BRING IT UP.
STAY BACK, ALL OF YOU!
BUT THEY HAVE NO WEAPONS--SHOUTS BLAZING PUDDLE, YOUNG AND OVER-CONFIDENT.
THEY NEED NO WEAPONS--I ALMOST SAY--
AKKK-CHH-CH
THEY ARE THE WEAPONS...
THEIRS THE SICKNESS.
OURS THE MEDICINE.

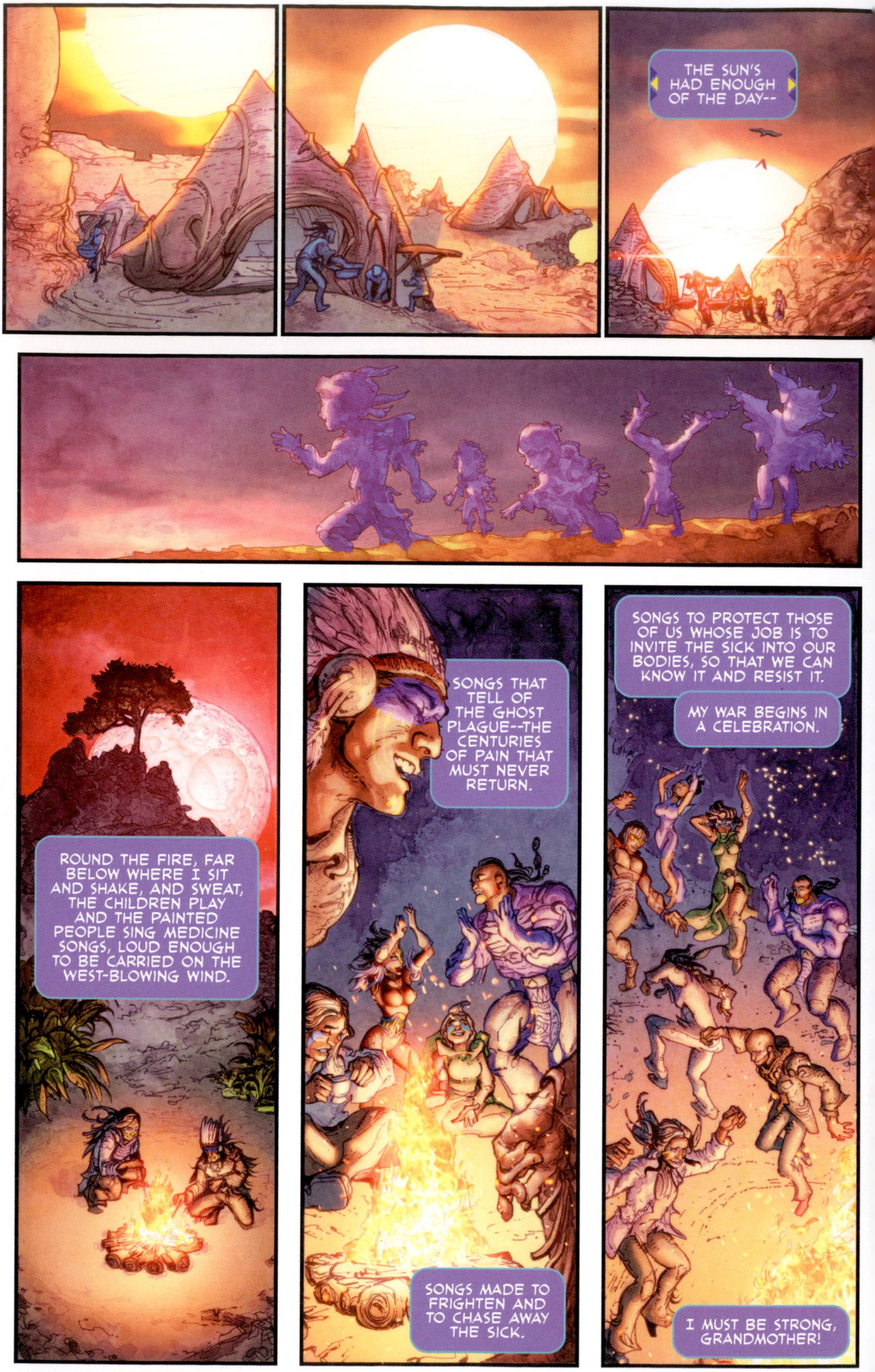
THE SUN'S HAD ENOUGH OF THE DAY--
ROUND THE FIRE, FAR BELOW WHERE I SIT AND SHAKE, AND SWEAT, THE CHILDREN PLAY AND THE PAINTED PEOPLE SING MEDICINE SONGS, LOUD ENOUGH TO BE CARRIED ON THE WEST-BLOWING WIND.
SONGS THAT TELL OF THE GHOST PLAGUE--THE CENTURIES OF PAIN THAT MUST NEVER RETURN.
SONGS MADE TO FRIGHTEN AND TO CHASE AWAY THE SICK.
SONGS TO PROTECT THOSE OF US WHOSE JOB IS TO INVITE THE SICK INTO OUR BODIES, SO THAT WE CAN KNOW IT AND RESIST IT.
MY WAR BEGINS IN A CELEBRATION.
I MUST BE STRONG, GRANDMOTHER!

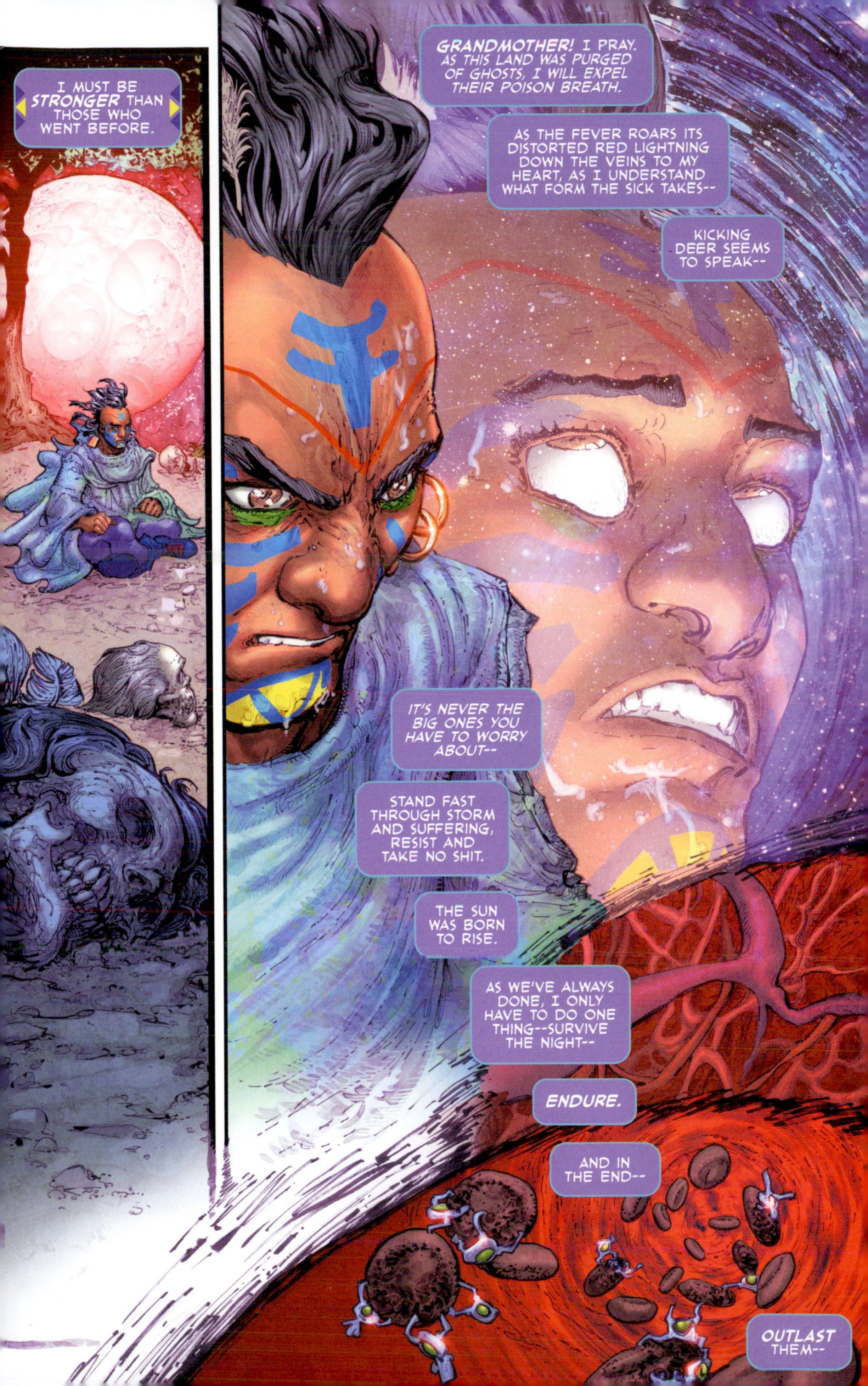
I MUST BE STRONGER THAN THOSE WHO WENT BEFORE.
GRANDMOTHER! I PRAY. AS THIS LAND WAS PURGED OF GHOSTS, I WILL EXPEL THEIR POISON BREATH.
AS THE FEVER ROARS ITS DISTORTED RED LIGHTNING DOWN THE VEINS TO MY HEART, AS I UNDERSTAND WHAT FORM THE SICK TAKES--
KICKING DEER SEEMS TO SPEAK--
IT'S NEVER THE BIG ONES YOU HAVE TO WORRY ABOUT--
STAND FAST THROUGH STORM AND SUFFERING, RESIST AND TAKE NO SHIT.
THE SUN WAS BORN TO RISE.
AS WE'VE ALWAYS DONE, I ONLY HAVE TO DO ONE THING--SURVIVE THE NIGHT--
ENDURE.
AND IN THE END--
OUTLAST THEM--

TRACK SEVEN

ONE WORLD

WRITTEN BY
FRANK
BELLO

ILLUSTRATED BY
ANDY
BELANGER

COLORED BY
TATTO
CABALLERO

BASED ON CHARACTERS INSPIRED BY BRANDON BELLO

"IT ONLY TAKES ONE DICKHEAD
TO RUIN ONE WORLD!"

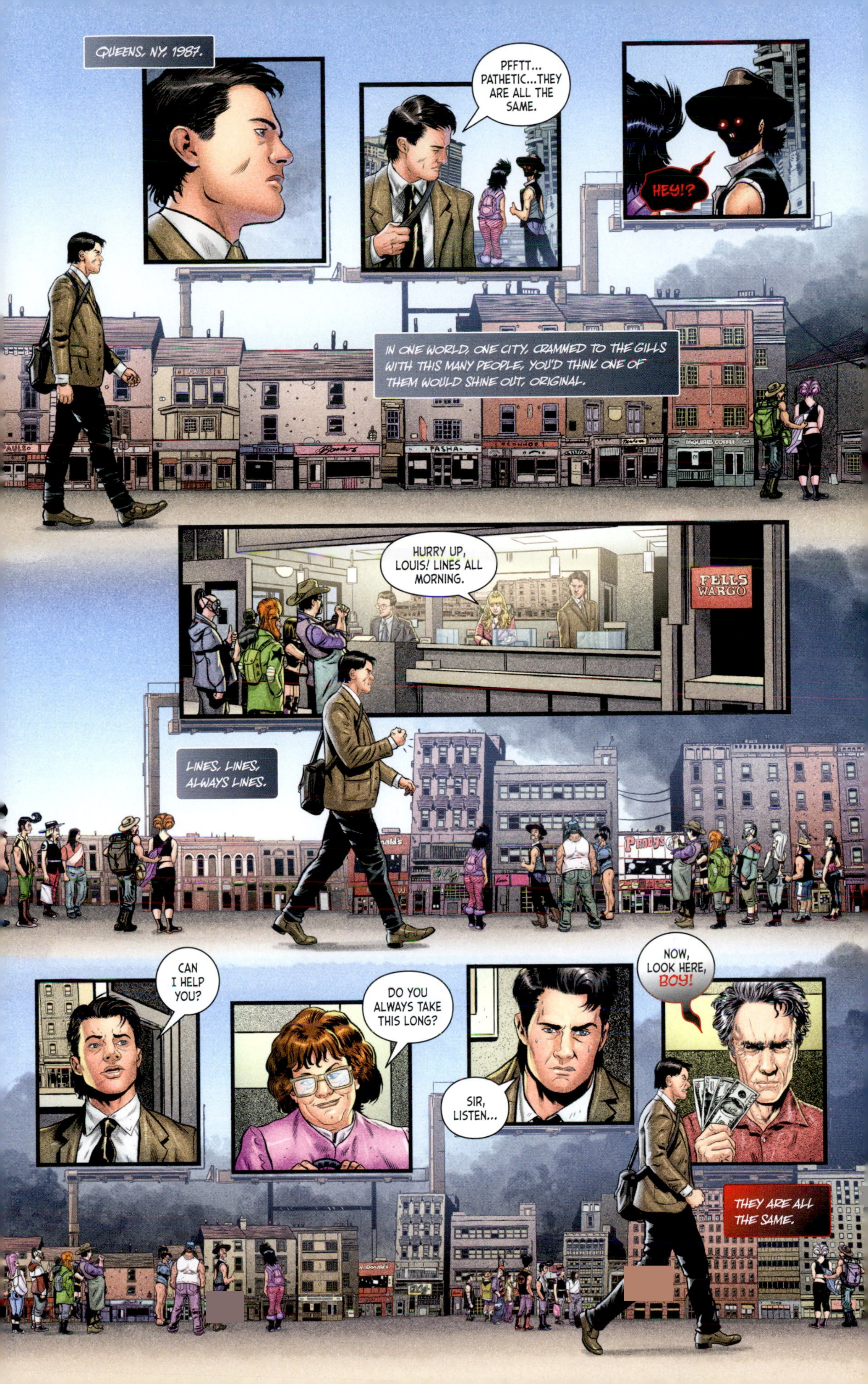
QUEENS, NY, 1987.
PFFTT... PATHETIC...THEY ARE ALL THE SAME.
HEY!?
IN ONE WORLD, ONE CITY, CRAMMED TO THE GILLS WITH THIS MANY PEOPLE, YOU'D THINK ONE OF THEM WOULD SHINE OUT, ORIGINAL.
HURRY UP, LOUIS! LINES ALL MORNING.
FELLS WARGO
LINES, LINES, ALWAYS LINES.
CAN I HELP YOU?
DO YOU ALWAYS TAKE THIS LONG?
SIR, LISTEN...
NOW, LOOK HERE, BOY!
THEY ARE ALL THE SAME.

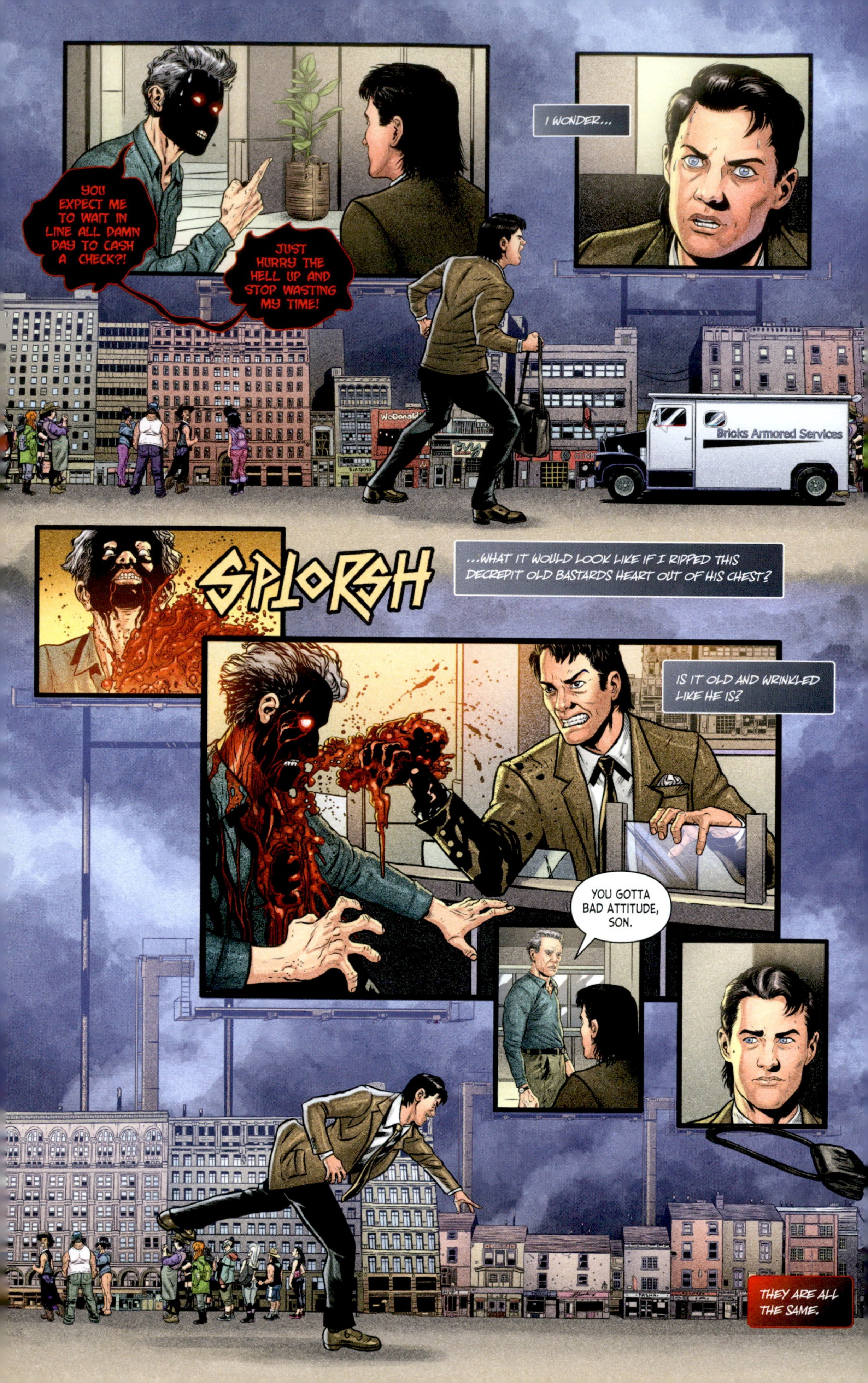
YOU EXPECT ME TO WAIT IN LINE ALL DAMN DAY TO CASH A CHECK?!
JUST HURRY THE HELL UP AND STOP WASTING MY TIME!
I WONDER...
Bricks Armored Services
SPLORSH
...WHAT IT WOULD LOOK LIKE IF I RIPPED THIS DECREPIT OLD BASTARDS HEART OUT OF HIS CHEST?
IS IT OLD AND WRINKLED LIKE HE IS?
YOU GOTTA BAD ATTITUDE, SON.
THEY ARE ALL THE SAME.

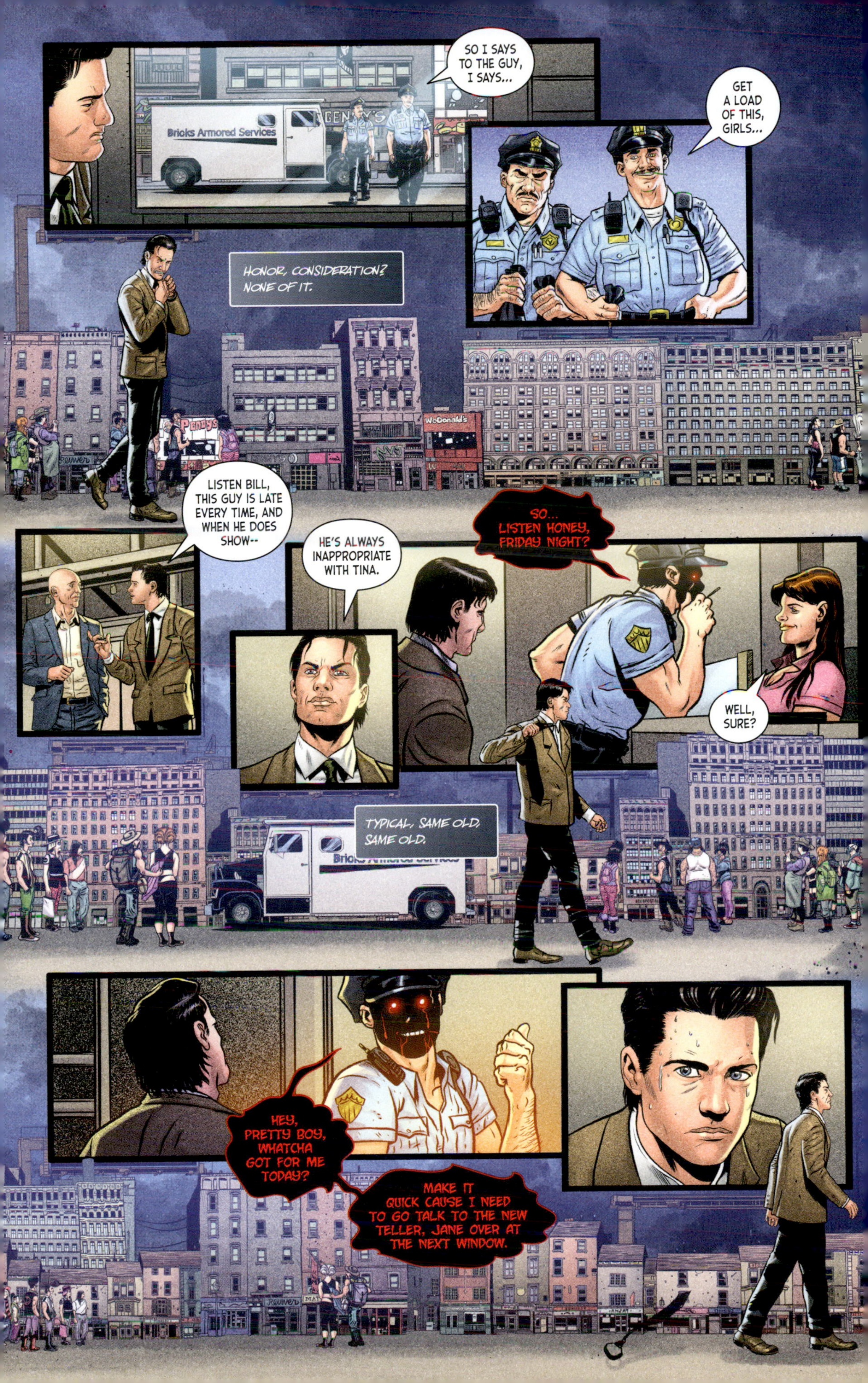
SO I SAYS TO THE GUY, I SAYS...
Bricks Armored Services
GET A LOAD OF THIS, GIRLS...
HONOR, CONSIDERATION? NONE OF IT.
McDonald's
LISTEN BILL, THIS GUY IS LATE EVERY TIME, AND WHEN HE DOES SHOW--
HE'S ALWAYS INAPPROPRIATE WITH TINA.
SO... LISTEN HONEY, FRIDAY NIGHT?
WELL, SURE?
TYPICAL, SAME OLD, SAME OLD.
HEY, PRETTY BOY, WHATCHA GOT FOR ME TODAY?
MAKE IT QUICK CAUSE I NEED TO GO TALK TO THE NEW TELLER, JANE OVER AT THE NEXT WINDOW.

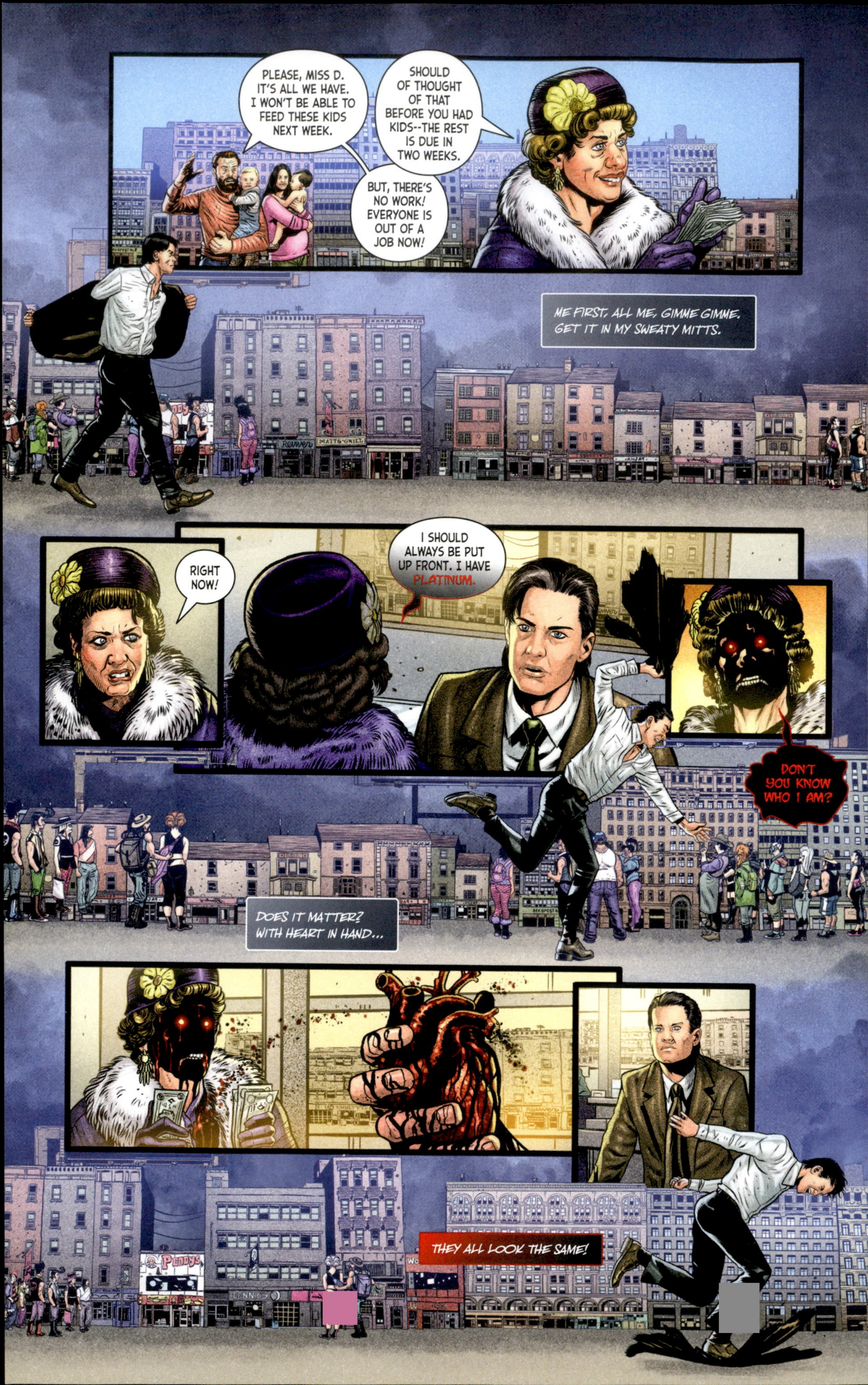

PLEASE, MISS D. IT'S ALL WE HAVE. I WON'T BE ABLE TO FEED THESE KIDS NEXT WEEK.
SHOULD OF THOUGHT OF THAT BEFORE YOU HAD KIDS--THE REST IS DUE IN TWO WEEKS.
BUT, THERE'S NO WORK! EVERYONE IS OUT OF A JOB NOW!
ME FIRST. ALL ME. GIMME GIMME. GET IT IN MY SWEATY MITTS.
RIGHT NOW!
I SHOULD ALWAYS BE PUT UP FRONT. I HAVE PLATINUM.
DON'T YOU KNOW WHO I AM?
DOES IT MATTER? WITH HEART IN HAND...
THEY ALL LOOK THE SAME!

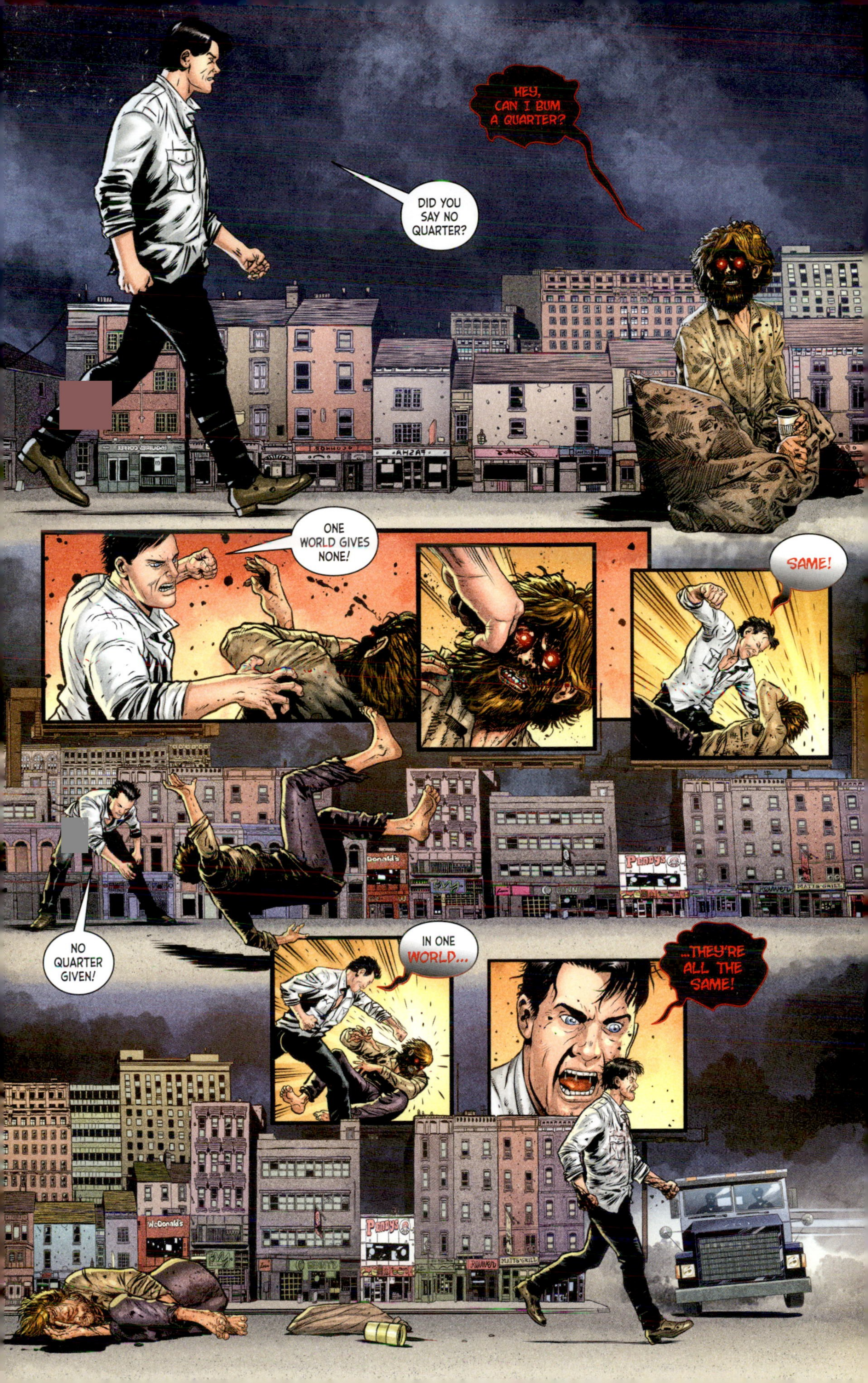
HEY, CAN I BUM A QUARTER?
DID YOU SAY NO QUARTER?
ONE WORLD GIVES NONE!
SAME!
NO QUARTER GIVEN!
IN ONE WORLD...
...THEY'RE ALL THE SAME!

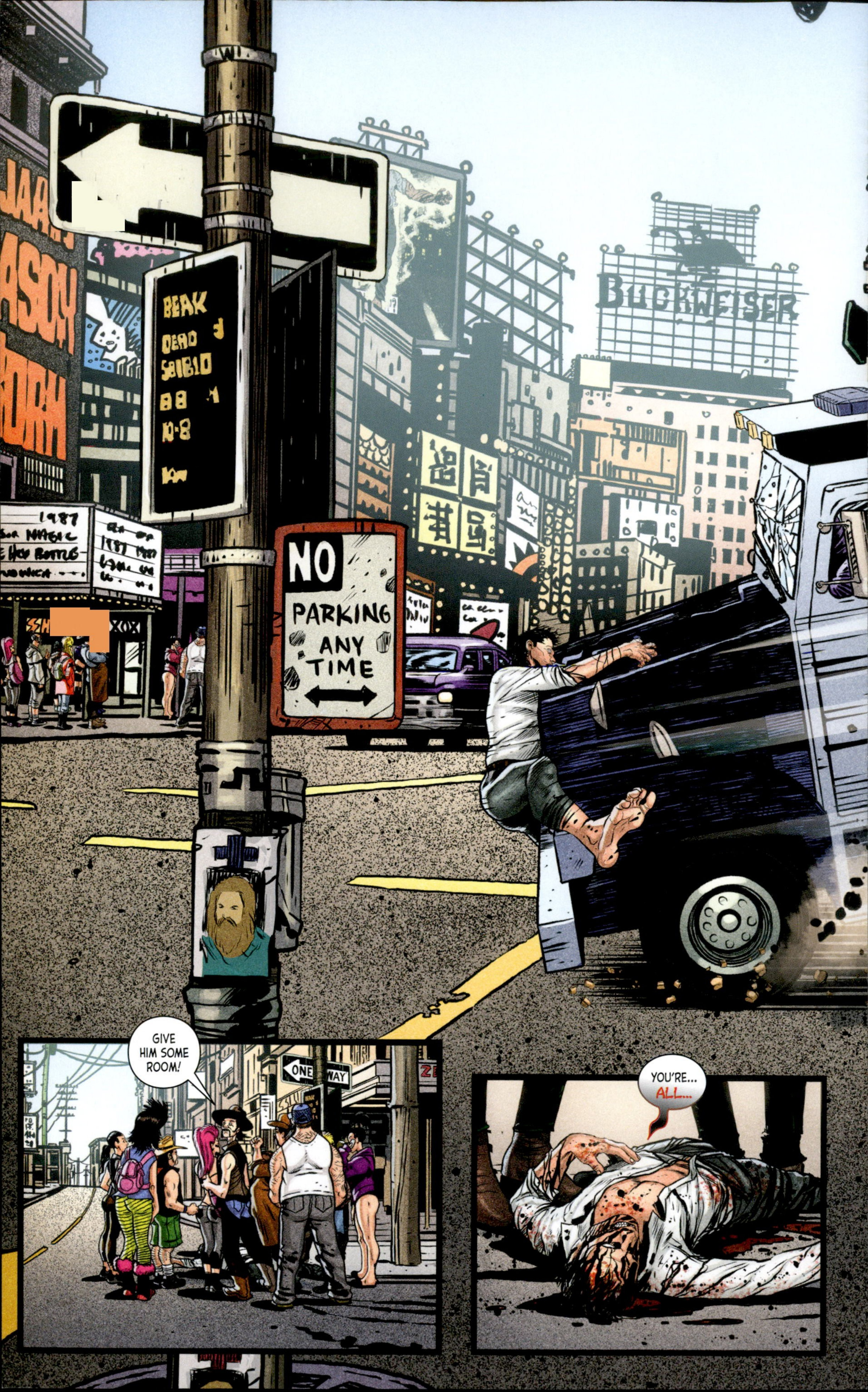
BUCKWEISER
NO PARKING ANY TIME
GIVE HIM SOME ROOM!
ONE WAY
YOU'RE... ALL...

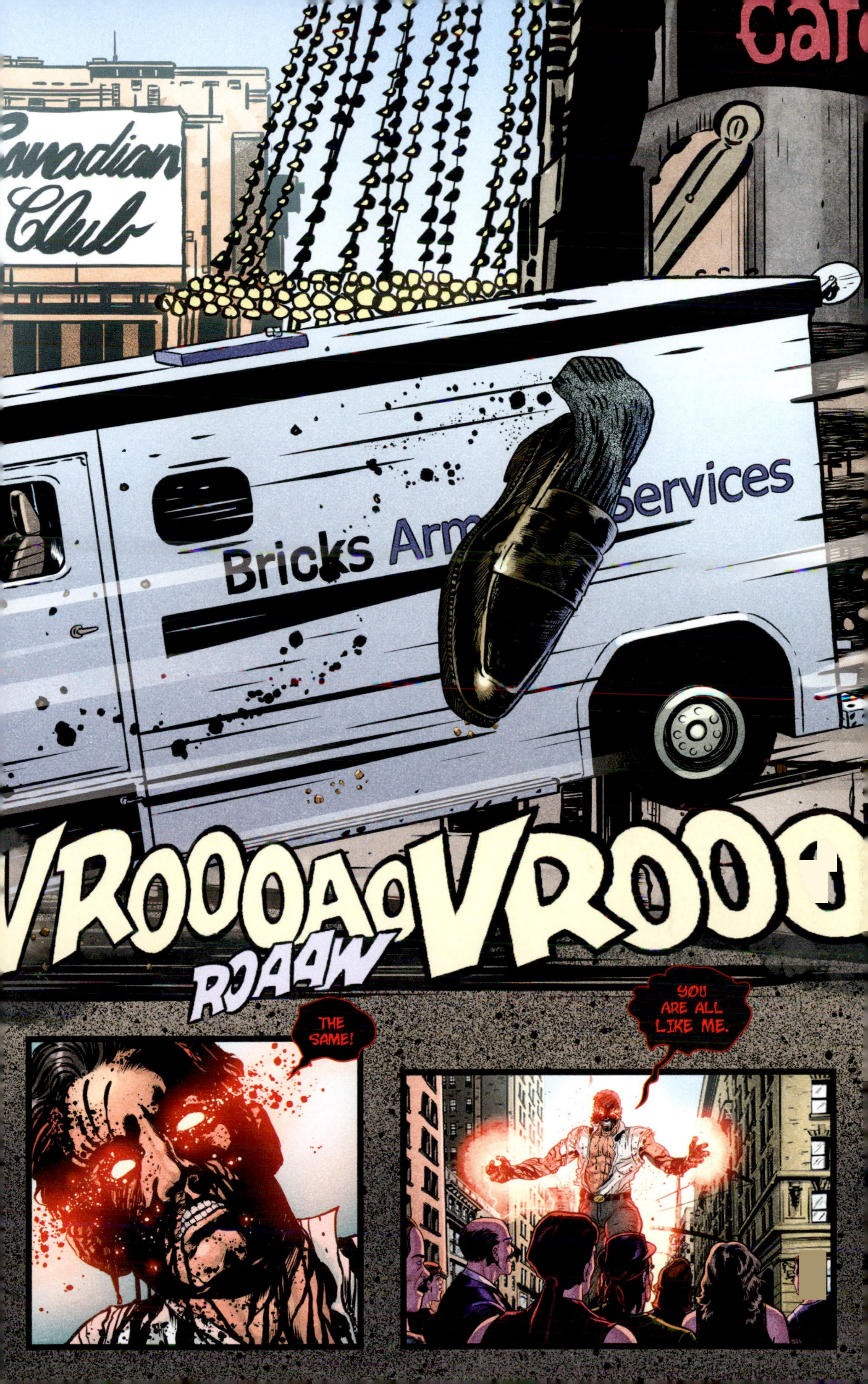
Bricks Arm
Services
VROOOAO
ROAAW
VROOO
THE SAME!
YOU ARE ALL LIKE ME.

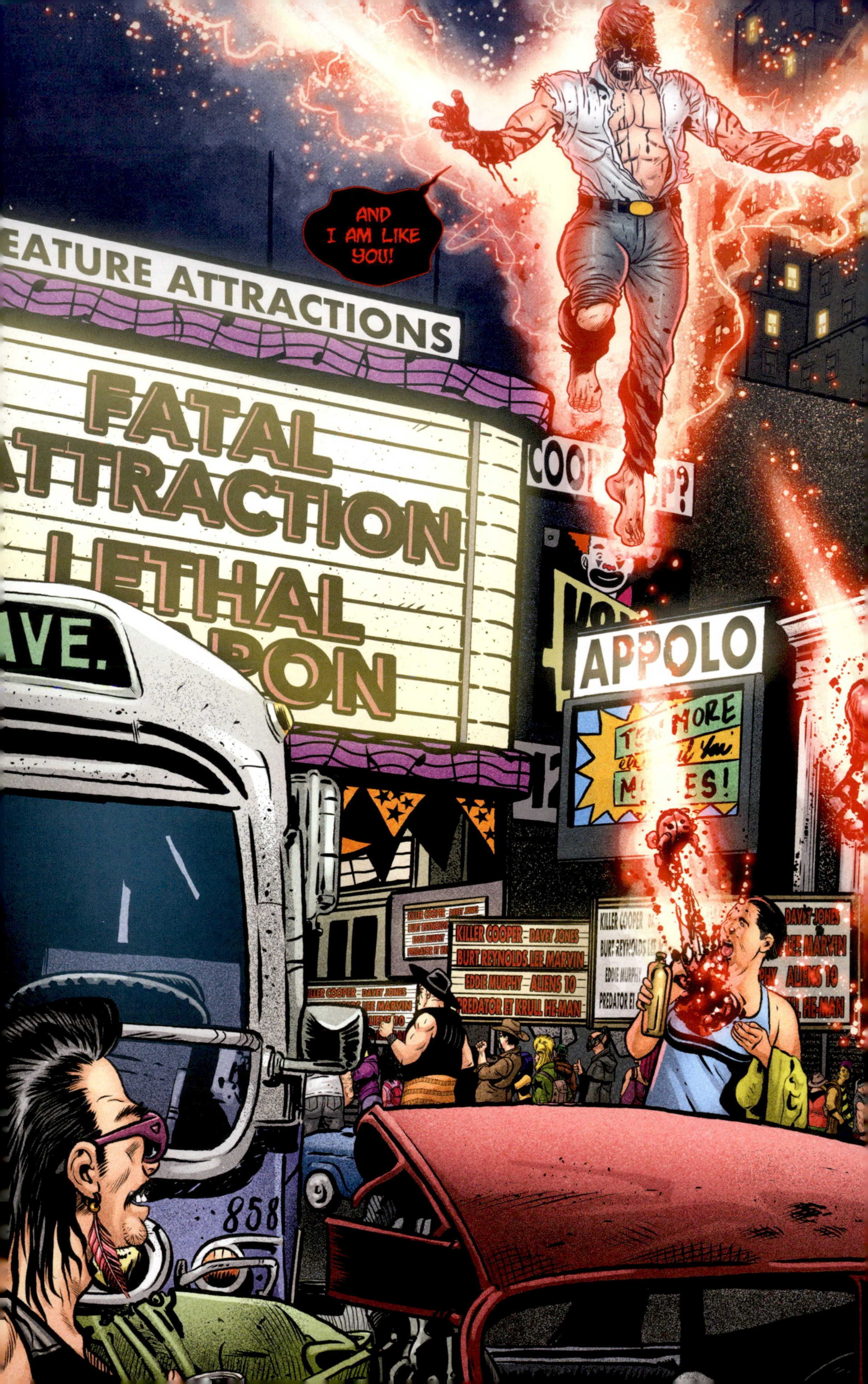
AND I AM LIKE YOU!
EATURE ATTRACTIONS
FATAL
TTRACTION
ETHAL
APPOLO
KILLER COOPER — DAVEY JONES
BURT REYNOLDS LEE MARVIN
EDDIE MURPHY — ALIENS 10
PREDATOR ET KRULL HE-MAN
858

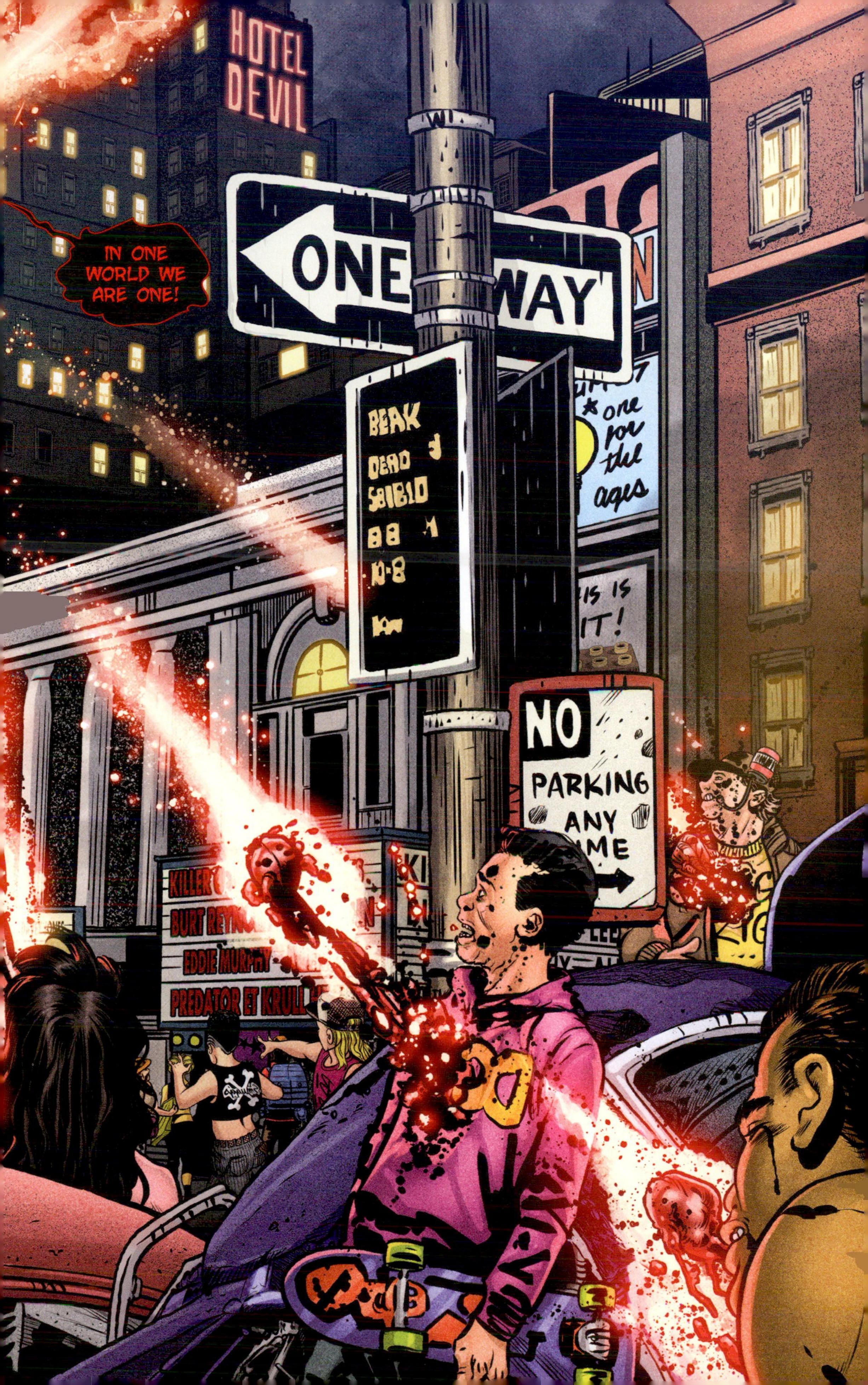
IN ONE WORLD WE ARE ONE!
HOTEL DEVIL
ONE WAY
one for the ages
NO PARKING ANY
EDDIE MURPHY
PREDATOR ET KRULL

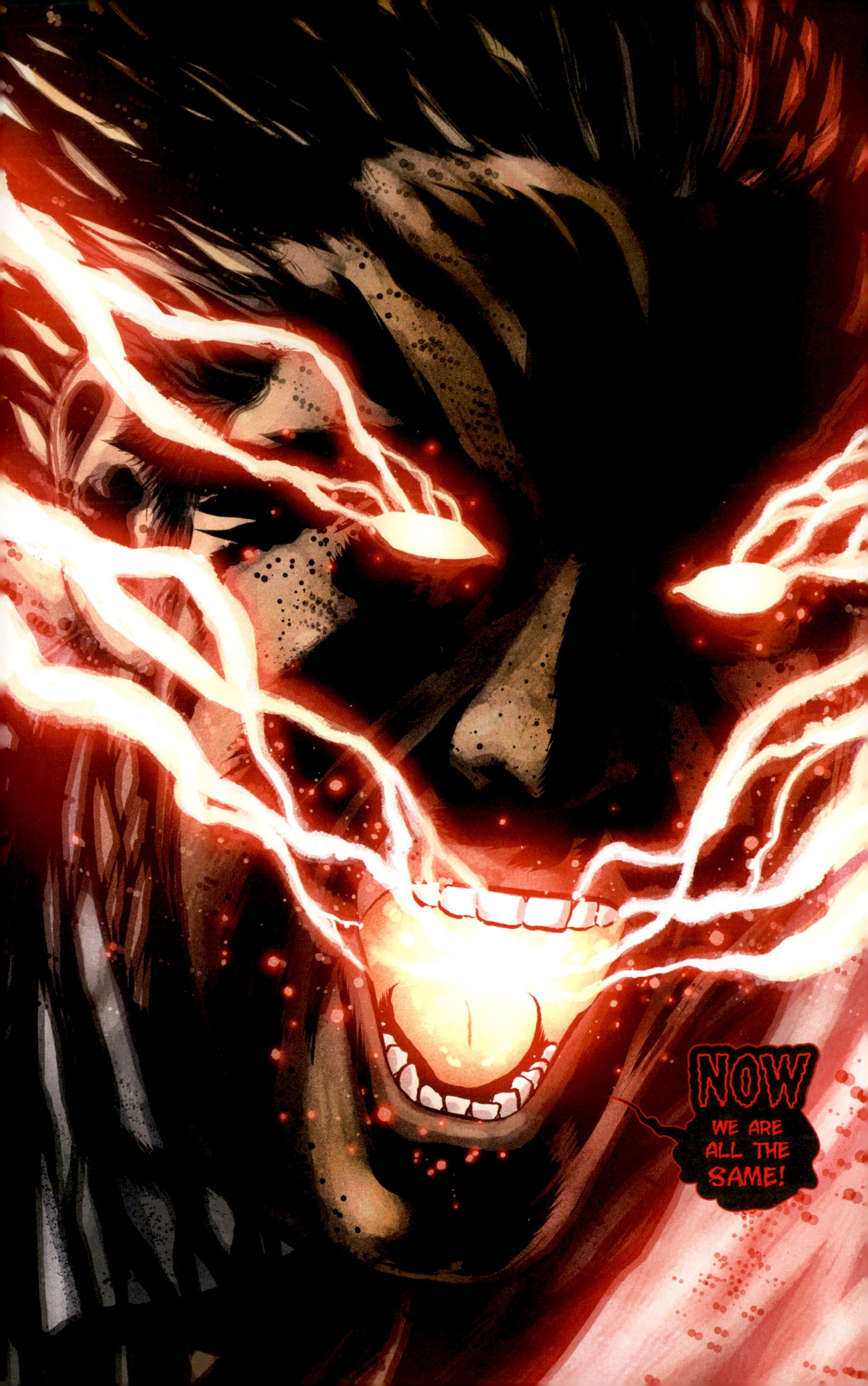
NOW
WE ARE ALL THE SAME!

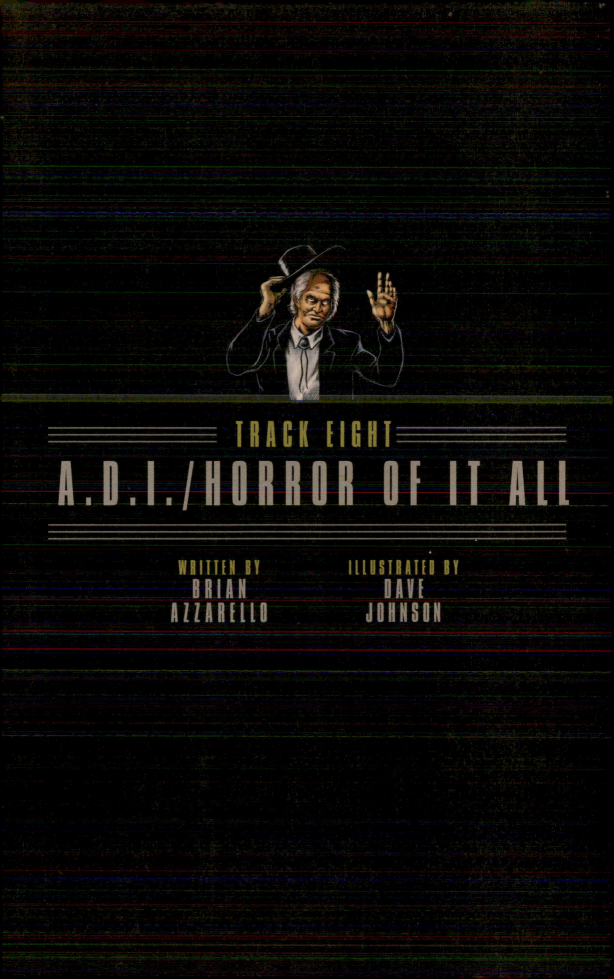

TRACK EIGHT

A.D.I./HORROR OF IT ALL

WRITTEN BY
**BRIAN
AZZARELLO**

ILLUSTRATED BY
**DAVE
JOHNSON**

"IN SPACE...NO ONE CAN HEAR YOUR GUITAR SOLO...OR HEAR YOU DIE!"

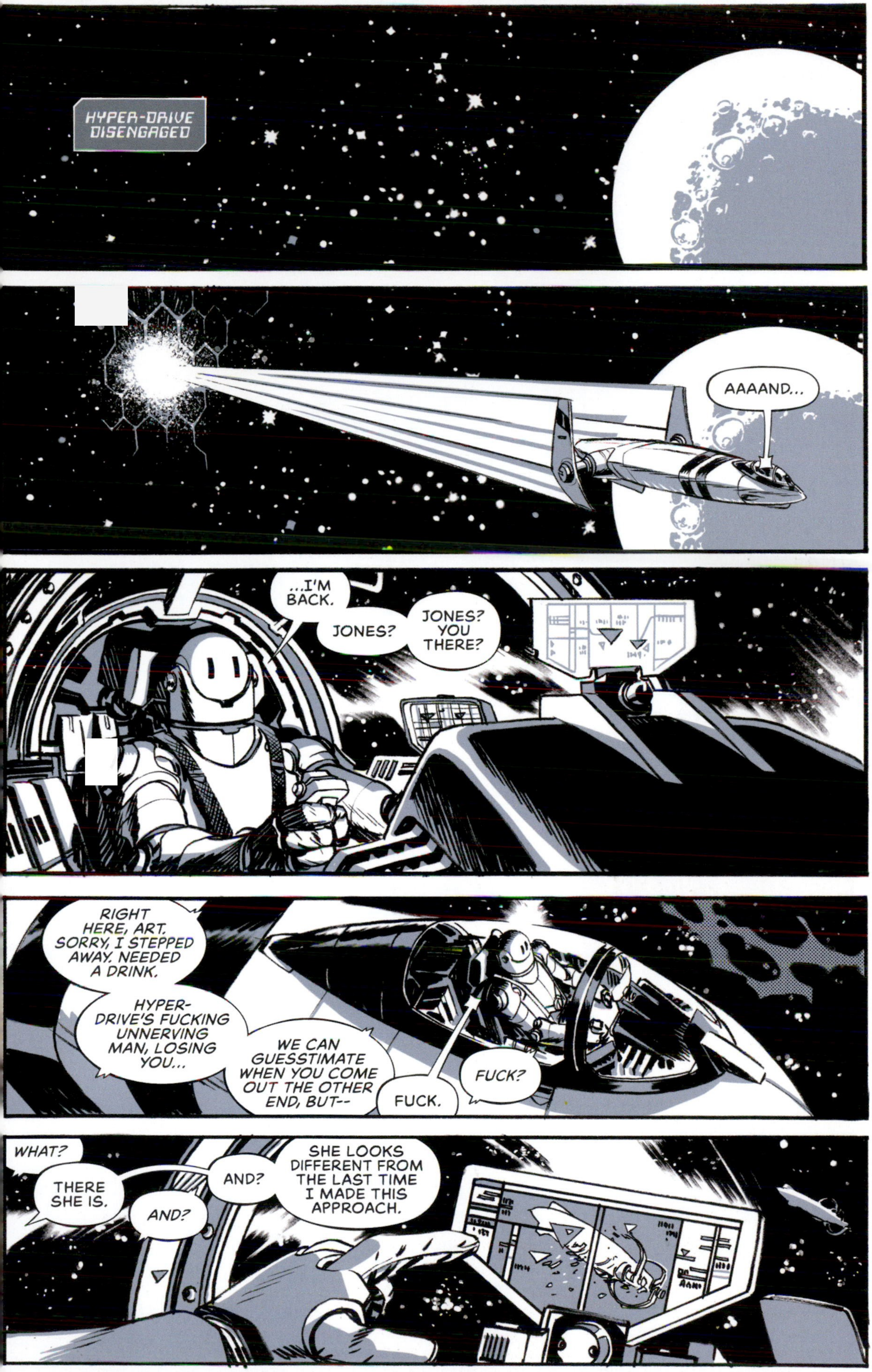
HYPER-DRIVE DISENGAGED
AAAAND...
...I'M BACK.
JONES?
JONES? YOU THERE?
RIGHT HERE, ART. SORRY, I STEPPED AWAY. NEEDED A DRINK.
HYPER-DRIVE'S FUCKING UNNERVING MAN, LOSING YOU...
WE CAN GUESSTIMATE WHEN YOU COME OUT THE OTHER END, BUT--
FUCK.
FUCK?
WHAT?
THERE SHE IS.
AND?
AND?
SHE LOOKS DIFFERENT FROM THE LAST TIME I MADE THIS APPROACH.

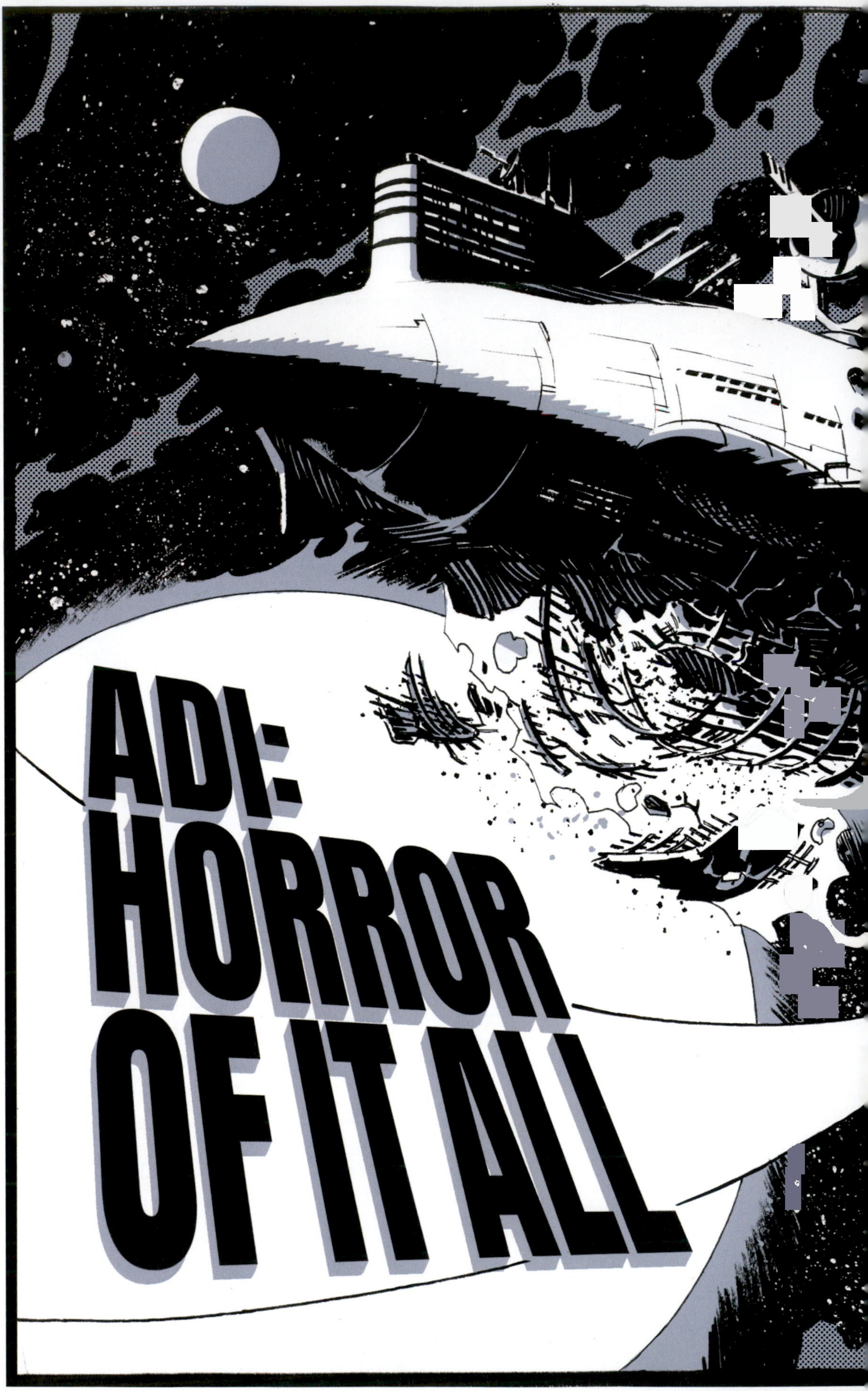
ADI:
HORROR
OF IT ALL

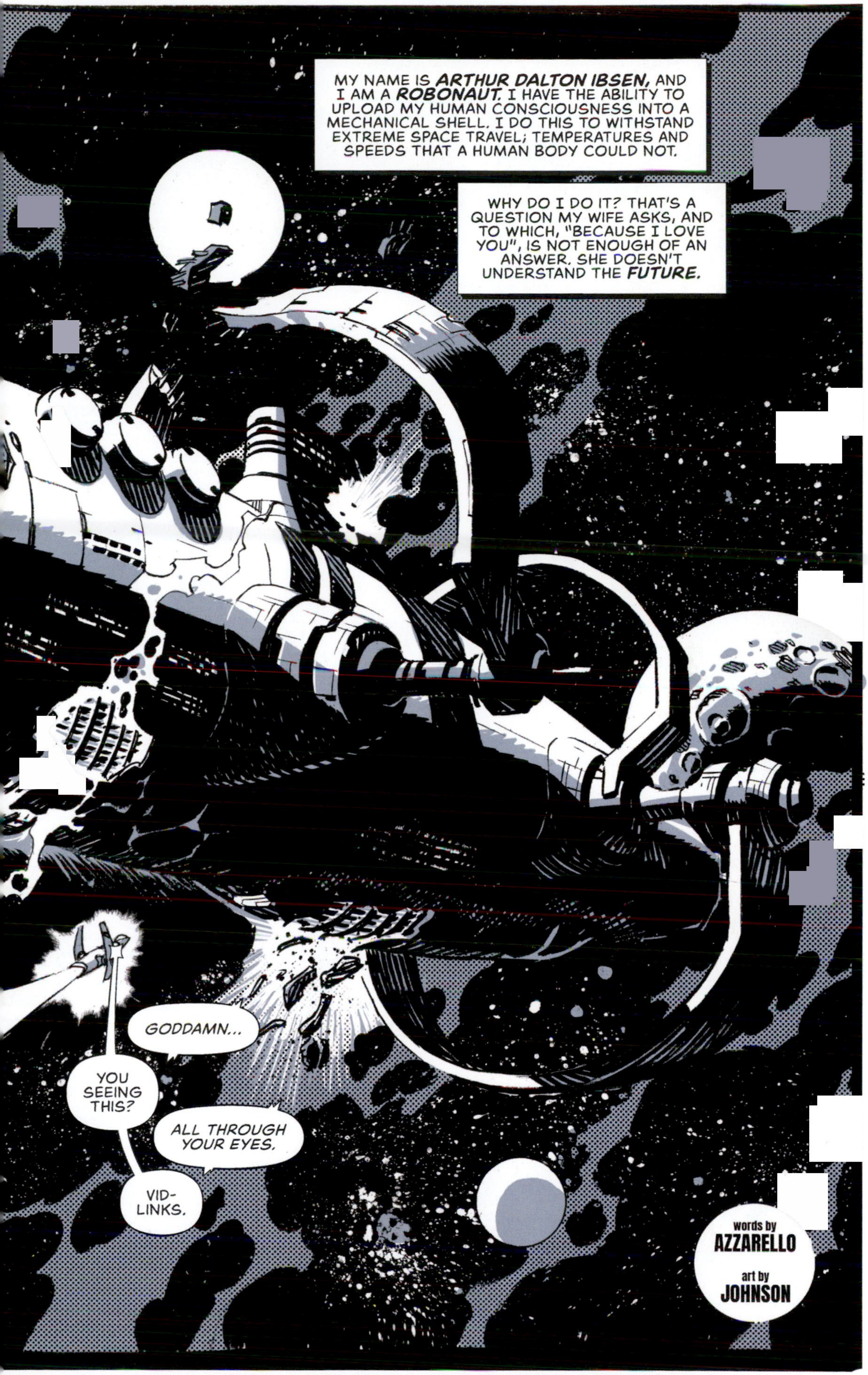
MY NAME IS ARTHUR DALTON IBSEN, AND I AM A ROBONAUT. I HAVE THE ABILITY TO UPLOAD MY HUMAN CONSCIOUSNESS INTO A MECHANICAL SHELL. I DO THIS TO WITHSTAND EXTREME SPACE TRAVEL; TEMPERATURES AND SPEEDS THAT A HUMAN BODY COULD NOT.
WHY DO I DO IT? THAT'S A QUESTION MY WIFE ASKS, AND TO WHICH, "BECAUSE I LOVE YOU", IS NOT ENOUGH OF AN ANSWER. SHE DOESN'T UNDERSTAND THE FUTURE.
GODDAMN...
YOU SEEING THIS?
ALL THROUGH YOUR EYES.
VID-LINKS.
words by AZZARELLO
art by JOHNSON

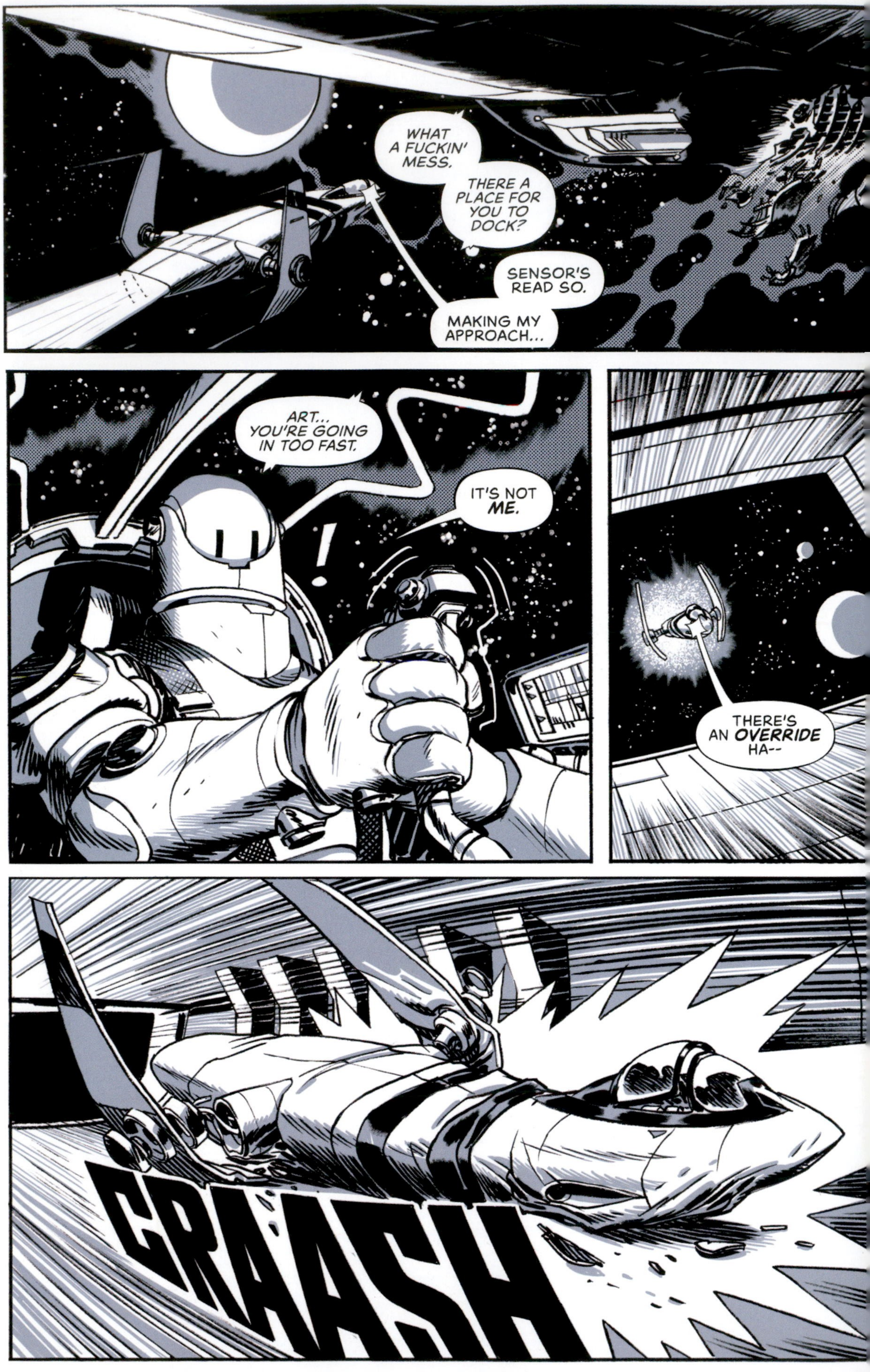
WHAT A FUCKIN' MESS.
THERE A PLACE FOR YOU TO DOCK?
SENSOR'S READ SO.
MAKING MY APPROACH...
ART... YOU'RE GOING IN TOO FAST.
IT'S NOT ME.
!
THERE'S AN OVERRIDE HA--
CRAASH

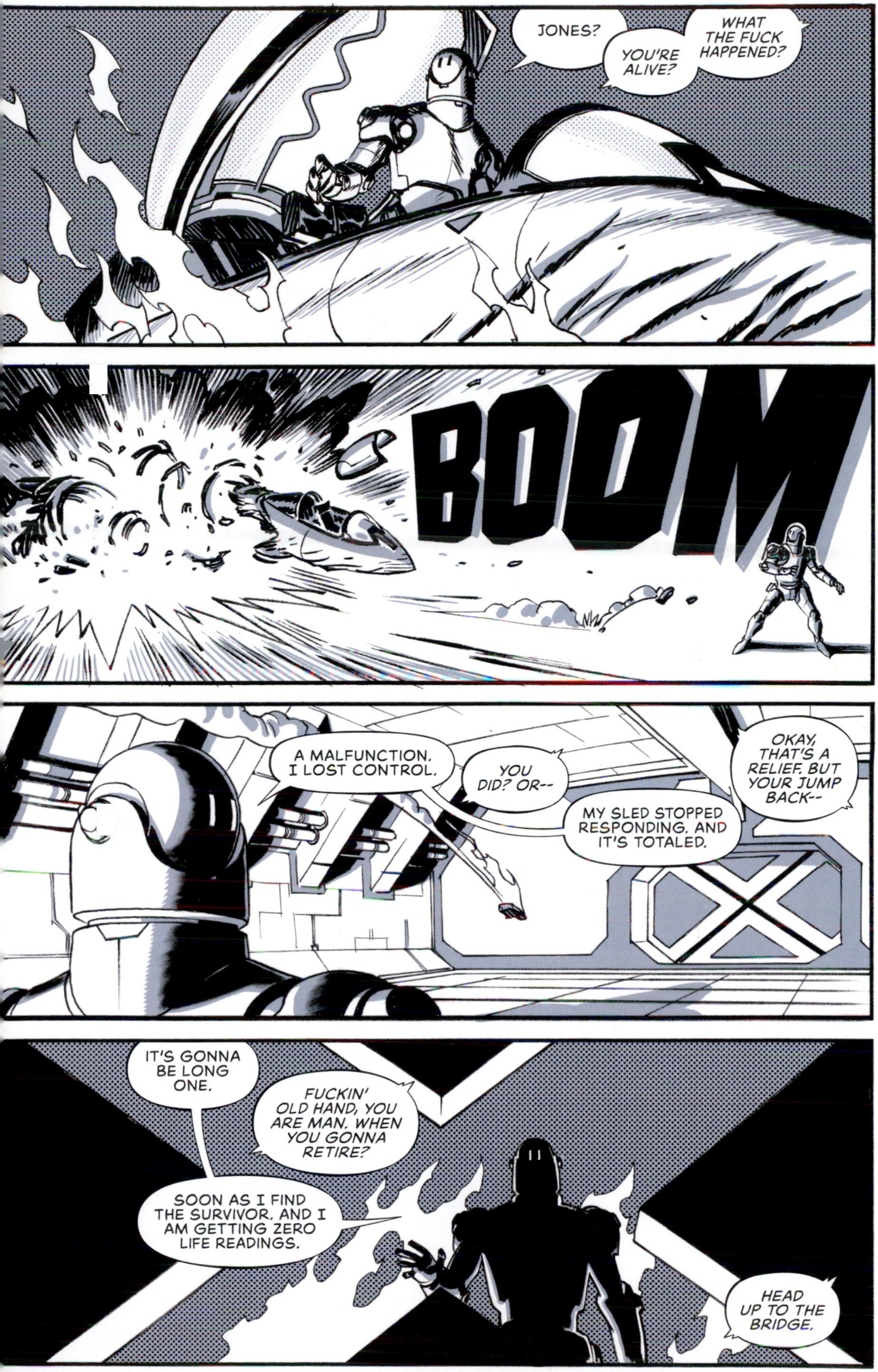
JONES?
YOU'RE ALIVE?
WHAT THE FUCK HAPPENED?
BOOM
A MALFUNCTION. I LOST CONTROL.
YOU DID? OR--
MY SLED STOPPED RESPONDING. AND IT'S TOTALED.
OKAY, THAT'S A RELIEF. BUT YOUR JUMP BACK--
IT'S GONNA BE LONG ONE.
FUCKIN' OLD HAND, YOU ARE MAN. WHEN YOU GONNA RETIRE?
SOON AS I FIND THE SURVIVOR. AND I AM GETTING ZERO LIFE READINGS.
HEAD UP TO THE BRIDGE.

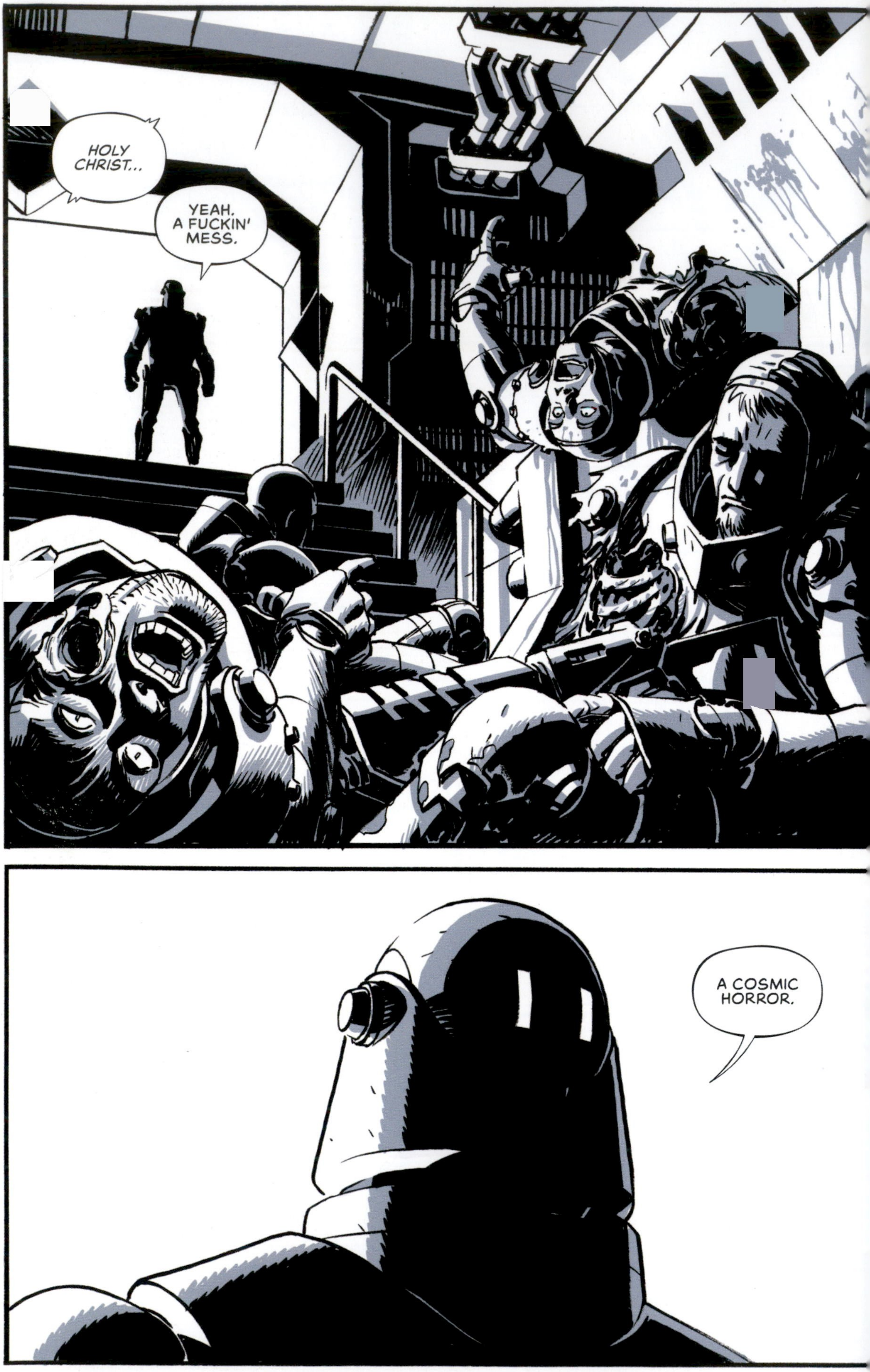
HOLY CHRIST...
YEAH, A FUCKIN' MESS.
A COSMIC HORROR.

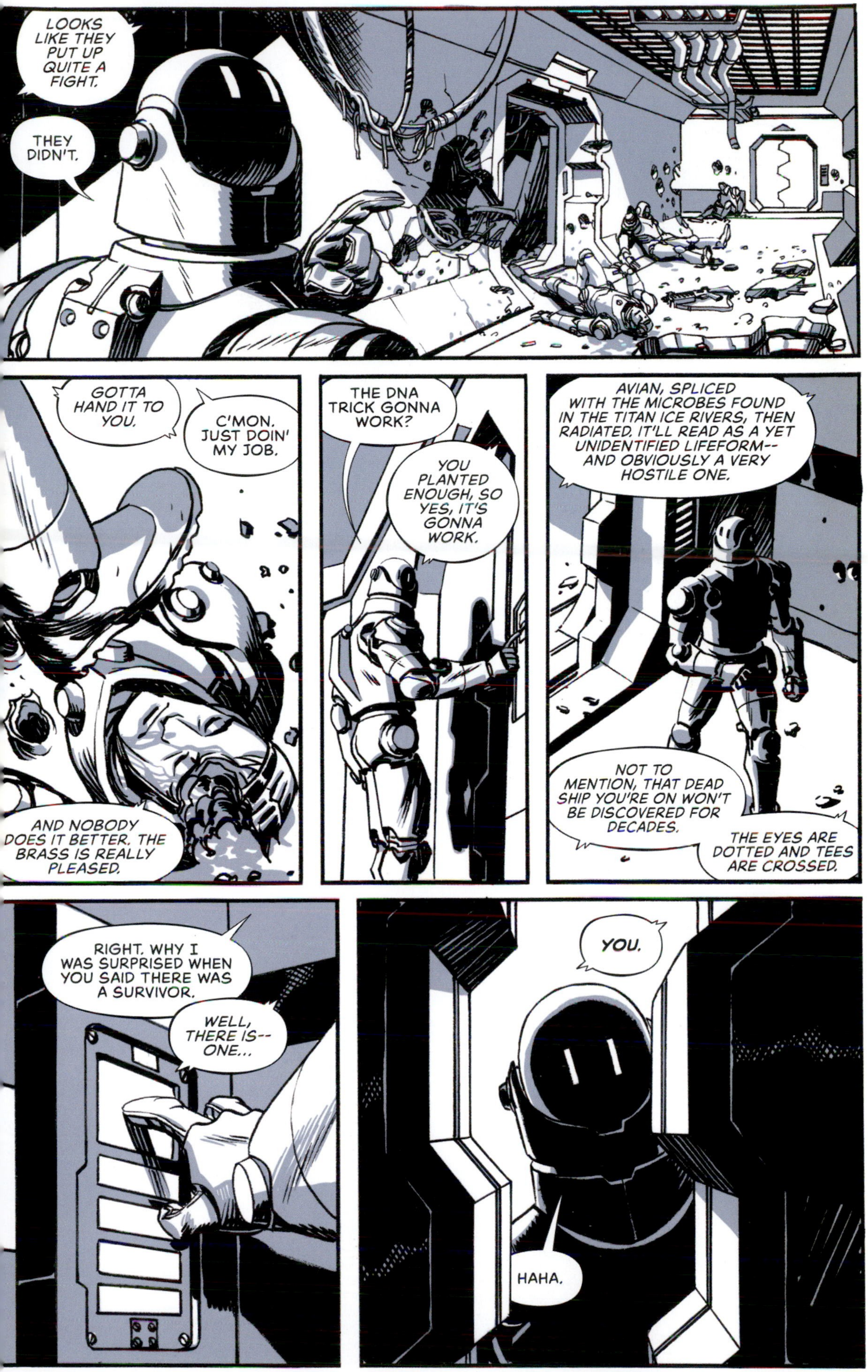
LOOKS LIKE THEY PUT UP QUITE A FIGHT.
THEY DIDN'T.
GOTTA HAND IT TO YOU.
C'MON. JUST DOIN' MY JOB.
AND NOBODY DOES IT BETTER. THE BRASS IS REALLY PLEASED.
THE DNA TRICK GONNA WORK?
YOU PLANTED ENOUGH, SO YES, IT'S GONNA WORK.
AVIAN, SPLICED WITH THE MICROBES FOUND IN THE TITAN ICE RIVERS, THEN RADIATED. IT'LL READ AS A YET UNIDENTIFIED LIFEFORM-- AND OBVIOUSLY A VERY HOSTILE ONE.
NOT TO MENTION, THAT DEAD SHIP YOU'RE ON WON'T BE DISCOVERED FOR DECADES.
THE EYES ARE DOTTED AND TEES ARE CROSSED.
RIGHT. WHY I WAS SURPRISED WHEN YOU SAID THERE WAS A SURVIVOR.
WELL, THERE IS-- ONE...
YOU.
HAHA.

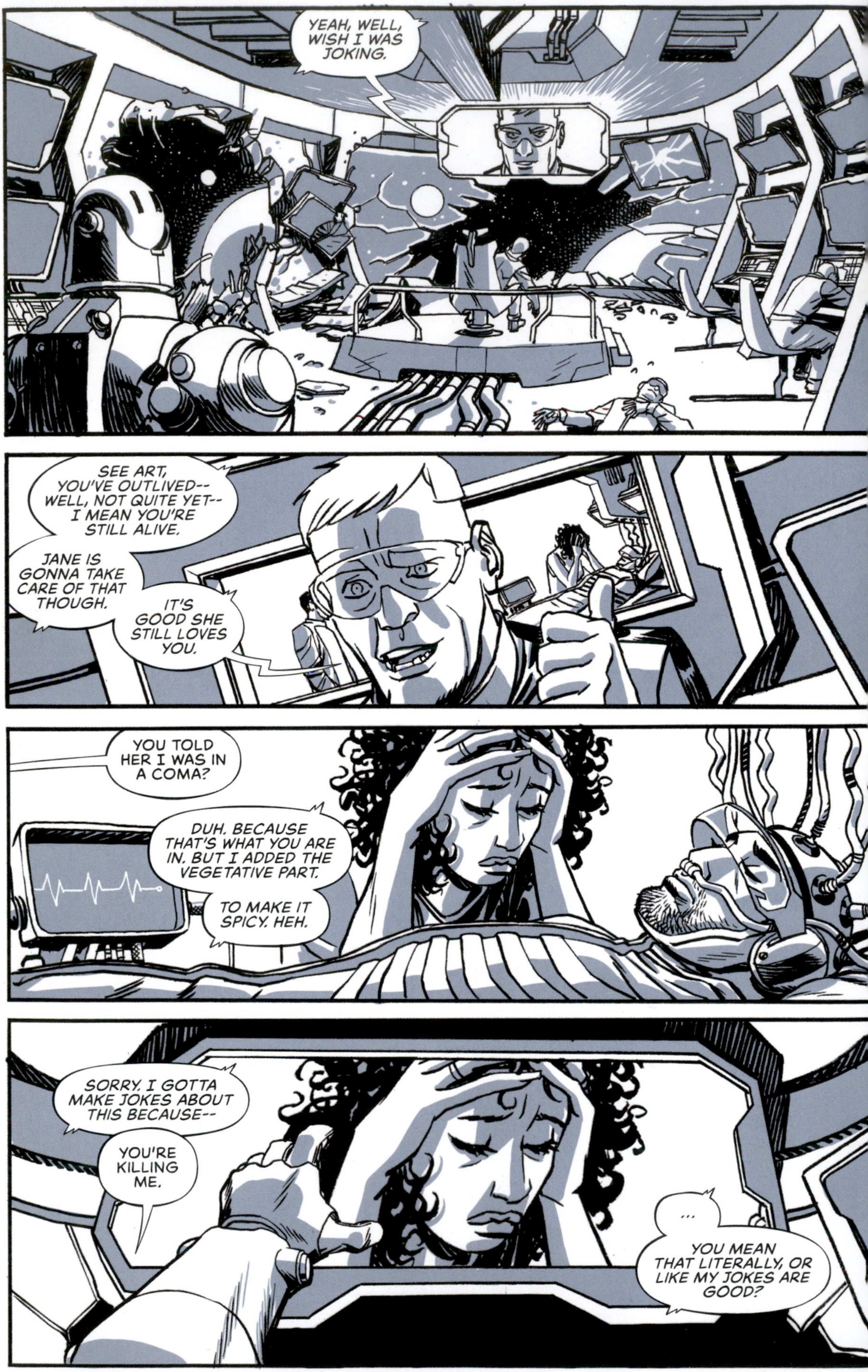
YEAH, WELL, WISH I WAS JOKING.
SEE ART, YOU'VE OUTLIVED-- WELL, NOT QUITE YET-- I MEAN YOU'RE STILL ALIVE.
JANE IS GONNA TAKE CARE OF THAT THOUGH.
IT'S GOOD SHE STILL LOVES YOU.
YOU TOLD HER I WAS IN A COMA?
DUH. BECAUSE THAT'S WHAT YOU ARE IN. BUT I ADDED THE VEGETATIVE PART.
TO MAKE IT SPICY. HEH.
SORRY. I GOTTA MAKE JOKES ABOUT THIS BECAUSE--
YOU'RE KILLING ME.
...
YOU MEAN THAT LITERALLY, OR LIKE MY JOKES ARE GOOD?

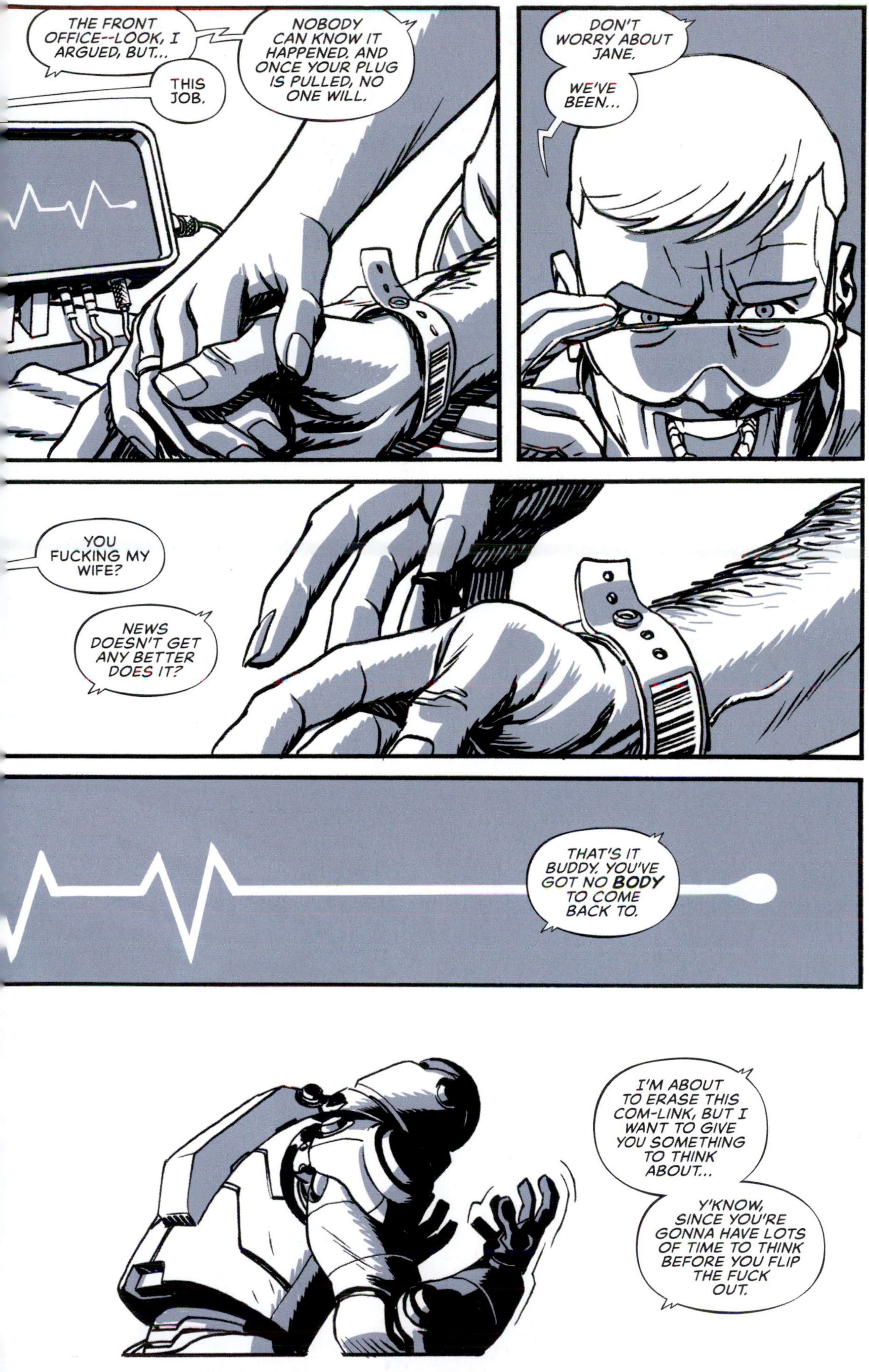
THE FRONT OFFICE--LOOK, I ARGUED, BUT...
THIS JOB.
NOBODY CAN KNOW IT HAPPENED. AND ONCE YOUR PLUG IS PULLED, NO ONE WILL.
DON'T WORRY ABOUT JANE.
WE'VE BEEN...
YOU FUCKING MY WIFE?
NEWS DOESN'T GET ANY BETTER DOES IT?
THAT'S IT BUDDY. YOU'VE GOT NO BODY TO COME BACK TO.
I'M ABOUT TO ERASE THIS COM-LINK, BUT I WANT TO GIVE YOU SOMETHING TO THINK ABOUT...
Y'KNOW, SINCE YOU'RE GONNA HAVE LOTS OF TIME TO THINK BEFORE YOU FLIP THE FUCK OUT.

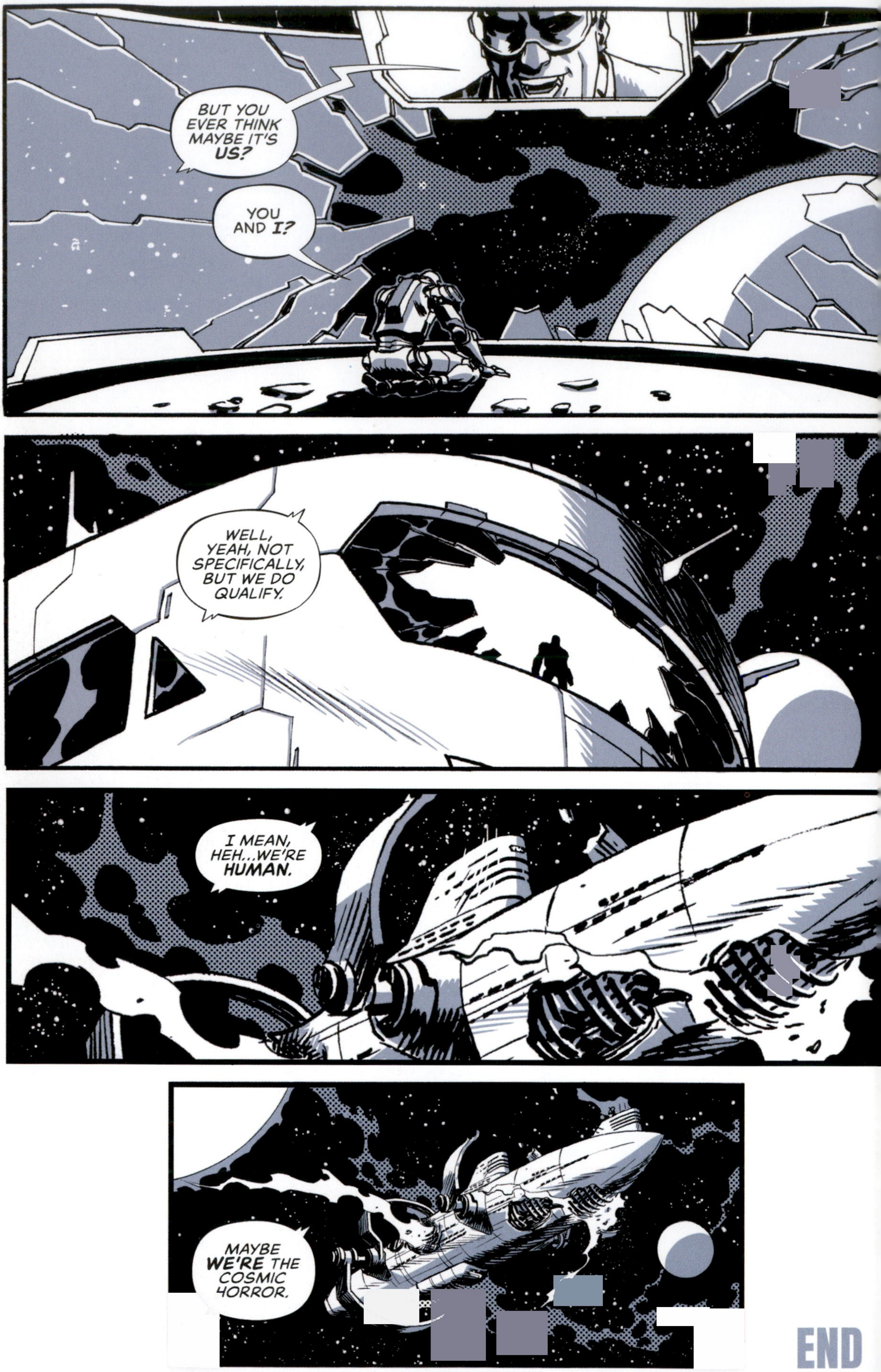
BUT YOU EVER THINK MAYBE IT'S **US?**
YOU AND ***I?***
WELL, YEAH, NOT SPECIFICALLY, BUT WE DO QUALIFY.
I MEAN, HEH...WE'RE **HUMAN.**
MAYBE **WE'RE** THE COSMIC HORROR.
END

TRACK NINE

IMITATION OF LIFE

WRITTEN BY
ROB ZOMBIE

ILLUSTRATED BY
ERIK RODRIGUEZ

COLORED BY
STEVE CHANKS

"JEEZ! THIS LAST STORY IS F'D UP!
WHAT'S WRONG WITH THIS GUY?"

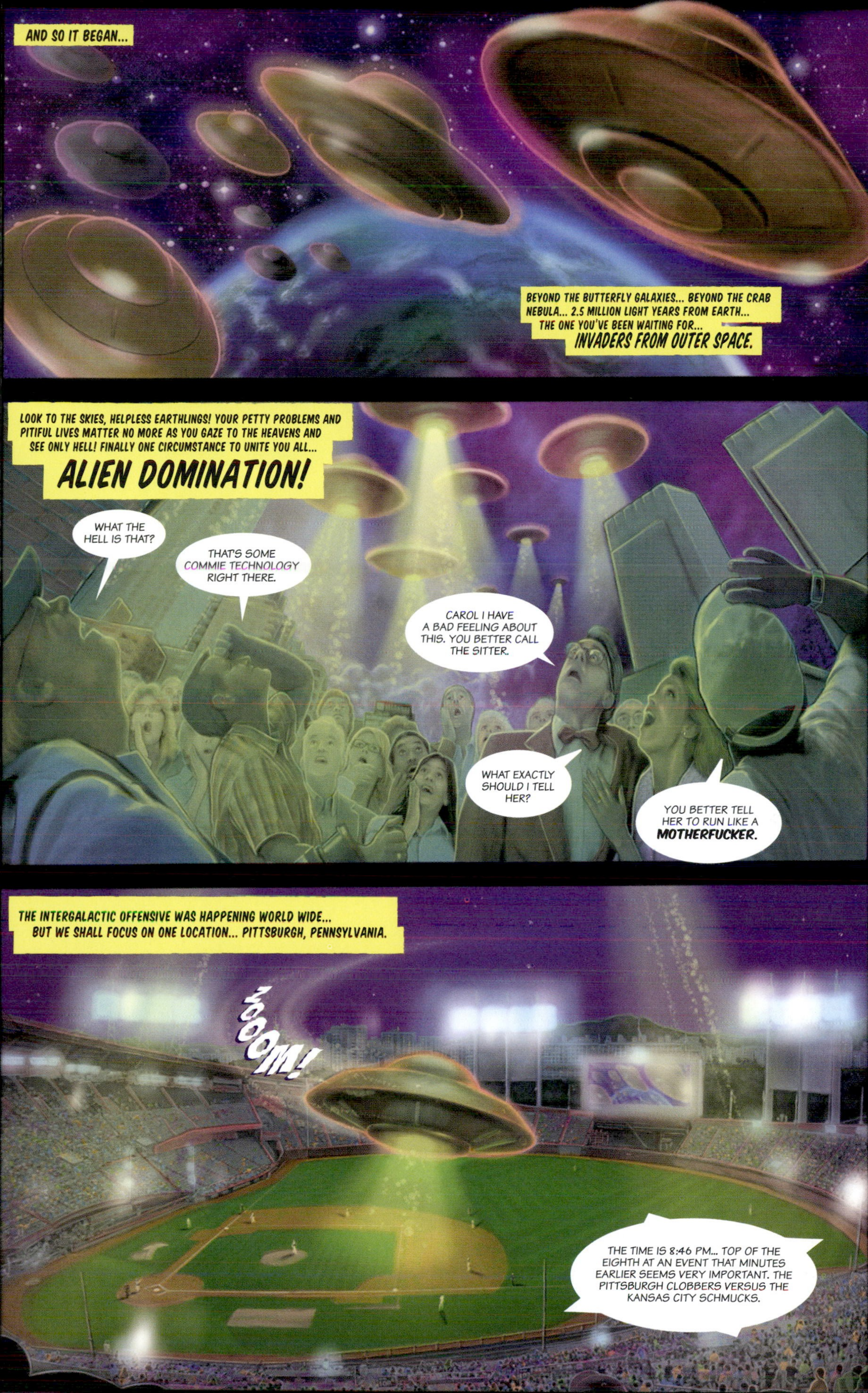
AND SO IT BEGAN...
BEYOND THE BUTTERFLY GALAXIES... BEYOND THE CRAB NEBULA... 2.5 MILLION LIGHT YEARS FROM EARTH... THE ONE YOU'VE BEEN WAITING FOR... INVADERS FROM OUTER SPACE.
LOOK TO THE SKIES, HELPLESS EARTHLINGS! YOUR PETTY PROBLEMS AND PITIFUL LIVES MATTER NO MORE AS YOU GAZE TO THE HEAVENS AND SEE ONLY HELL! FINALLY ONE CIRCUMSTANCE TO UNITE YOU ALL... ALIEN DOMINATION!
WHAT THE HELL IS THAT?
THAT'S SOME COMMIE TECHNOLOGY RIGHT THERE.
CAROL I HAVE A BAD FEELING ABOUT THIS. YOU BETTER CALL THE SITTER.
WHAT EXACTLY SHOULD I TELL HER?
YOU BETTER TELL HER TO RUN LIKE A **MOTHERFUCKER.**
THE INTERGALACTIC OFFENSIVE WAS HAPPENING WORLD WIDE... BUT WE SHALL FOCUS ON ONE LOCATION... PITTSBURGH, PENNSYLVANIA.
ZOOOM!
THE TIME IS 8:46 PM... TOP OF THE EIGHTH AT AN EVENT THAT MINUTES EARLIER SEEMS VERY IMPORTANT. THE PITTSBURGH CLOBBERS VERSUS THE KANSAS CITY SCHMUCKS.

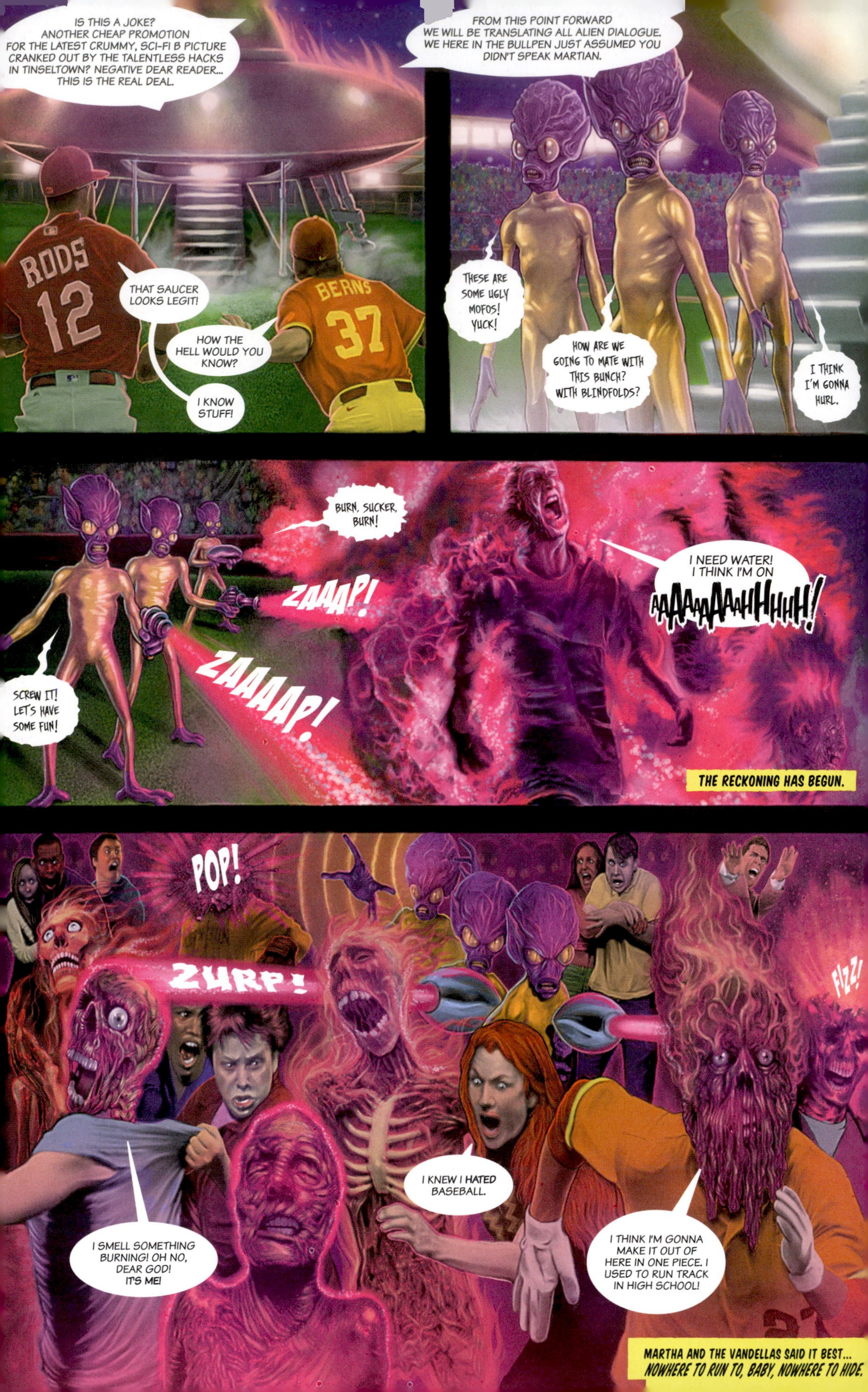

IS THIS A JOKE? ANOTHER CHEAP PROMOTION FOR THE LATEST CRUMMY, SCI-FI B PICTURE CRANKED OUT BY THE TALENTLESS HACKS IN TINSELTOWN? NEGATIVE DEAR READER... THIS IS THE REAL DEAL.
RODS 12
BERNS 37
THAT SAUCER LOOKS LEGIT!
HOW THE HELL WOULD YOU KNOW?
I KNOW STUFF!
FROM THIS POINT FORWARD WE WILL BE TRANSLATING ALL ALIEN DIALOGUE. WE HERE IN THE BULLPEN JUST ASSUMED YOU DIDN'T SPEAK MARTIAN.
THESE ARE SOME UGLY MOFOS! YUCK!
HOW ARE WE GOING TO MATE WITH THIS BUNCH? WITH BLINDFOLDS?
I THINK I'M GONNA HURL.
BURN, SUCKER, BURN!
I NEED WATER! I THINK I'M ON AAAAAAAAHHHHH!
ZAAAP!
ZAAAAAP!
SCREW IT! LET'S HAVE SOME FUN!
THE RECKONING HAS BEGUN.
POP!
ZURP!
FIZZ!
I KNEW I HATED BASEBALL.
I SMELL SOMETHING BURNING! OH NO, DEAR GOD! IT'S ME!
I THINK I'M GONNA MAKE IT OUT OF HERE IN ONE PIECE. I USED TO RUN TRACK IN HIGH SCHOOL!
MARTHA AND THE VANDELLAS SAID IT BEST... NOWHERE TO RUN TO, BABY, NOWHERE TO HIDE.

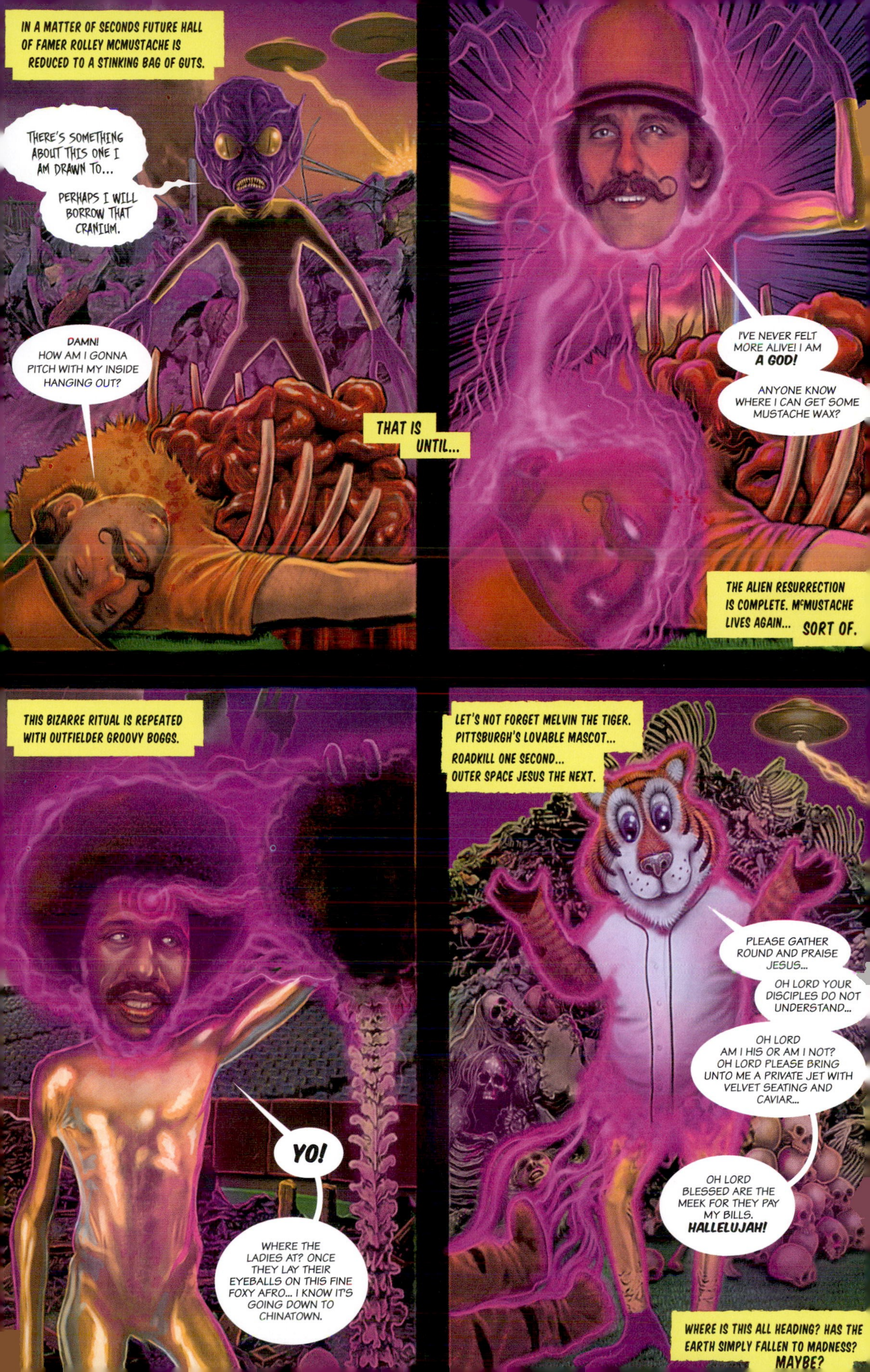

IN A MATTER OF SECONDS FUTURE HALL OF FAMER ROLLEY MCMUSTACHE IS REDUCED TO A STINKING BAG OF GUTS.
THERE'S SOMETHING ABOUT THIS ONE I AM DRAWN TO...
PERHAPS I WILL BORROW THAT CRANIUM.
DAMN! HOW AM I GONNA PITCH WITH MY INSIDE HANGING OUT?
THAT IS UNTIL...
I'VE NEVER FELT MORE ALIVE! I AM A GOD!
ANYONE KNOW WHERE I CAN GET SOME MUSTACHE WAX?
THE ALIEN RESURRECTION IS COMPLETE. McMUSTACHE LIVES AGAIN... SORT OF.
THIS BIZARRE RITUAL IS REPEATED WITH OUTFIELDER GROOVY BOGGS.
YO!
WHERE THE LADIES AT? ONCE THEY LAY THEIR EYEBALLS ON THIS FINE FOXY AFRO... I KNOW IT'S GOING DOWN TO CHINATOWN.
LET'S NOT FORGET MELVIN THE TIGER. PITTSBURGH'S LOVABLE MASCOT...
ROADKILL ONE SECOND... OUTER SPACE JESUS THE NEXT.
PLEASE GATHER ROUND AND PRAISE JESUS...
OH LORD YOUR DISCIPLES DO NOT UNDERSTAND...
OH LORD AM I HIS OR AM I NOT? OH LORD PLEASE BRING UNTO ME A PRIVATE JET WITH VELVET SEATING AND CAVIAR...
OH LORD BLESSED ARE THE MEEK FOR THEY PAY MY BILLS. HALLELUJAH!
WHERE IS THIS ALL HEADING? HAS THE EARTH SIMPLY FALLEN TO MADNESS? MAYBE?

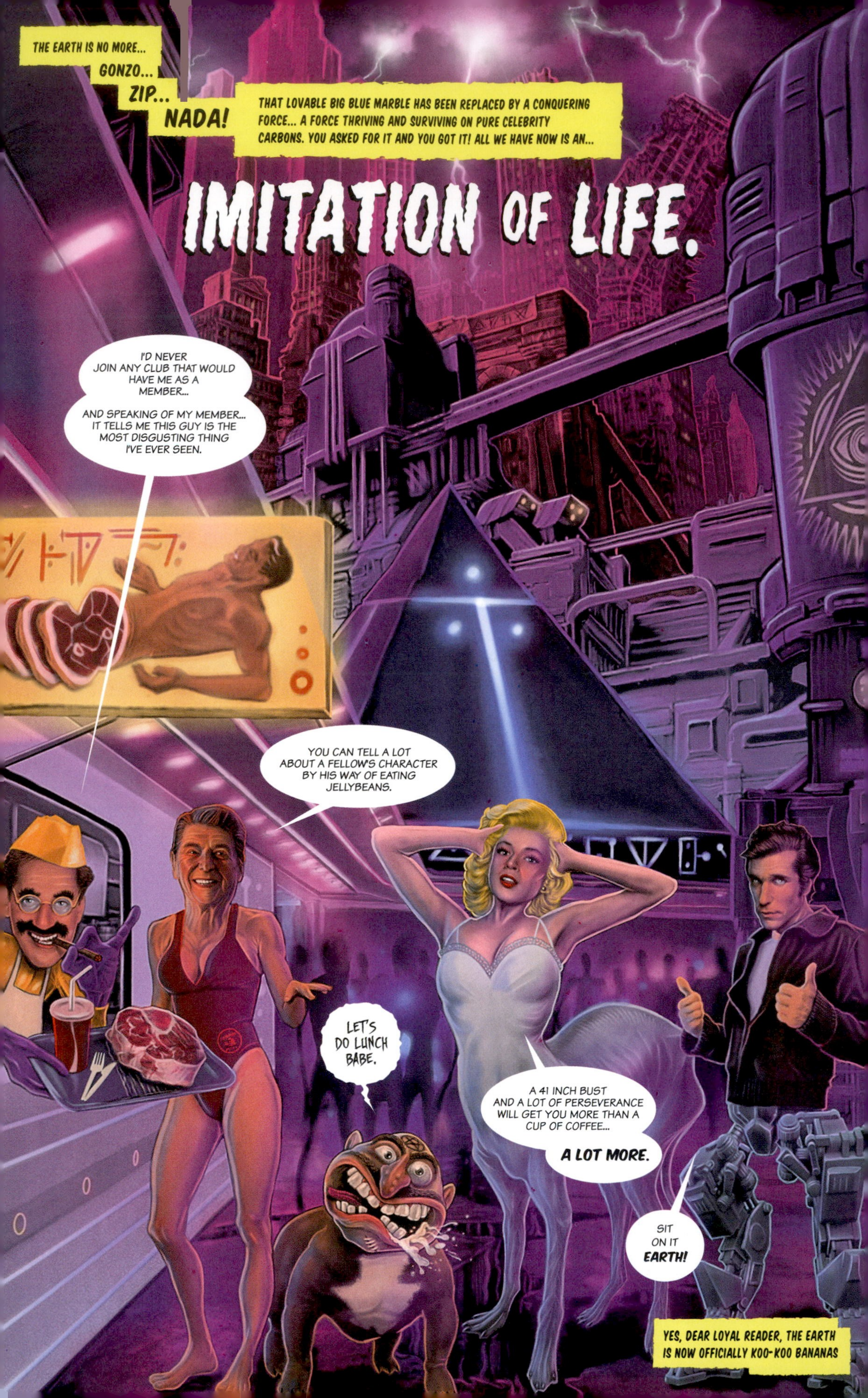
THE EARTH IS NO MORE...
GONZO...
ZIP...
NADA!
THAT LOVABLE BIG BLUE MARBLE HAS BEEN REPLACED BY A CONQUERING FORCE... A FORCE THRIVING AND SURVIVING ON PURE CELEBRITY CARBONS. YOU ASKED FOR IT AND YOU GOT IT! ALL WE HAVE NOW IS AN...
IMITATION OF LIFE.
I'D NEVER JOIN ANY CLUB THAT WOULD HAVE ME AS A MEMBER...
AND SPEAKING OF MY MEMBER... IT TELLS ME THIS GUY IS THE MOST DISGUSTING THING I'VE EVER SEEN.
YOU CAN TELL A LOT ABOUT A FELLOW'S CHARACTER BY HIS WAY OF EATING JELLYBEANS.
LET'S DO LUNCH BABE.
A 41 INCH BUST AND A LOT OF PERSEVERANCE WILL GET YOU MORE THAN A CUP OF COFFEE...
A LOT MORE.
SIT ON IT EARTH!
YES, DEAR LOYAL READER, THE EARTH IS NOW OFFICIALLY KOO-KOO BANANAS

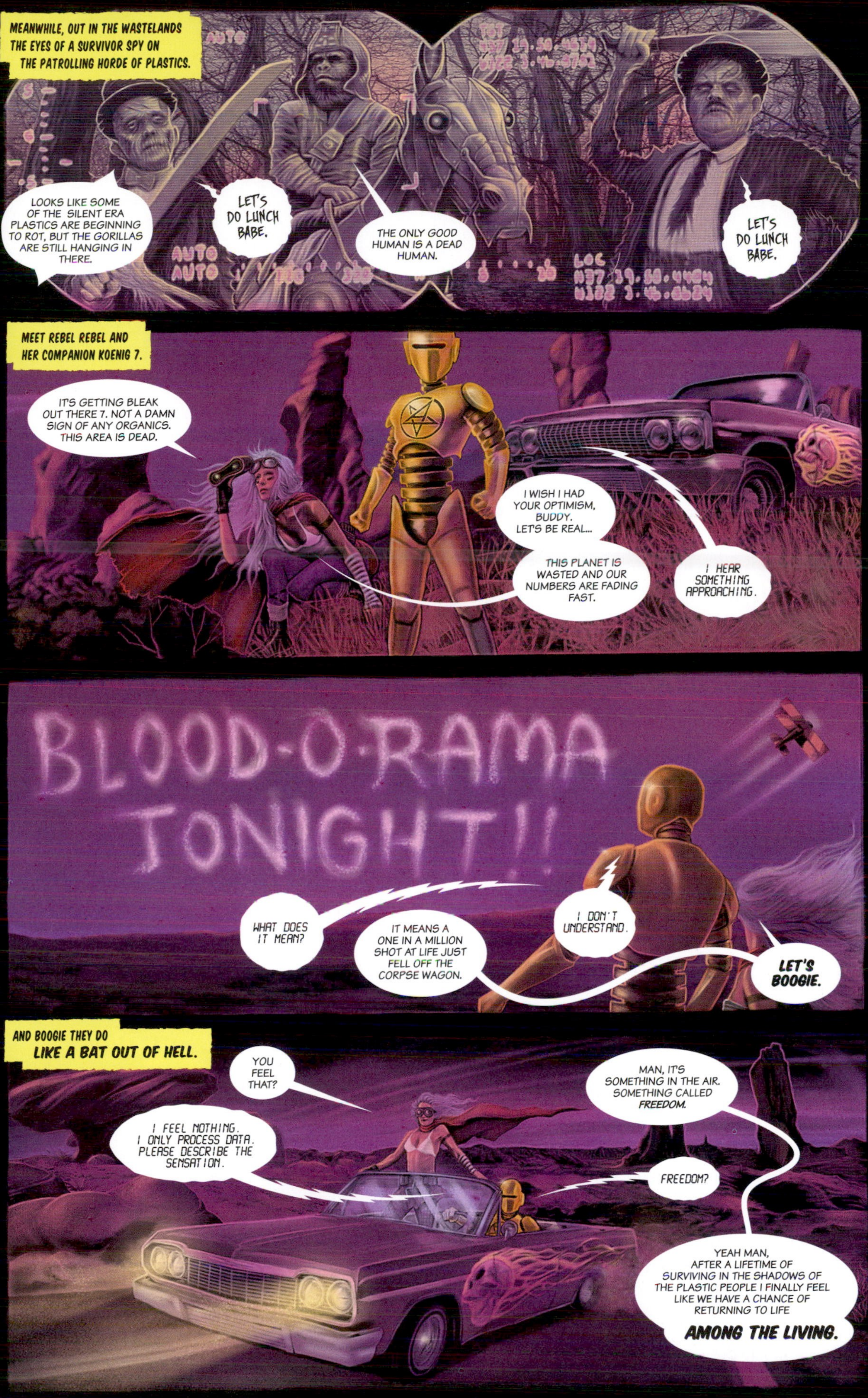
MEANWHILE, OUT IN THE WASTELANDS THE EYES OF A SURVIVOR SPY ON THE PATROLLING HORDE OF PLASTICS.
LOOKS LIKE SOME OF THE SILENT ERA PLASTICS ARE BEGINNING TO ROT, BUT THE GORILLAS ARE STILL HANGING IN THERE.
LET'S DO LUNCH BABE.
THE ONLY GOOD HUMAN IS A DEAD HUMAN.
LET'S DO LUNCH BABE.
MEET REBEL REBEL AND HER COMPANION KOENIG 7.
IT'S GETTING BLEAK OUT THERE 7. NOT A DAMN SIGN OF ANY ORGANICS. THIS AREA IS DEAD.
I WISH I HAD YOUR OPTIMISM, BUDDY. LET'S BE REAL...
THIS PLANET IS WASTED AND OUR NUMBERS ARE FADING FAST.
I HEAR SOMETHING APPROACHING.
BLOOD-O-RAMA TONIGHT!!
WHAT DOES IT MEAN?
IT MEANS A ONE IN A MILLION SHOT AT LIFE JUST FELL OFF THE CORPSE WAGON.
I DON'T UNDERSTAND.
LET'S BOOGIE.
AND BOOGIE THEY DO LIKE A BAT OUT OF HELL.
YOU FEEL THAT?
I FEEL NOTHING. I ONLY PROCESS DATA. PLEASE DESCRIBE THE SENSATION.
MAN, IT'S SOMETHING IN THE AIR. SOMETHING CALLED FREEDOM.
FREEDOM?
YEAH MAN, AFTER A LIFETIME OF SURVIVING IN THE SHADOWS OF THE PLASTIC PEOPLE I FINALLY FEEL LIKE WE HAVE A CHANCE OF RETURNING TO LIFE AMONG THE LIVING.

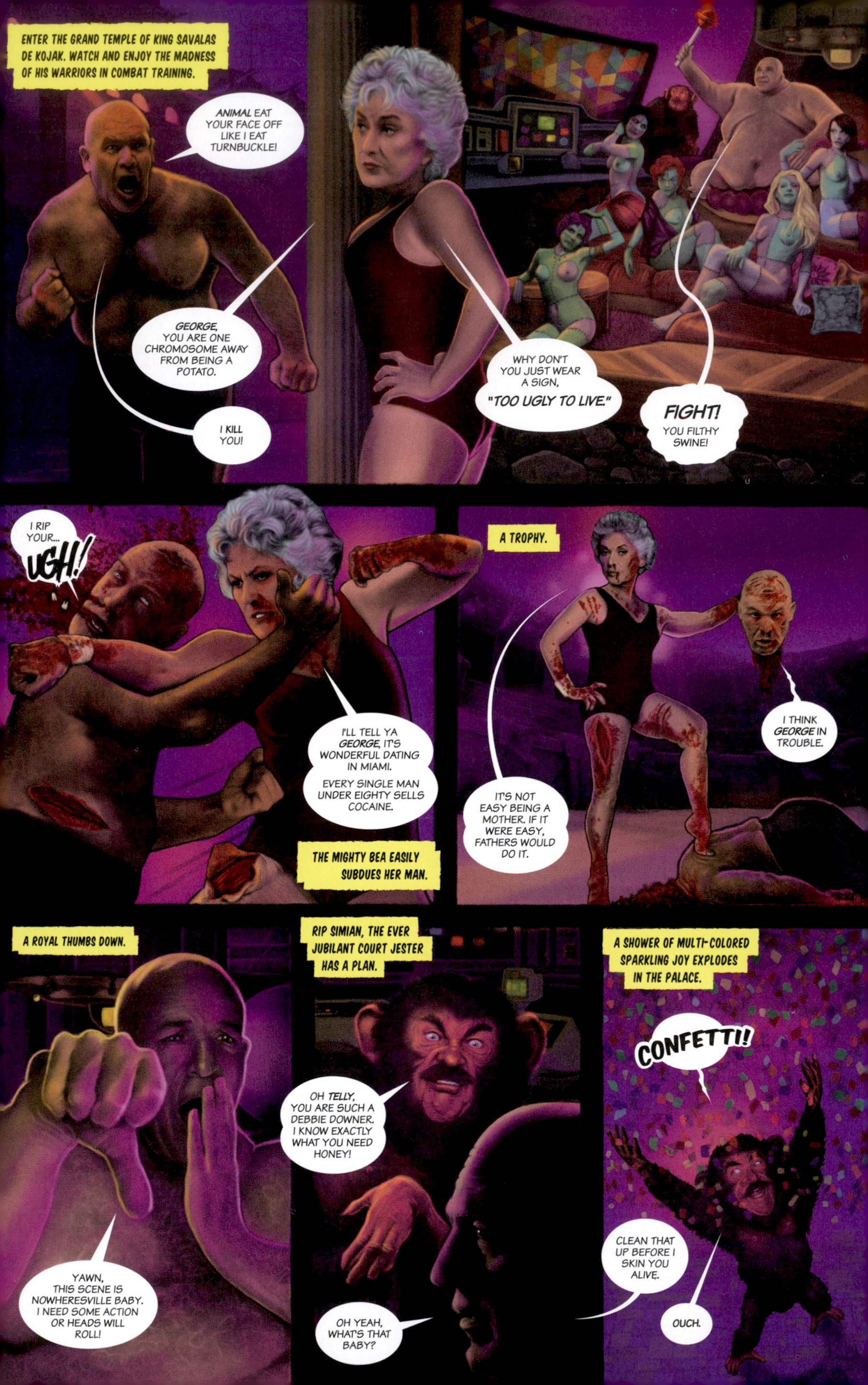
ENTER THE GRAND TEMPLE OF KING SAVALAS DE KOJAK. WATCH AND ENJOY THE MADNESS OF HIS WARRIORS IN COMBAT TRAINING.
ANIMAL EAT YOUR FACE OFF LIKE I EAT TURNBUCKLE!
GEORGE, YOU ARE ONE CHROMOSOME AWAY FROM BEING A POTATO.
I KILL YOU!
WHY DON'T YOU JUST WEAR A SIGN, "TOO UGLY TO LIVE."
FIGHT! YOU FILTHY SWINE!
I RIP YOUR... UGH!
I'LL TELL YA GEORGE, IT'S WONDERFUL DATING IN MIAMI.
EVERY SINGLE MAN UNDER EIGHTY SELLS COCAINE.
THE MIGHTY BEA EASILY SUBDUES HER MAN.
A TROPHY.
I THINK GEORGE IN TROUBLE.
IT'S NOT EASY BEING A MOTHER. IF IT WERE EASY, FATHERS WOULD DO IT.
A ROYAL THUMBS DOWN.
YAWN, THIS SCENE IS NOWHERESVILLE BABY. I NEED SOME ACTION OR HEADS WILL ROLL!
RIP SIMIAN, THE EVER JUBILANT COURT JESTER HAS A PLAN.
OH TELLY, YOU ARE SUCH A DEBBIE DOWNER. I KNOW EXACTLY WHAT YOU NEED HONEY!
OH YEAH, WHAT'S THAT BABY?
A SHOWER OF MULTI-COLORED SPARKLING JOY EXPLODES IN THE PALACE.
CONFETTI!!
CLEAN THAT UP BEFORE I SKIN YOU ALIVE.
OUCH.

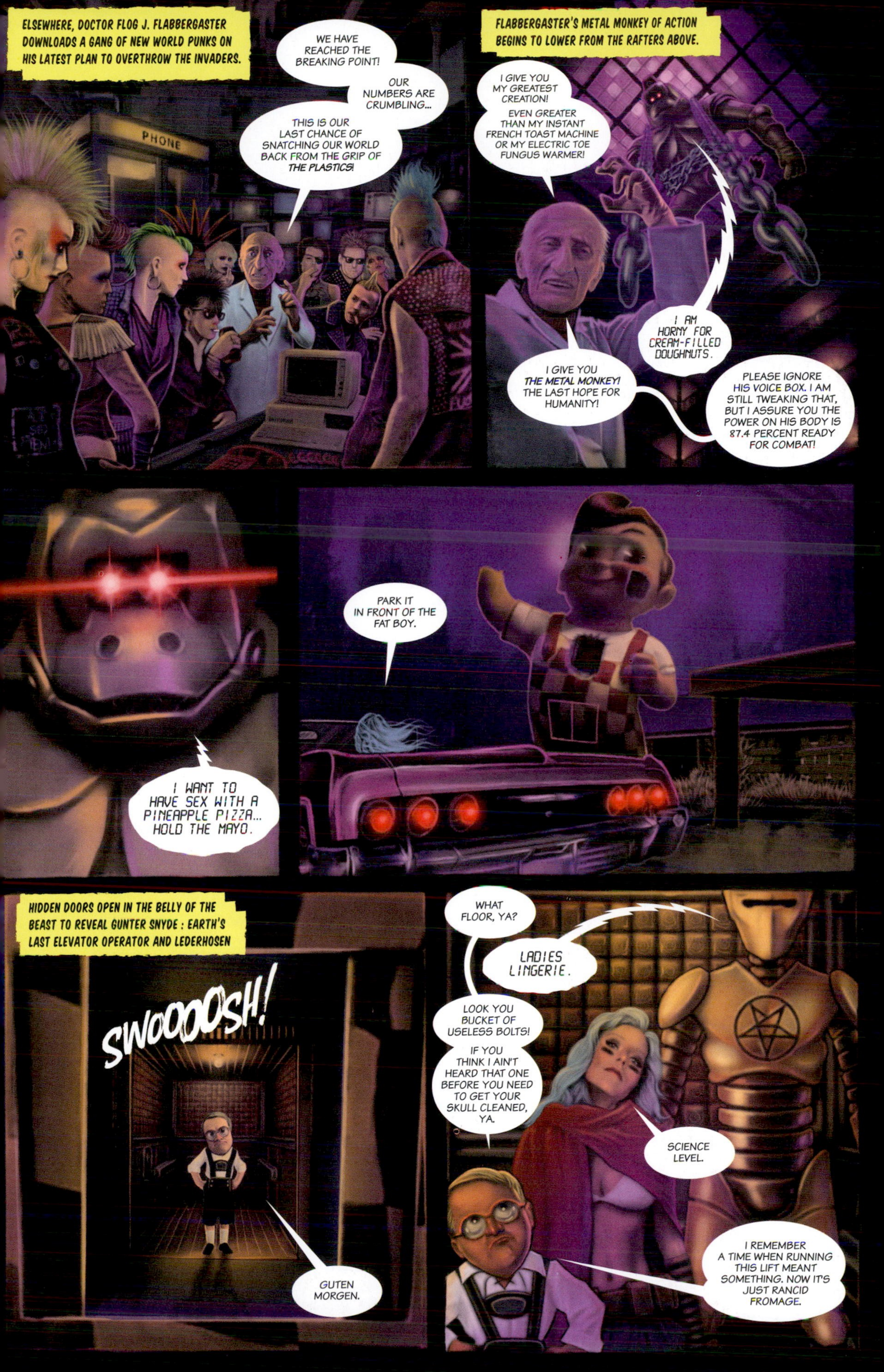
ELSEWHERE, DOCTOR FLOG J. FLABBERGASTER DOWNLOADS A GANG OF NEW WORLD PUNKS ON HIS LATEST PLAN TO OVERTHROW THE INVADERS.
WE HAVE REACHED THE BREAKING POINT!
OUR NUMBERS ARE CRUMBLING...
THIS IS OUR LAST CHANCE OF SNATCHING OUR WORLD BACK FROM THE GRIP OF THE PLASTICS!
PHONE
FLABBERGASTER'S METAL MONKEY OF ACTION BEGINS TO LOWER FROM THE RAFTERS ABOVE.
I GIVE YOU MY GREATEST CREATION!
EVEN GREATER THAN MY INSTANT FRENCH TOAST MACHINE OR MY ELECTRIC TOE FUNGUS WARMER!
I AM HORNY FOR CREAM-FILLED DOUGHNUTS.
I GIVE YOU THE METAL MONKEY! THE LAST HOPE FOR HUMANITY!
PLEASE IGNORE HIS VOICE BOX. I AM STILL TWEAKING THAT, BUT I ASSURE YOU THE POWER ON HIS BODY IS 87.4 PERCENT READY FOR COMBAT!
I WANT TO HAVE SEX WITH A PINEAPPLE PIZZA... HOLD THE MAYO.
PARK IT IN FRONT OF THE FAT BOY.
HIDDEN DOORS OPEN IN THE BELLY OF THE BEAST TO REVEAL GUNTER SNYDE : EARTH'S LAST ELEVATOR OPERATOR AND LEDERHOSEN
SWOOOOSH!
GUTEN MORGEN.
WHAT FLOOR, YA?
LADIES LINGERIE.
LOOK YOU BUCKET OF USELESS BOLTS!
IF YOU THINK I AIN'T HEARD THAT ONE BEFORE YOU NEED TO GET YOUR SKULL CLEANED, YA.
SCIENCE LEVEL.
I REMEMBER A TIME WHEN RUNNING THIS LIFT MEANT SOMETHING. NOW IT'S JUST RANCID FROMAGE.

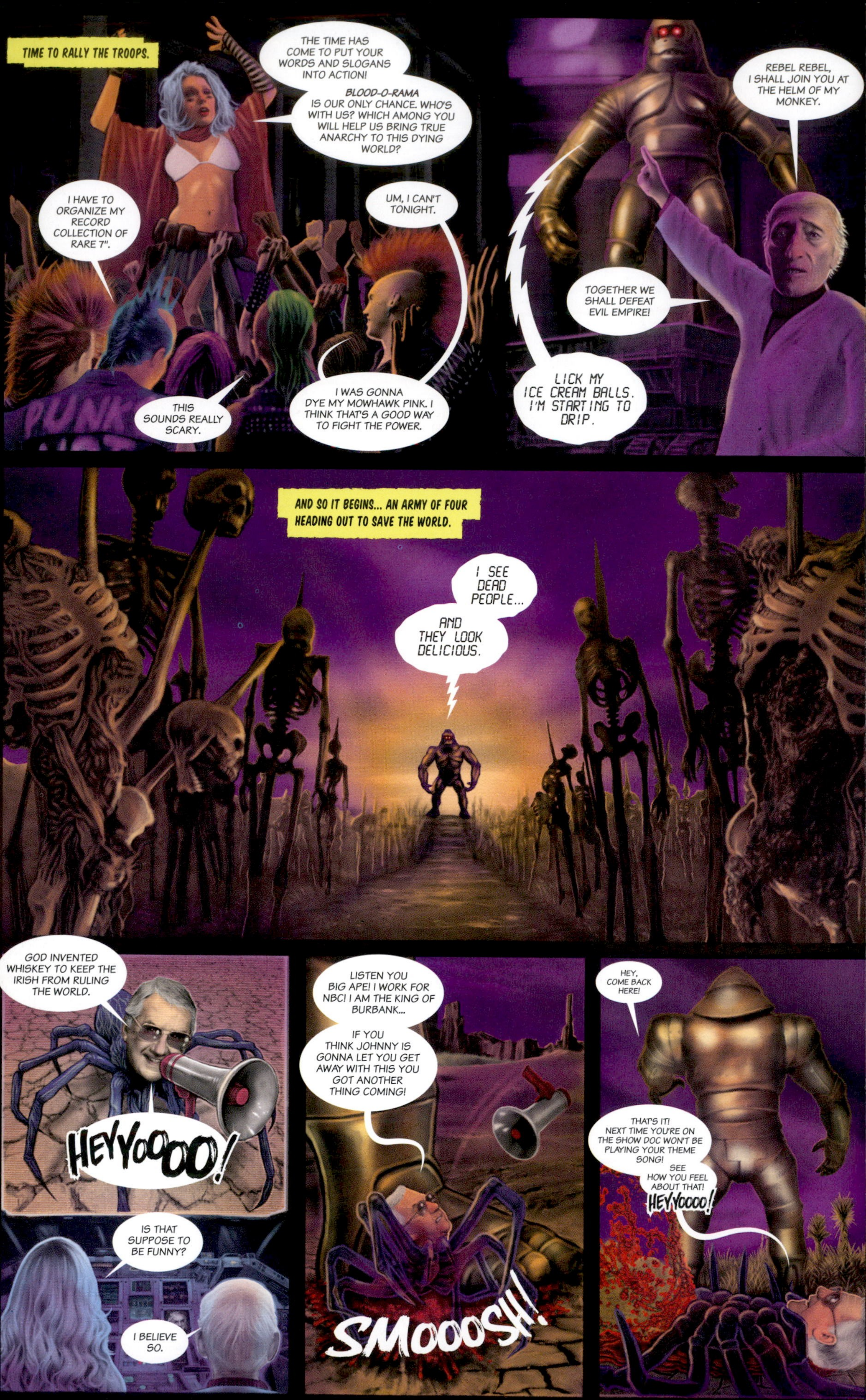

TIME TO RALLY THE TROOPS.
THE TIME HAS COME TO PUT YOUR WORDS AND SLOGANS INTO ACTION!
BLOOD-O-RAMA IS OUR ONLY CHANCE. WHO'S WITH US? WHICH AMONG YOU WILL HELP US BRING TRUE ANARCHY TO THIS DYING WORLD?
I HAVE TO ORGANIZE MY RECORD COLLECTION OF RARE 7".
UM, I CAN'T TONIGHT.
THIS SOUNDS REALLY SCARY.
I WAS GONNA DYE MY MOWHAWK PINK. I THINK THAT'S A GOOD WAY TO FIGHT THE POWER.
REBEL REBEL, I SHALL JOIN YOU AT THE HELM OF MY MONKEY.
TOGETHER WE SHALL DEFEAT EVIL EMPIRE!
LICK MY ICE CREAM BALLS. I'M STARTING TO DRIP.
AND SO IT BEGINS... AN ARMY OF FOUR HEADING OUT TO SAVE THE WORLD.
I SEE DEAD PEOPLE...
AND THEY LOOK DELICIOUS.
GOD INVENTED WHISKEY TO KEEP THE IRISH FROM RULING THE WORLD.
HEYYOOOOO!
IS THAT SUPPOSE TO BE FUNNY?
I BELIEVE SO.
LISTEN YOU BIG APE! I WORK FOR NBC! I AM THE KING OF BURBANK...
IF YOU THINK JOHNNY IS GONNA LET YOU GET AWAY WITH THIS YOU GOT ANOTHER THING COMING!
SMOOOSH!
HEY, COME BACK HERE!
THAT'S IT! NEXT TIME YOU'RE ON THE SHOW DOC WON'T BE PLAYING YOUR THEME SONG!
SEE HOW YOU FEEL ABOUT THAT! HEYYOOOO!

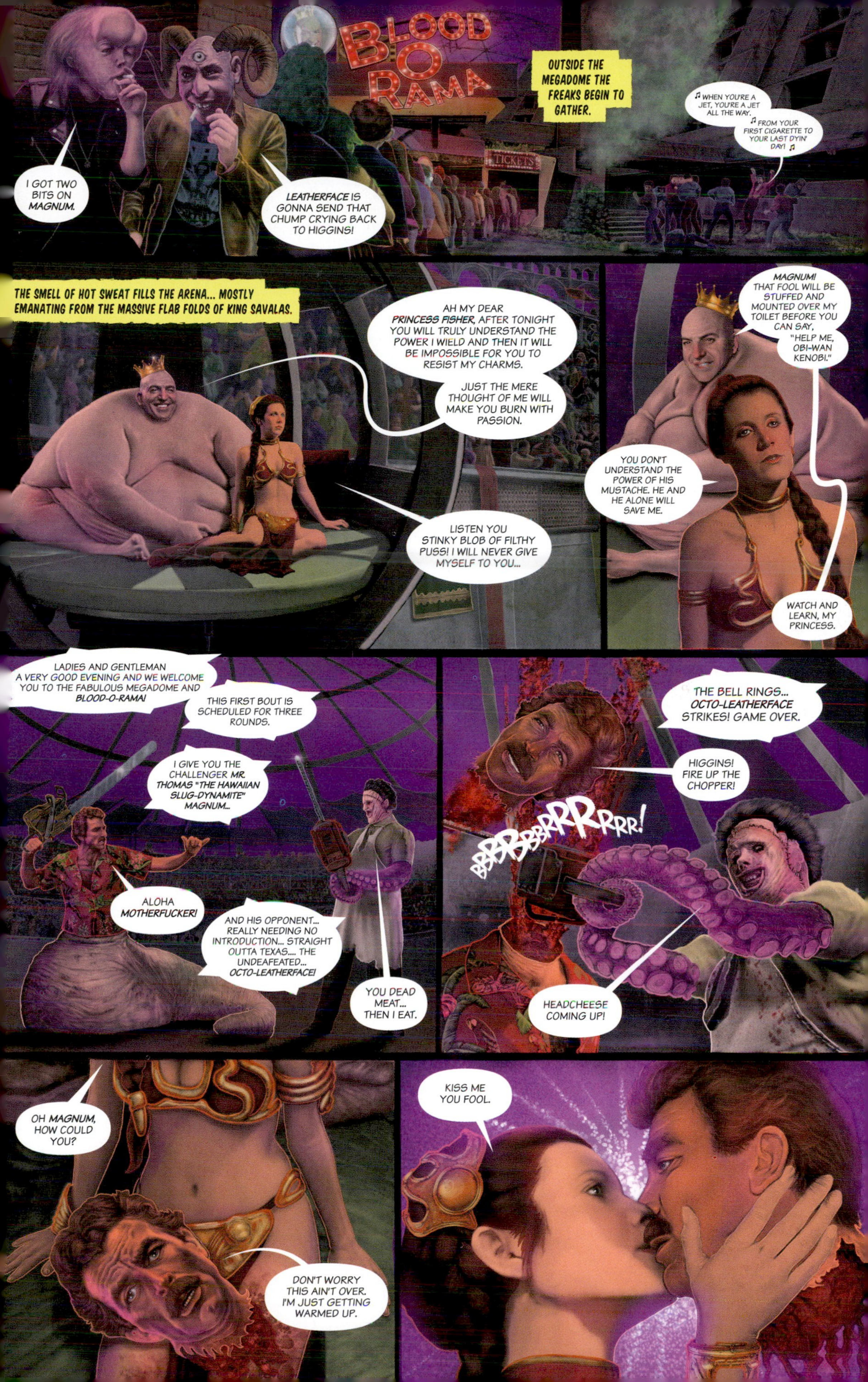

BLOOD O RAMA
TICKETS
OUTSIDE THE MEGADOME THE FREAKS BEGIN TO GATHER.
♪ WHEN YOU'RE A JET, YOU'RE A JET ALL THE WAY.
♪ FROM YOUR FIRST CIGARETTE TO YOUR LAST DYIN' DAY! ♪
I GOT TWO BITS ON MAGNUM.
LEATHERFACE IS GONNA SEND THAT CHUMP CRYING BACK TO HIGGINS!
THE SMELL OF HOT SWEAT FILLS THE ARENA... MOSTLY EMANATING FROM THE MASSIVE FLAB FOLDS OF KING SAVALAS.
AH MY DEAR PRINCESS FISHER, AFTER TONIGHT YOU WILL TRULY UNDERSTAND THE POWER I WIELD AND THEN IT WILL BE IMPOSSIBLE FOR YOU TO RESIST MY CHARMS.
JUST THE MERE THOUGHT OF ME WILL MAKE YOU BURN WITH PASSION.
LISTEN YOU STINKY BLOB OF FILTHY PUSS! I WILL NEVER GIVE MYSELF TO YOU...
MAGNUM! THAT FOOL WILL BE STUFFED AND MOUNTED OVER MY TOILET BEFORE YOU CAN SAY, "HELP ME, OBI-WAN KENOBI."
YOU DON'T UNDERSTAND THE POWER OF HIS MUSTACHE. HE AND HE ALONE WILL SAVE ME.
WATCH AND LEARN, MY PRINCESS.
LADIES AND GENTLEMAN A VERY GOOD EVENING AND WE WELCOME YOU TO THE FABULOUS MEGADOME AND BLOOD-O-RAMA!
THIS FIRST BOUT IS SCHEDULED FOR THREE ROUNDS.
I GIVE YOU THE CHALLENGER MR. THOMAS "THE HAWAIIAN SLUG-DYNAMITE" MAGNUM...
ALOHA MOTHERFUCKER!
AND HIS OPPONENT... REALLY NEEDING NO INTRODUCTION... STRAIGHT OUTTA TEXAS.... THE UNDEAFEATED... OCTO-LEATHERFACE!
YOU DEAD MEAT... THEN I EAT.
THE BELL RINGS... OCTO-LEATHERFACE STRIKES! GAME OVER.
HIGGINS! FIRE UP THE CHOPPER!
BBBBBBRRRRrrr!
HEADCHEESE COMING UP!
OH MAGNUM, HOW COULD YOU?
DON'T WORRY THIS AIN'T OVER. I'M JUST GETTING WARMED UP.
KISS ME YOU FOOL.

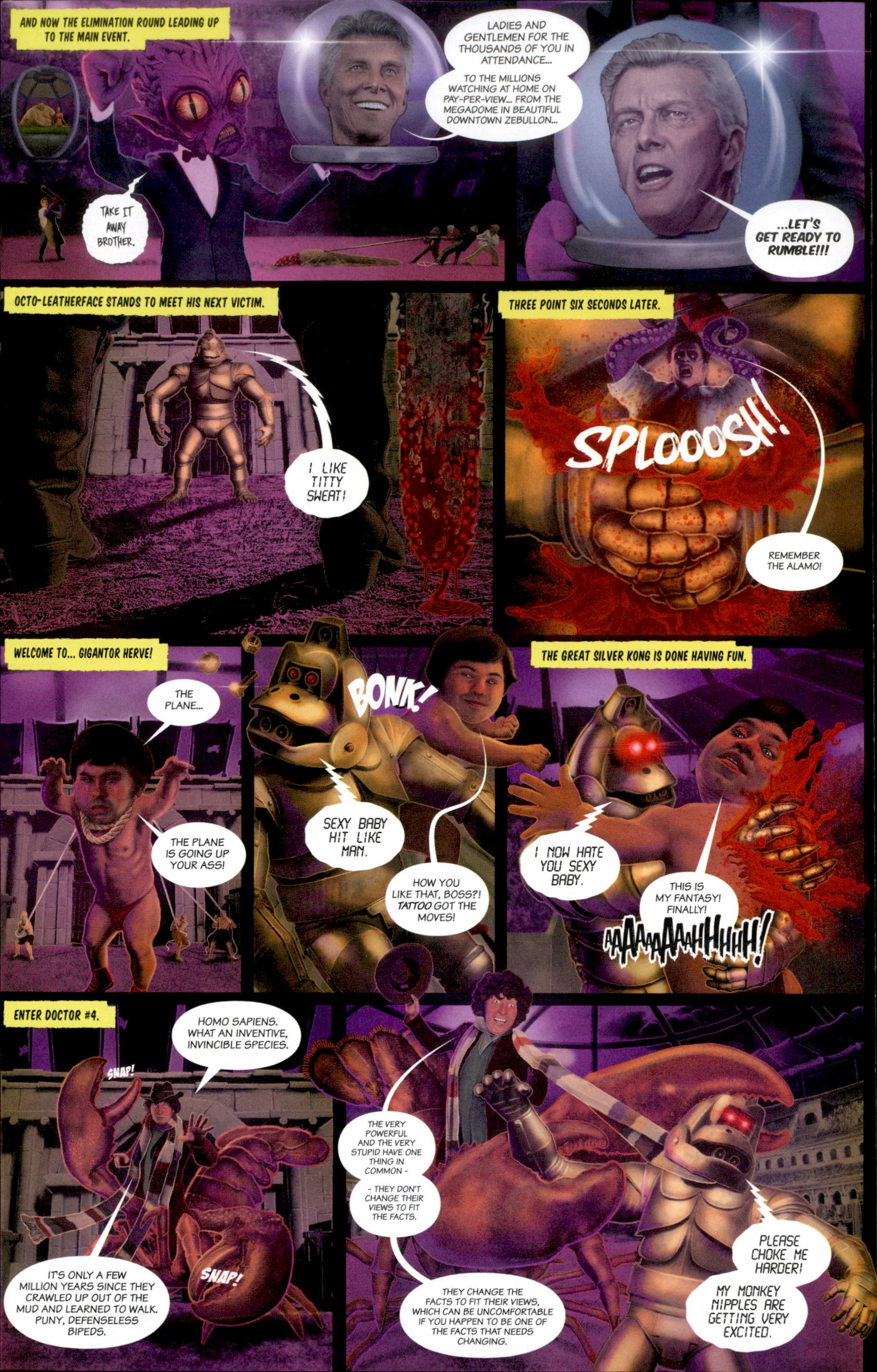
AND NOW THE ELIMINATION ROUND LEADING UP TO THE MAIN EVENT.
TAKE IT AWAY BROTHER.
LADIES AND GENTLEMEN FOR THE THOUSANDS OF YOU IN ATTENDANCE...
TO THE MILLIONS WATCHING AT HOME ON PAY-PER-VIEW... FROM THE MEGADOME IN BEAUTIFUL DOWNTOWN ZEBULLON...
...LET'S GET READY TO RUMBLE!!!
OCTO-LEATHERFACE STANDS TO MEET HIS NEXT VICTIM.
I LIKE TITTY SWEAT!
THREE POINT SIX SECONDS LATER.
SPLOOOSH!
REMEMBER THE ALAMO!
WELCOME TO... GIGANTOR HERVE!
THE PLANE...
THE PLANE IS GOING UP YOUR ASS!
BONK!
SEXY BABY HIT LIKE MAN.
HOW YOU LIKE THAT, BOSS?! TATTOO GOT THE MOVES!
THE GREAT SILVER KONG IS DONE HAVING FUN.
I NOW HATE YOU SEXY BABY.
THIS IS MY FANTASY! FINALLY!
AAAAAAAAHHHHH!
ENTER DOCTOR #4.
HOMO SAPIENS. WHAT AN INVENTIVE, INVINCIBLE SPECIES.
SNAP!
IT'S ONLY A FEW MILLION YEARS SINCE THEY CRAWLED UP OUT OF THE MUD AND LEARNED TO WALK. PUNY, DEFENSELESS BIPEDS.
SNAP!
THE VERY POWERFUL AND THE VERY STUPID HAVE ONE THING IN COMMON -
- THEY DON'T CHANGE THEIR VIEWS TO FIT THE FACTS.
THEY CHANGE THE FACTS TO FIT THEIR VIEWS, WHICH CAN BE UNCOMFORTABLE IF YOU HAPPEN TO BE ONE OF THE FACTS THAT NEEDS CHANGING.
PLEASE CHOKE ME HARDER!
MY MONKEY NIPPLES ARE GETTING VERY EXCITED.

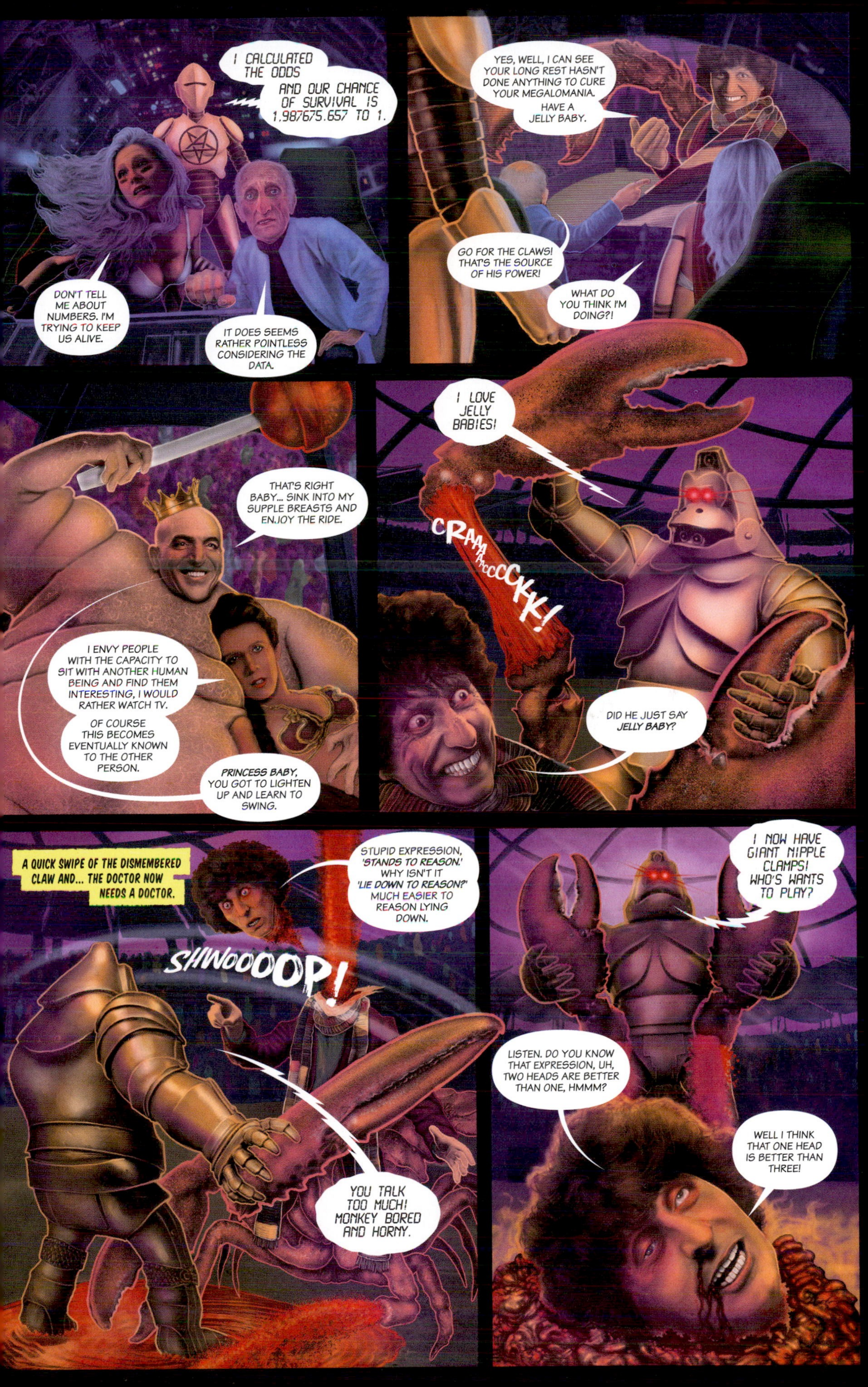

I CALCULATED THE ODDS
AND OUR CHANCE OF SURVIVAL IS 1.987675.657 TO 1.
DON'T TELL ME ABOUT NUMBERS. I'M TRYING TO KEEP US ALIVE.
IT DOES SEEMS RATHER POINTLESS CONSIDERING THE DATA.
YES, WELL, I CAN SEE YOUR LONG REST HASN'T DONE ANYTHING TO CURE YOUR MEGALOMANIA.
HAVE A JELLY BABY.
GO FOR THE CLAWS! THAT'S THE SOURCE OF HIS POWER!
WHAT DO YOU THINK I'M DOING?!
THAT'S RIGHT BABY... SINK INTO MY SUPPLE BREASTS AND ENJOY THE RIDE.
I ENVY PEOPLE WITH THE CAPACITY TO SIT WITH ANOTHER HUMAN BEING AND FIND THEM INTERESTING, I WOULD RATHER WATCH TV.
OF COURSE THIS BECOMES EVENTUALLY KNOWN TO THE OTHER PERSON.
PRINCESS BABY, YOU GOT TO LIGHTEN UP AND LEARN TO SWING.
I LOVE JELLY BABIES!
CRAAACCCKK!
DID HE JUST SAY JELLY BABY?
A QUICK SWIPE OF THE DISMEMBERED CLAW AND... THE DOCTOR NOW NEEDS A DOCTOR.
STUPID EXPRESSION, 'STANDS TO REASON.' WHY ISN'T IT 'LIE DOWN TO REASON?' MUCH EASIER TO REASON LYING DOWN.
SHWOOOOP!
YOU TALK TOO MUCH! MONKEY BORED AND HORNY.
I NOW HAVE GIANT NIPPLE CLAMPS! WHO'S WANTS TO PLAY?
LISTEN. DO YOU KNOW THAT EXPRESSION, UH, TWO HEADS ARE BETTER THAN ONE, HMMM?
WELL I THINK THAT ONE HEAD IS BETTER THAN THREE!

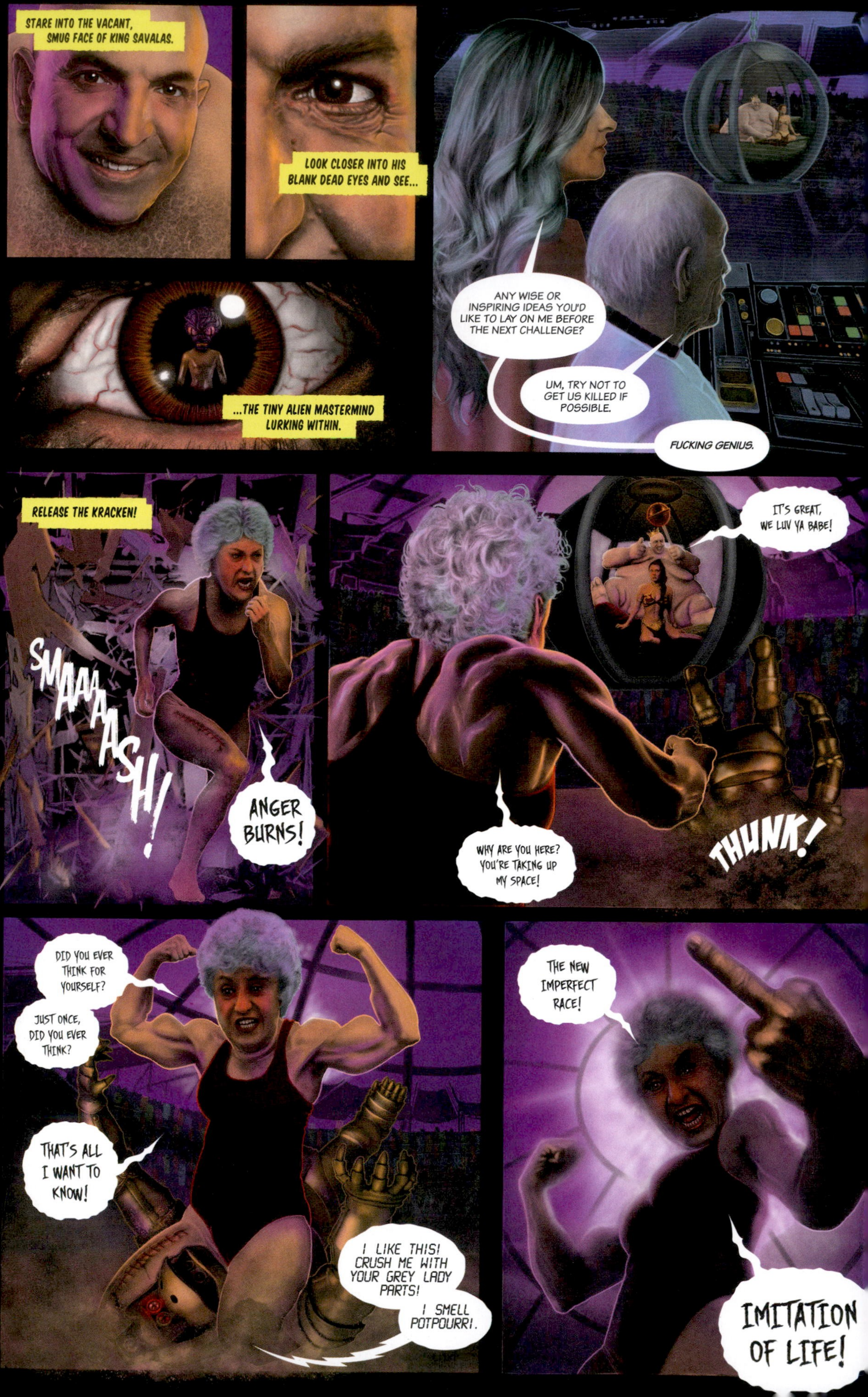
STARE INTO THE VACANT, SMUG FACE OF KING SAVALAS.
LOOK CLOSER INTO HIS BLANK DEAD EYES AND SEE...
...THE TINY ALIEN MASTERMIND LURKING WITHIN.
ANY WISE OR INSPIRING IDEAS YOU'D LIKE TO LAY ON ME BEFORE THE NEXT CHALLENGE?
UM, TRY NOT TO GET US KILLED IF POSSIBLE.
FUCKING GENIUS.
RELEASE THE KRACKEN!
SMAAAAASH!
ANGER BURNS!
IT'S GREAT, WE LUV YA BABE!
WHY ARE YOU HERE? YOU'RE TAKING UP MY SPACE!
THUNK!
DID YOU EVER THINK FOR YOURSELF?
JUST ONCE, DID YOU EVER THINK?
THAT'S ALL I WANT TO KNOW!
I LIKE THIS! CRUSH ME WITH YOUR GREY LADY PARTS!
I SMELL POTPOURRI.
THE NEW IMPERFECT RACE!
IMITATION OF LIFE!

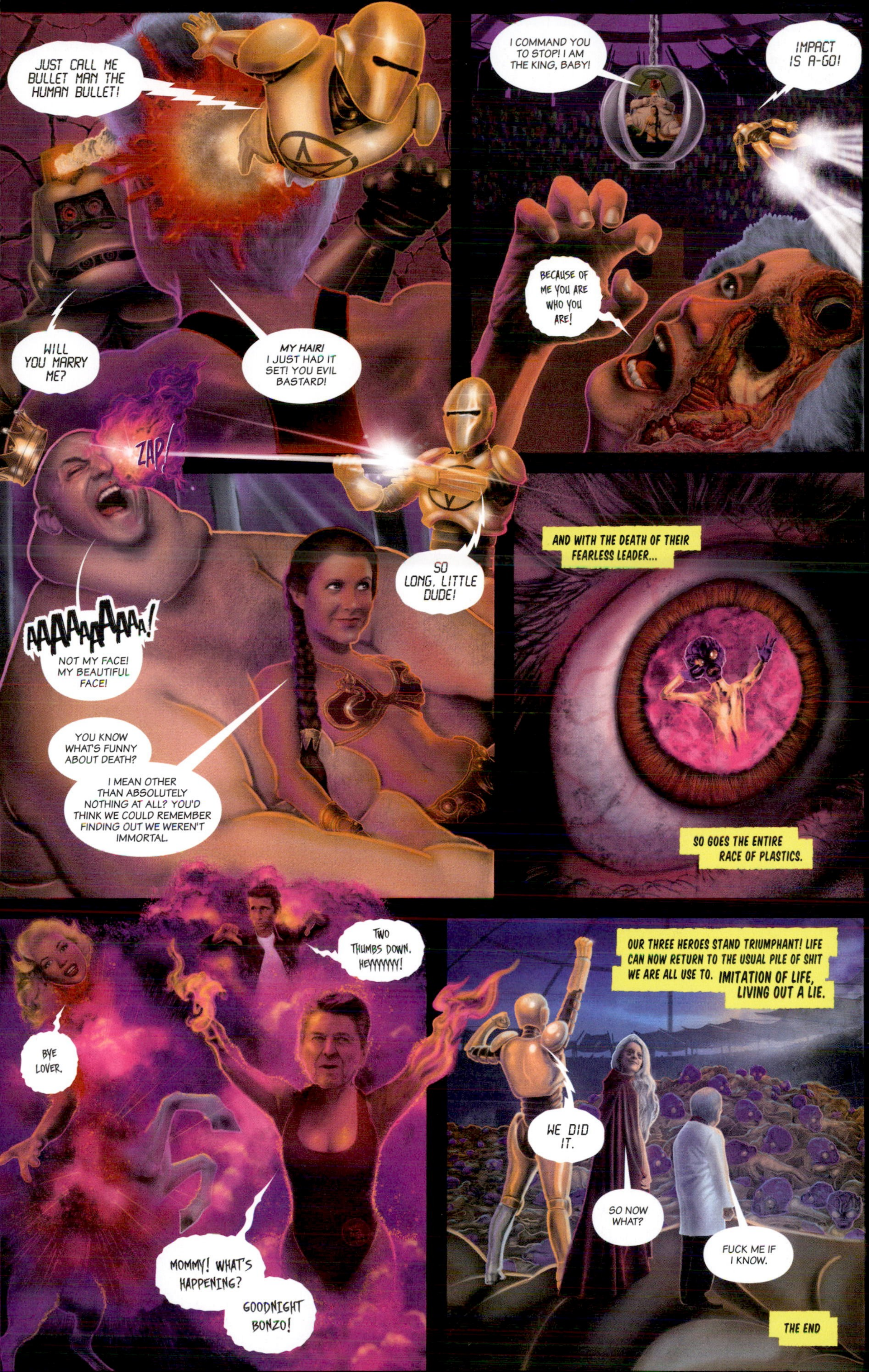
JUST CALL ME BULLET MAN THE HUMAN BULLET!
WILL YOU MARRY ME?
MY HAIR! I JUST HAD IT SET! YOU EVIL BASTARD!
I COMMAND YOU TO STOP! I AM THE KING, BABY!
IMPACT IS A-GO!
BECAUSE OF ME YOU ARE WHO YOU ARE!
ZAP!
AAAAAAAAAA!
NOT MY FACE! MY BEAUTIFUL FACE!
SO LONG, LITTLE DUDE!
YOU KNOW WHAT'S FUNNY ABOUT DEATH?
I MEAN OTHER THAN ABSOLUTELY NOTHING AT ALL? YOU'D THINK WE COULD REMEMBER FINDING OUT WE WEREN'T IMMORTAL.
AND WITH THE DEATH OF THEIR FEARLESS LEADER...
SO GOES THE ENTIRE RACE OF PLASTICS.
TWO THUMBS DOWN. HEYYYYYY!
BYE LOVER.
MOMMY! WHAT'S HAPPENING?
GOODNIGHT BONZO!
OUR THREE HEROES STAND TRIUMPHANT! LIFE CAN NOW RETURN TO THE USUAL PILE OF SHIT WE ARE ALL USE TO. IMITATION OF LIFE, LIVING OUT A LIE.
WE DID IT.
SO NOW WHAT?
FUCK ME IF I KNOW.
THE END

BACK PAGES

COVER AND PRINT GALLERY

THE FOLLWING ARTWORK BY

J.G. JONES + ERIC POWELL + CHARLIE BENANTE

BRIAN EWING + JOSH BERNSTEIN

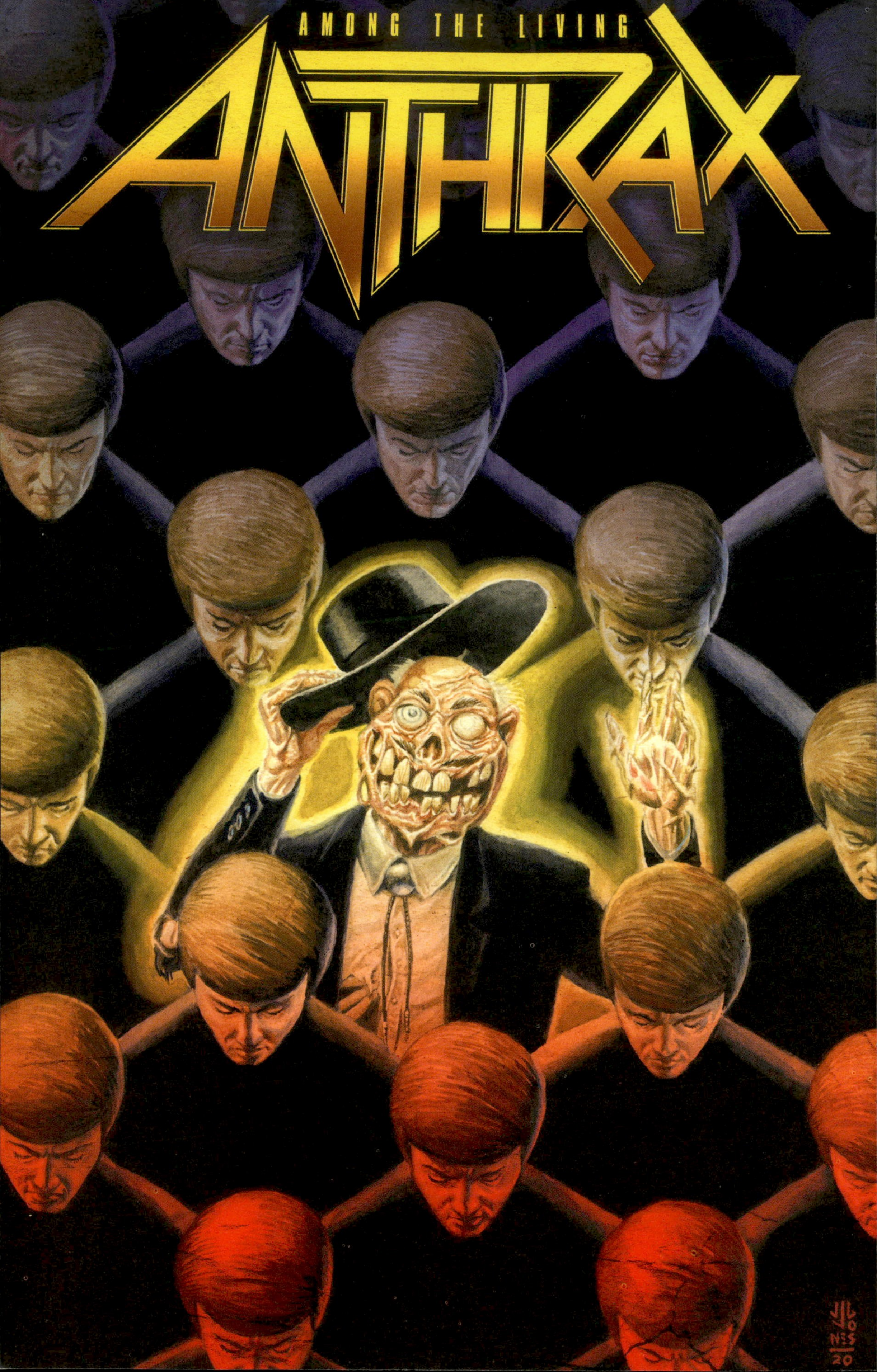

AMONG THE LIVING
ANTHRAX

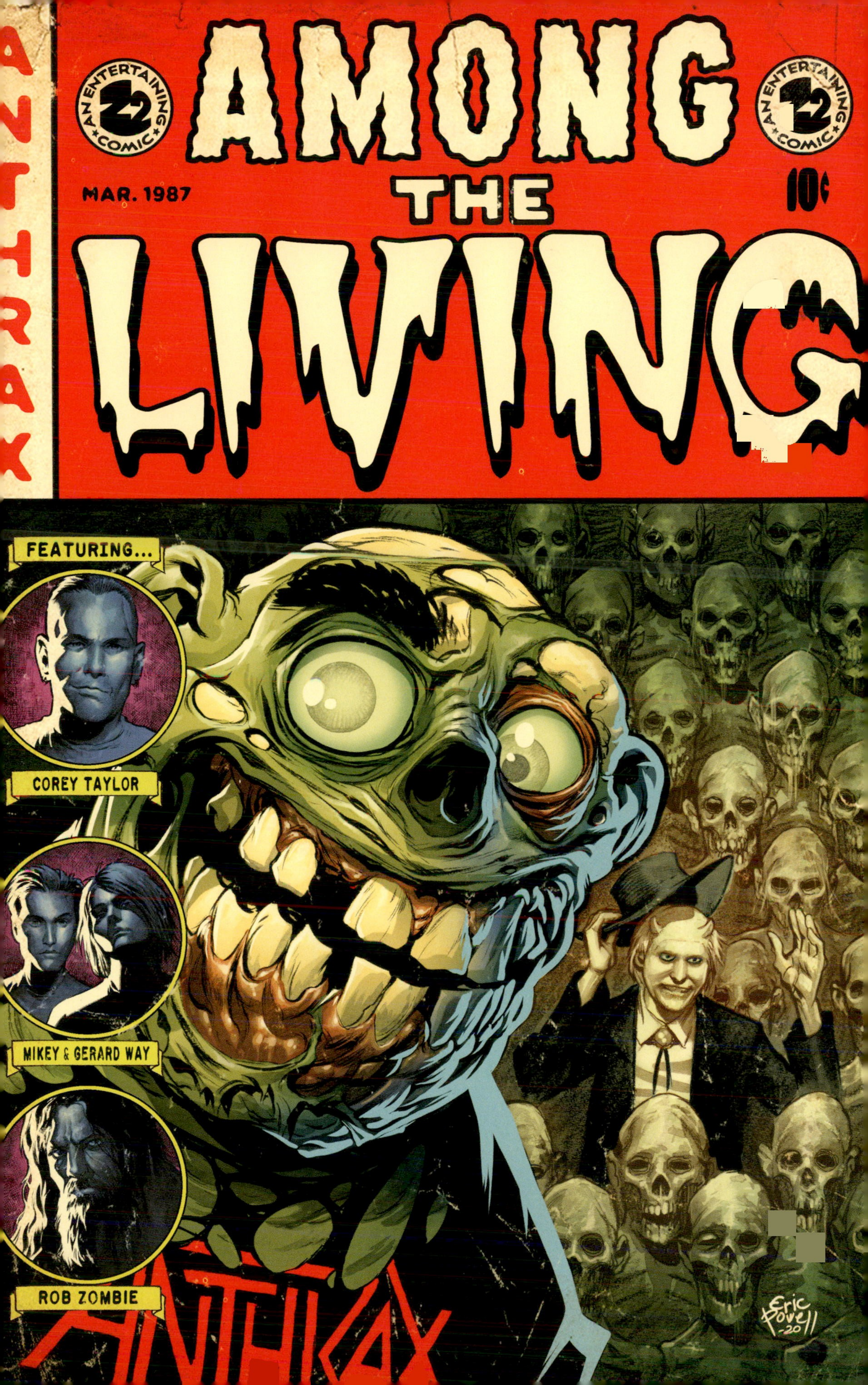
ANTHRAX
AN ENTERTAINING COMIC
AMONG
THE
LIVING
MAR. 1987
10¢
FEATURING...
COREY TAYLOR
MIKEY & GERARD WAY
ROB ZOMBIE
ANTHRAX
Eric Powell -2011

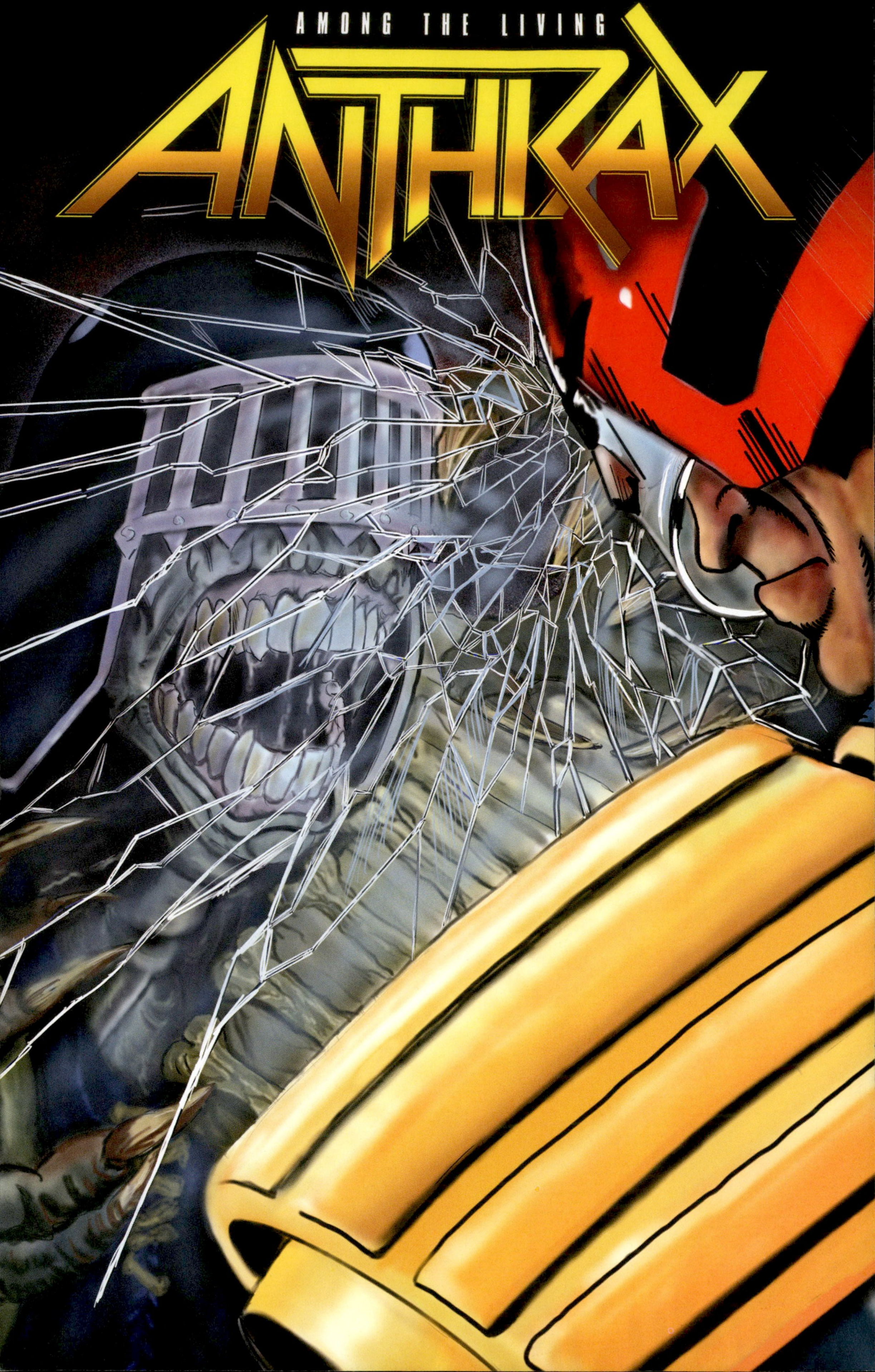
AMONG THE LIVING
ANTHRAX

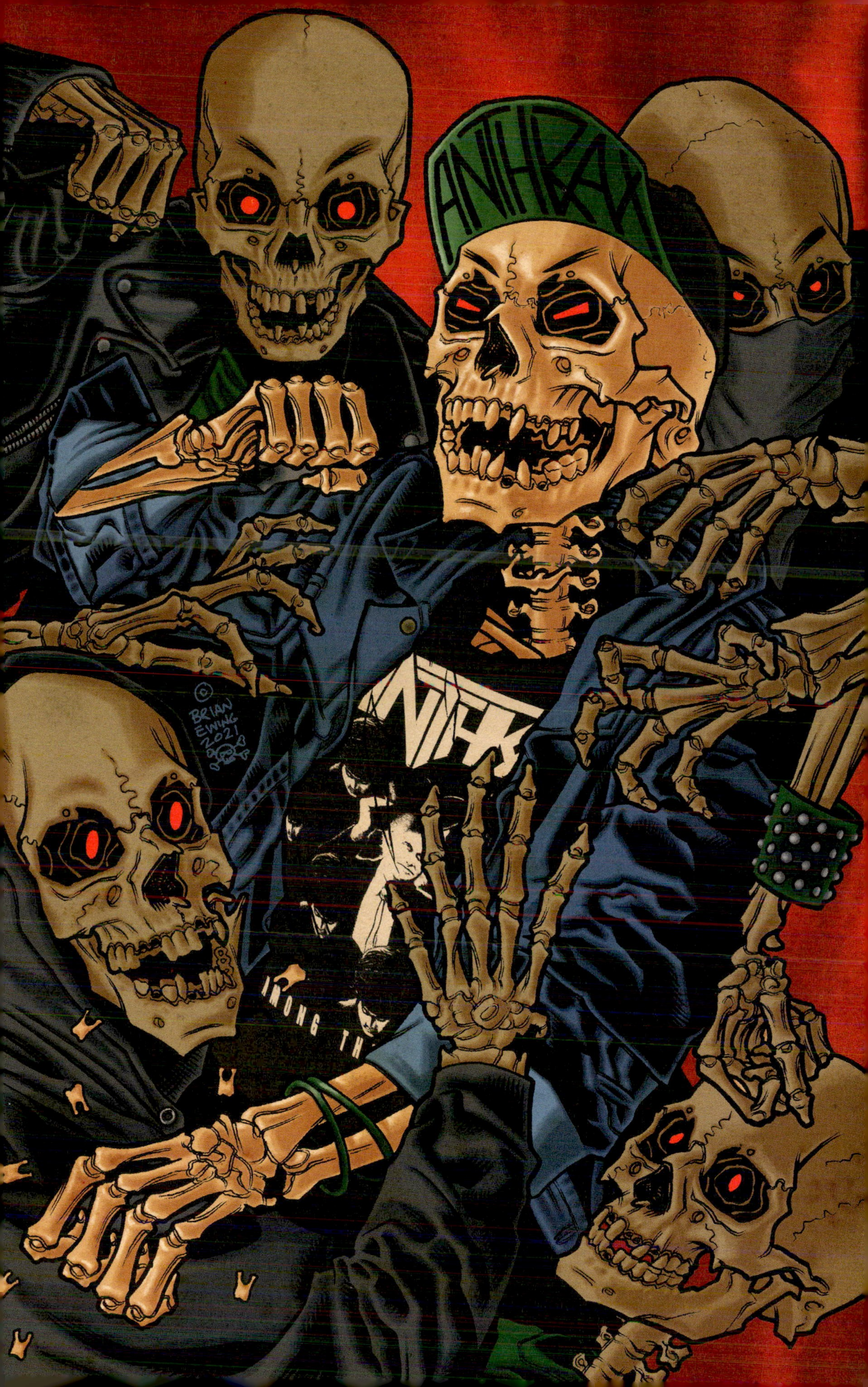
ANTHRAX
© BRIAN EWING 2021

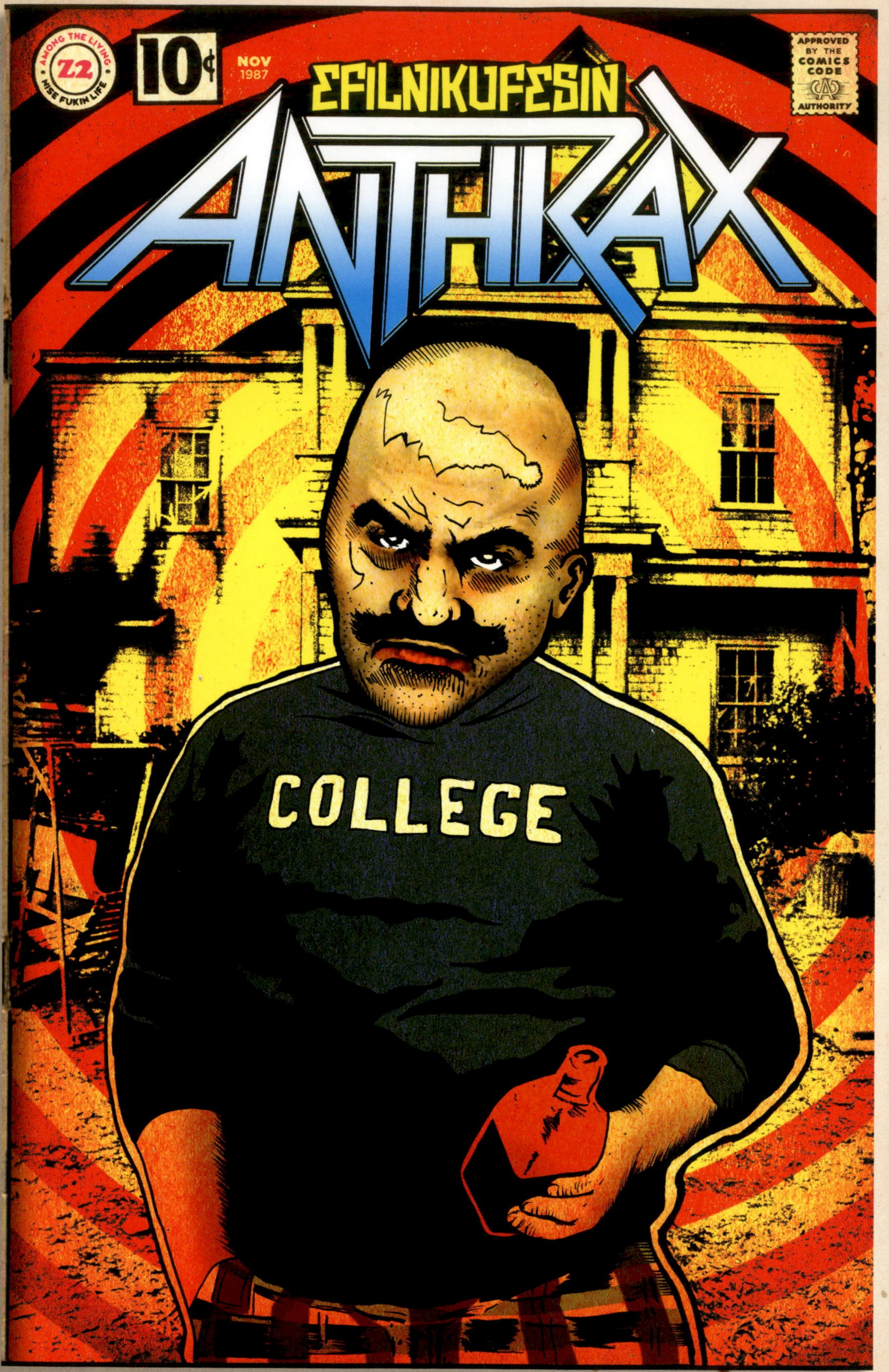
AMONG THE LIVING
Z2
NISE FUKIN LIFE
10¢
NOV
1987
ƎFILNIKUFƎSIN
ANTHRAX
APPROVED BY THE COMICS CODE AUTHORITY
COLLEGE

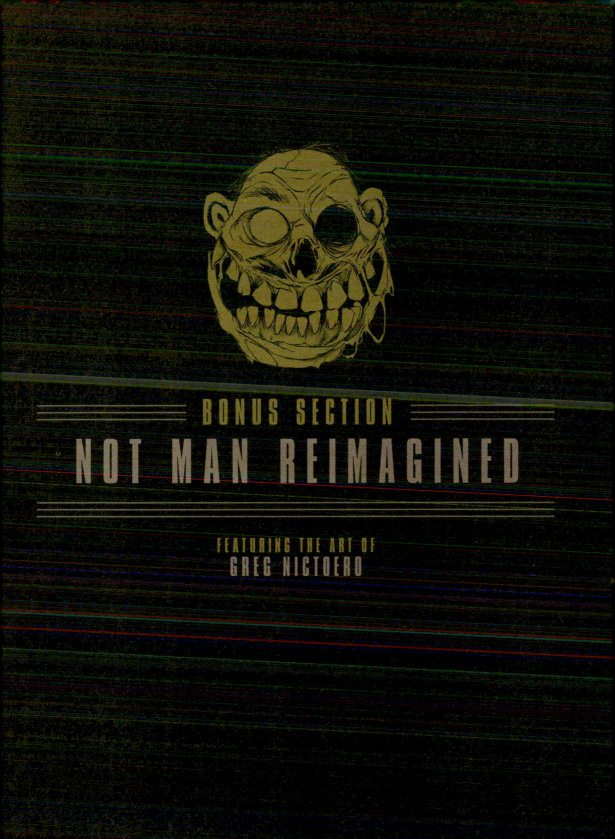

BONUS SECTION
NOT MAN REIMAGINED

FEATURING THE ART OF
GREG NICTOERO

GREG NICOTERO ILLUSTRATION BY STEVE CHANKS

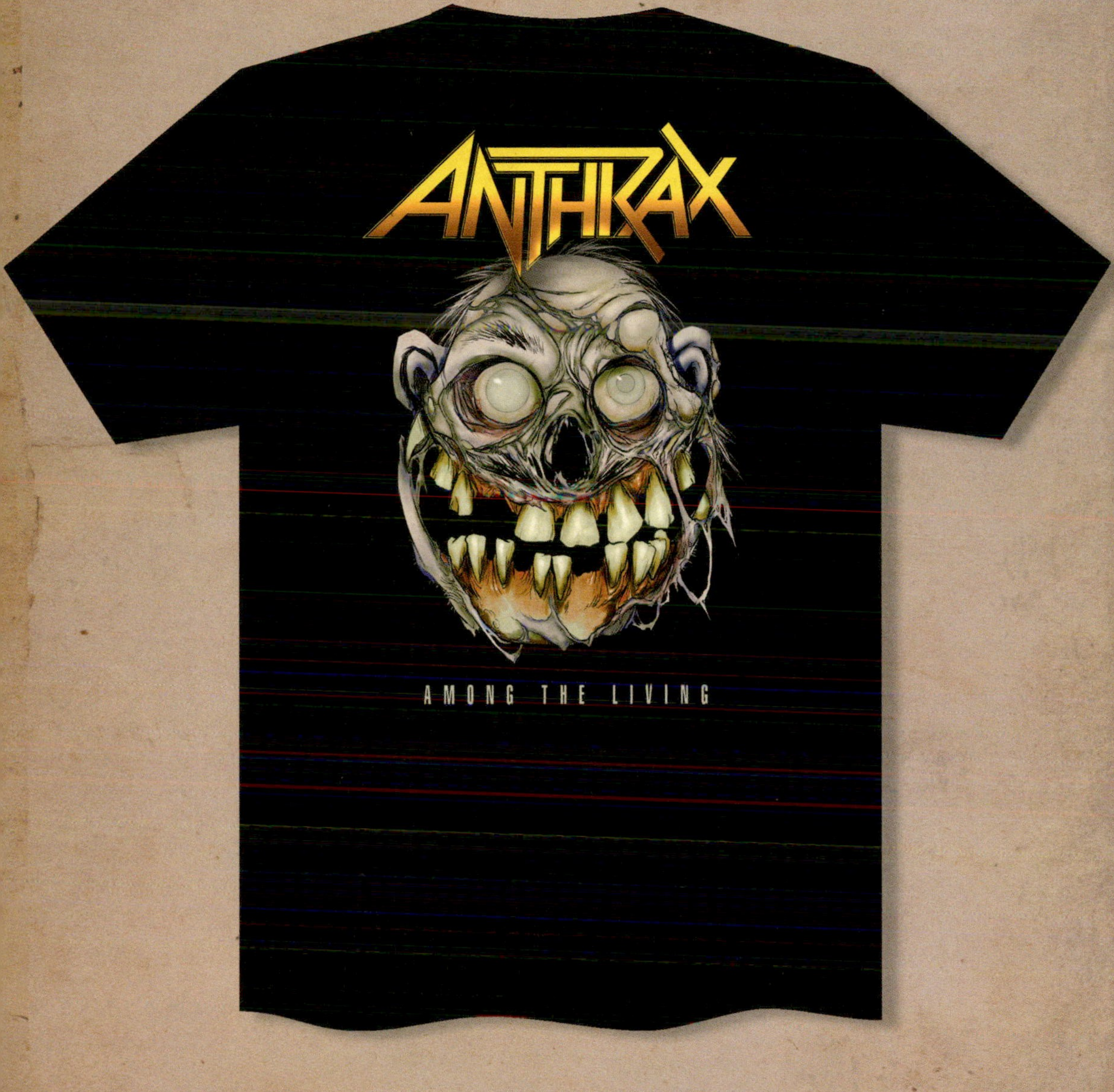
ANTHRAX
AMONG THE LIVING

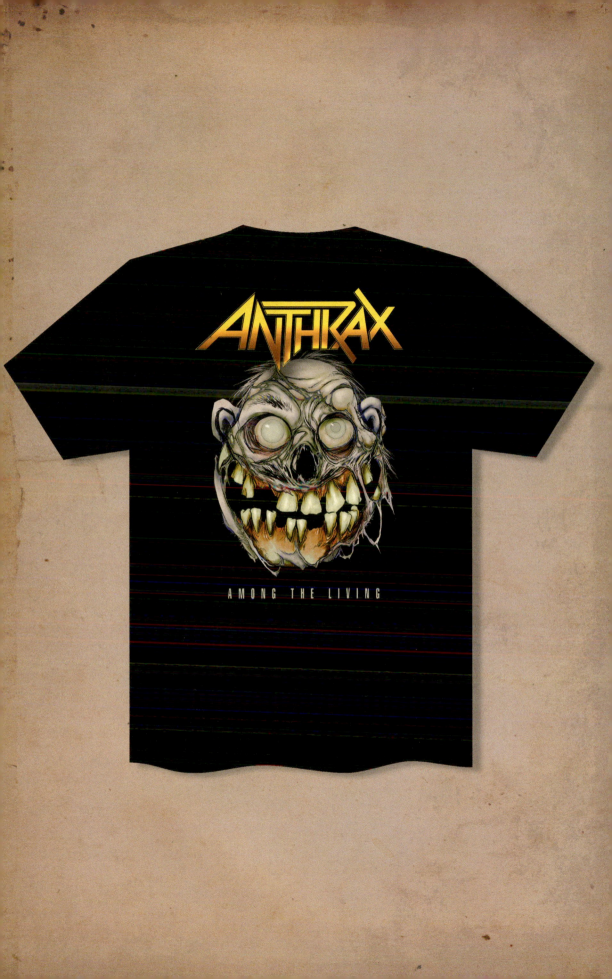

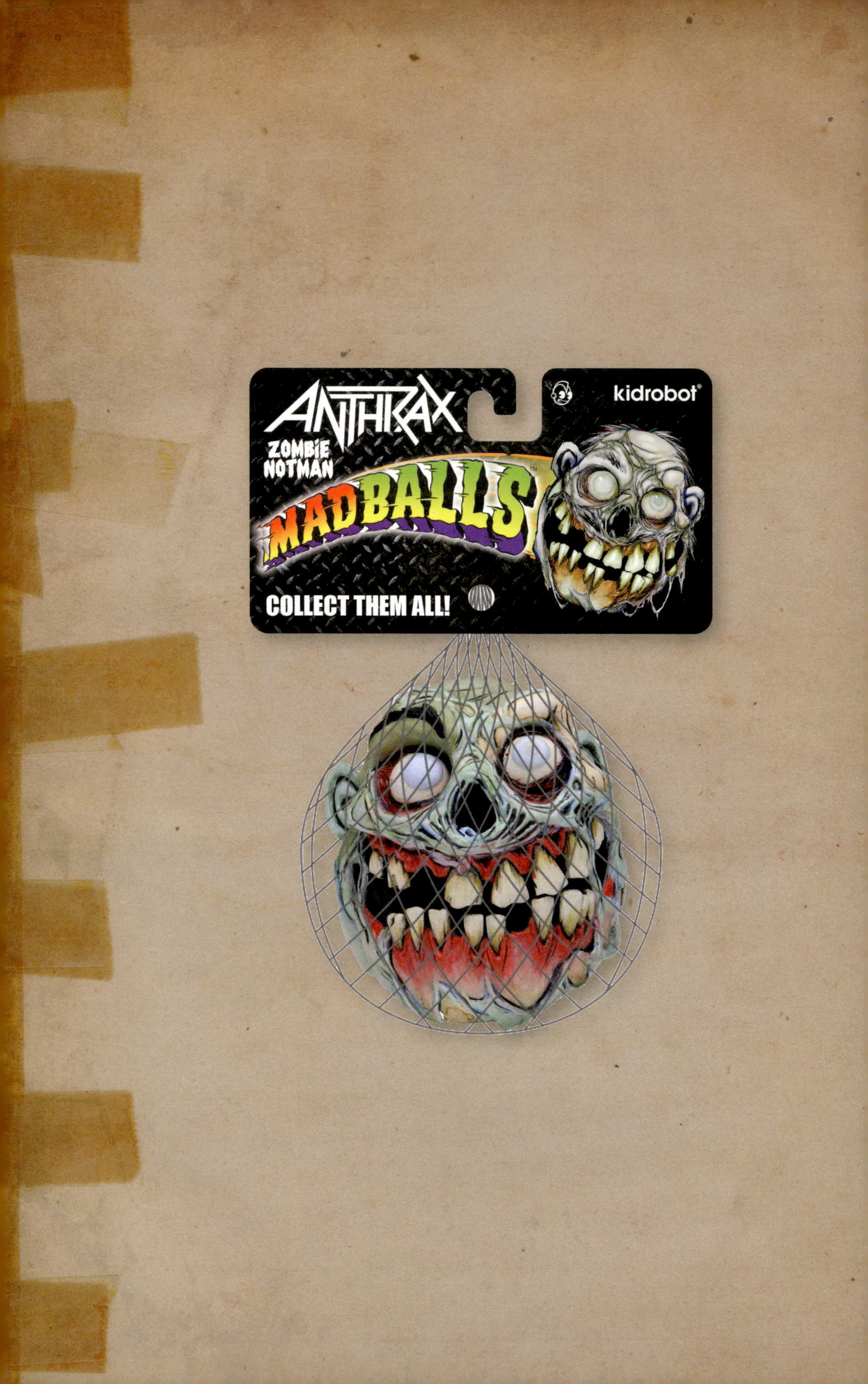
ANTHRAX
ZOMBIE NOTMAN
MADBALLS
kidrobot
COLLECT THEM ALL!

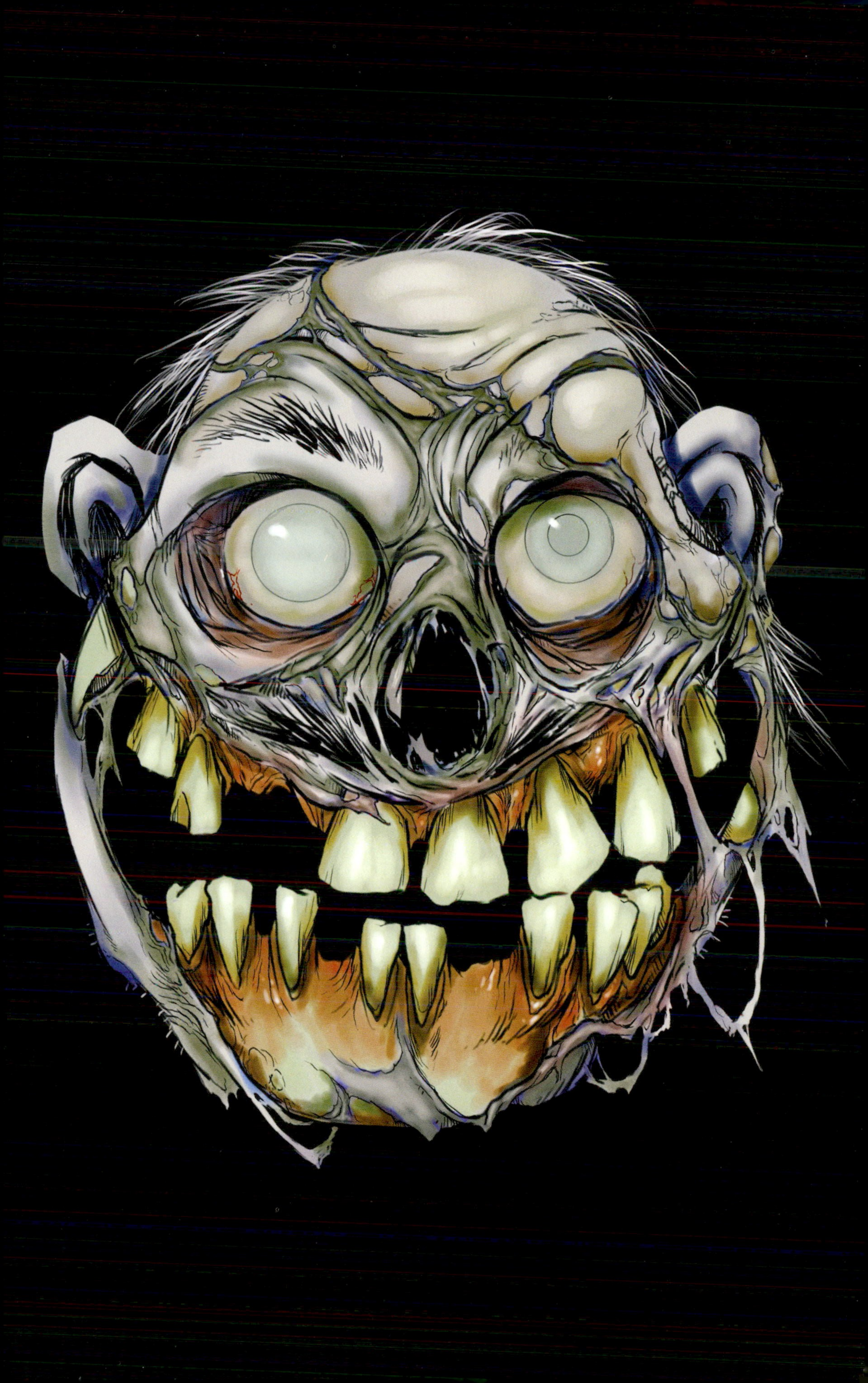